STANDARD

ETHNIC RELATIONS AND SCHOOLING

Ethnic Relations and Schooling

Policy and Practice in the 1990s

Edited by

Sally Tomlinson & Maurice Craft

ATHLONE
London and Atlantic Highlands, NJ

First published 1995 by
THE ATHLONE PRESS
1 Park Drive, London NW11 7SG
and 165 First Avenue,
Atlantic Highlands, NJ 07716

British Library Cataloguing in Publication Data
*A catalogue record for this book is available
from the British Library*

ISBN 0 485 11456 9   hb
0 485 12108 5   pb

Library of Congress Cataloging in Publication Data

Ethnic relations and schooling : policy and practice in the 1990s
/ edited by Sally Tomlinson, Maurice Craft.
   p.   cm.
Includes bibliographical references and index.
ISBN 0-485-11456-9. -- ISBN 0-485-12108-5 (pbk.)
  1. Education and state--Great Britain. 2. Multiculturalism--
Great Britains.   I. Tomlinson, Sally.   II. Craft, Maurice, 1932–   .
LC93.G7E79   1995
379.41--dc20   94-46798
                                                                         CIP

Typeset by
Bibloset, Chester

Printed and bound in Great Britain by
Bookcraft (Bath) Ltd

Contents

Foreword

The last decade has seen some major changes in both the philosophy and implementation of an education appropriate for all children in an ethnically diverse society. The national policy objectives of the early 1980s regarding diversity in education, which embodied both an idealistic preoccupation with social justice and a pragmatic concern for social order, were expressed most fully in the Swann Report of 1985. But by the beginning of the 1990s they had been by-passed by a broader, mainstream drive to raise educational productivity through a return to the marketplace, and by a weakening of the advocacy of equal opportunities.

In this collection of papers we have sought to examine the practical outcomes and foreseeable implications of these policy changes, and our contributors have respectively addressed a number of the major dimensions. It will be some time before their full impact is felt; indeed, the changes themselves are still in process of modification. But it is our hope that the long-established consensus on the school's role in maximizing individuals' talents and promoting positive ethnic relations will be seen to have survived; and that the fulfilment of all citizens within a plural, democratic society will continue to be a major objective of the British educational system.

Our warm thanks to our contributors, and to Mr Brian Southam, Chairman of The Athlone Press, for his kind invitation to assemble this symposium on ethnic relations in schools in the 1990s.

Sally Tomlinson
Maurice Craft

Acknowledgements

The authors and editors would like to thank the following publishers for their permission to reproduce copyright material:

David Fulton (Publishers) for extracts from Cecile Wright, *Race Relations in the Primary School*, 1992.

The Falmer Press for the reproduction of extracts from G.K. Verma, P. Zec and G.D. Skinner, *The Ethnic Crucible*, 1994.

CHAPTER 1

Education for All in the 1990s

Sally Tomlinson and Maurice Craft

This opening chapter reviews the concept of an appropriate education for all children in a plural society as it has evolved during the last decade, setting subsequent chapters in this context.

In the 1990s, inter-ethnic tensions and conflicts are still apparent in many countries around the world, but some, notably South Africa, have made significant progress towards equal opportunities. In Britain, there is a growing acceptance that the nation is ethnically diverse, and that ethnic minority communities are part of a citizenry with equal rights and responsibilities who should be accorded equal respect. Although statistics of racial harassment, documentation of discrimination on ethnic or racial grounds, and the persistence of racist political groups, are constant reminders that there is still a long way to go, there has been over the past twenty years a steady movement towards what the Committee of Inquiry into the Education of Children from Ethnic Minority Groups chaired by Lord Swann described as 'the "assimilation" of *all* groups within a redefined concept of what it means to live in British society today' (DES, 1985, p. 8). Education has played, and continues to play, a crucial role in facilitating that redefinition. Schools have attempted, however haltingly, to educate *all* groups of children together. There have been significant attempts – certainly up to the later 1980s – to develop a curriculum relevant to the needs of an ethnically diverse society. Teachers have become much more aware of their responsibilities to help majority and minority pupils to respect and accept each other, and to understand the changing nature of our society and of what it means to be British.

A DECADE OF CHANGE

For some years but particularly during the past decade there has been an increasing awarenesss of racial, ethnic, cultural, linguistic and religious issues among politicians, the media and the general public. Despite the attempts of those on the 'new right' to define a British heritage and culture which appears to exclude non-white citizens, and the timidity of some politicians who have failed to offer leadership, there has nonetheless been much central and local political support for schools and teachers who recognize the need for education to give a lead in combating ignorance and the stereotyping of other cultures and nations. Some of this support has stemmed from humanitarian, moral and egalitarian concerns, but social and economic considerations have undoubtedly played a part. There has been a concern for public order; and the interdependence of the world economy and trade, mutual investment and joint ventures with former colonies have simply made it 'uneconomic' to hold arrogant or hostile attitudes towards non-white people both in Britain and abroad.

The emergence of a government view that education for an ethnically diverse society is important can be traced in official documents from 1977. This was the year that a Labour Government's Green Paper on education stated clearly that 'our society is a multicultural and multi-racial one, and the curriculum should reflect a sympathetic understanding of the different cultures and races that now make up our society' (DES, 1977, p. 41). A Conservative Government elected in 1979 continued to support a policy of curriculum development for a post-imperial society, particularly through HMI documents (e.g. DES, 1981a) which asserted that learning in a multicultural society should help pupils to develop respect for religious values, tolerance of other races and ways of life, and knowledge of the interdependence of individuals and nations. The Committee of Inquiry into the Education of Ethnic Minority Children (which later became an inquiry into the education of *all* children in Britain) sat from 1979 to 1985, noting in an interim report that accurate information on the historical and economic reasons for migration to Britain should be offered to all pupils (DES, 1981a); and recommending in their final report that the curriculum should help to bring about 'the fundamental reorientation of attitudes which were needed in an ethnically diverse society' (DES, 1985, p. 324).

During his period of office as Secretary of State for Education, 1981–85, Sir Keith Joseph set up CATE, the Council for the Accreditation of Teacher Education, whose provisions included the requirement that all student teachers should receive some training for teaching in a multicultural society. He also extended grant-related in-service training courses for teachers, to cover 'teaching and the curriculum in a multi-ethnic society' – these courses being made a national priority in 1986 and 1987; and he required the new GCSE examining boards, set up from 1986, to have regard for cultural and linguistic diversity. He reviewed the Section 11 grants given by the Home Office under the 1966 Local Government Act for language and other assistance for the education of minorities, and decided they should remain; and he initiated the Education Support Grant projects, by which central government money was given to support projects on curriculum development for an ethnically diverse society, 120 such projects eventually being funded in all areas of the country between 1985 and 1990. On leaving office, Sir Keith restated that Britain was an ethnically mixed society, and reaffirmed his belief that minority cultures should be acknowledged in schools and that racial prejudice should be eliminated (Joseph, 1985).

During the 1980s, Local Education Authorities (LEAs) and some schools began to produce written policy statements with the theme of education for a multi-ethnic, non-racist society. By 1987, over two-thirds of all LEAs had some such statement, and these acted as a bench-mark to improve professional practice.

The activities of some LEAs were undoubtedly over-zealous, and the development of multicultural/anti-racist policies were hindered by the media who seized on tragedies such as the 1986 murder of an Asian boy at Burnage School, Manchester (MacDonald, 1988), to belittle written policy statements. Overall, however, the 1980s partnership between central government commitment and Local Education Authority support did produce a growing awareness of the political, social and economic reasons for developing an education system relevant to an ethnically diverse society, and the need to encourage schools and teachers to develop constructive inter-ethnic perspectives whether or not the schools had ethnic minority pupils. After the 1988 Education Reform Act (ERA) had become law, Kenneth Baker, the then Secretary of State for Education, instructed his new National Curriculum Council as it began work on the development of a national curriculum, to 'take account of ethnic and cultural diversity, and the importance of the curriculum in promoting equal opportunity for all pupils regardless of ethnic origin or gender' (DES, 1988).

POST-1988

Despite Baker's request to the National Curriculum Council, educational policies since 1988 have affected ethnic relations and cultural pluralism in schools in less than positive ways. The national and local policy objectives which previously embodied a concern for equal opportunities – raising the achievement levels of ethnic minorities, for example – and for a curriculum which offered new knowledge about minorities and redefined the concept of 'being British', disappeared abruptly. A broad mainstream drive to raise standards in education and training by introducing market competition between schools, developing a tightly regulated National Curriculum with an associated testing programme and reducing the influence of Local Education Authorities, has been accompanied by a rejection of the rhetoric of equal opportunities. Chapter 7 in this volume begins with Prime Minister John Major's blunt statement at the 1992 Conservative Party Conference that 'Primary teachers should learn how to teach children to read, not waste their time on the politics of gender, race and class.' This seemed to diverge from what had hitherto been a bipartisan commitment to equal opportunities. In 1989, for example, the Labour Party had published a document re-affirming the importance of education for racial justice and equal opportunity. It stated that

> Britain is manifestly a multiracial society. We believe that the education system must – working within a plurality of cultures – set itself two objectives. First, it must ensure that all children in our schools develop an understanding of the plurality of cultures and traditions, and must guarantee that all cultures are accorded legitimacy and respect . . . and secondly, it must ensure that all pupils develop their full potential. (Labour Party, 1989, p. 2)

Meanwhile, the parental right of choice of school, embodied in the 1980 and 1988 Education Acts, was exacerbating 'white flight' from schools attended by minority children. Rights to choose a school conflicted with the 1976 Race Relations Act, if parents, as in a case in Cleveland Local Authority, were too frank about the racial reasons for their choice (Commission for Racial Equality, 1989). The possibility of increasing ethnic segregation in education, by parental choice but also on religious grounds, as Muslim groups have continued to press for state-supported Islamic schools, has become greater in the 1990s.

The *Times Educational Supplement* noted in June 1990 that

> unspoken anxieties about ethnic differences underlie several different bits of educational policy, all of which are beginning to show a pattern. There seems to be a definite though unformulated intent to starve multicultural education of resources and let it wither on the vine. (*TES*, 1990, p. A.23)

In fact, the intent was not 'unformulated'. Duncan Graham, the first Chief Executive of the National Curriculum Council, has documented specific Ministerial instructions to remove references to multicultural education from the National Curriculum (Graham, 1993); and the report of a multicultural task group, set up by the Council in 1989 to consider ways in which the national curriculum could broaden the horizons of all pupils and address the needs of minority – especially bilingual – pupils, was never published nor were its recommendations put into operation (Tomlinson, 1993). There was considerably political direction of the work of the original task groups which were set up to produce the 'first' National Curriculum (Cox, 1991); and although the 1994 review and production of a second National Curriculum (Dearing, 1994) has less political steer there is still no overt mention of curricular initiatives or teacher support for an ethnically diverse society. The revised National Curriculum, produced in May 1994, appears to be further minimising the multicultural aspect. The then Secretary of State, John Patten, was reported as 'calming fears that children will not learn about British heritage' by promising that under the new history curriculum, 'children will learn about British history from the invasion of this land by Julius Caesar up until D-day' (Smith, 1994), which excludes the more recent history of migration and post-colonialism.

In the new market-oriented climate and with the partnership between central and local government much weakened, there is no longer central nor local government commitment to, or financing of projects and programmes to improve relations in an ethnically diverse society, either in terms of curriculum projects, teacher in-service courses, or even bilingual support, with Section 11 grants being cut back. On the other hand, there is a commitment to a national curriculum to which *all* children are entitled; the regular publication of test results of *all* groups of pupils; an opening up of information on schools to *all* parents; the local management of schools to meet individual school needs, and much more parental and community involvement in school management via governing bodies and parent associations. Where do these contrary tendencies leave ethnic relations in schools in the 1990s?

CURRENT CONCERNS

In bringing together this collection of papers, the editors' main purpose has been to examine the *practical outcomes* and foreseeable implications of the last decade's educational policy changes as they affect ethnic relations and cultural pluralism in education, and the contributors to this volume have drawn upon a range of recent researches which seek to address these questions. The focus is generally micro rather than macro, and a number of relevant case studies are reported. Methodologically the contributions are eclectic, ranging from classroom ethnography to the large-scale survey and including a good deal of individual interviewing.

A central question continues to be how far the introduction of a national curriculum and programme of assessment will affect minority opportunities and the education of majority culture pupils for life in a plural society. The new pattern is still in process of establishment and modification, and in time may well come to offer equal entitlement for minority pupils; but in Chapter 2 Anna King feels this is still far from reality, and cites the 1992–93 Report of HM Chief Inspector of Schools which claimed that 'minority pupils were often insufficiently extended and challenged. In general, they were under-represented in the top ability sets'. Whether or not the National Curriculum provides *all* pupils with the wider perspective appropriate to life in modern Britain is less easy to establish. Some of the original subject working groups took this very seriously, others less so, and the eventual implementation of these proposals in the National Curriculum has often been ambiguous and confused. As King indicates at several points, much will depend upon the ability and enthusiasm of teachers to exploit the opportunities, but equally a good deal will turn on the way the new assessment patterns are operated. Overall, there seems to have been a significant drawing back from the original instructions of the former Secretary of State, Kenneth Baker, to the new National Curriculum Council in 1988 (cited above).

A second question in relation to the practical outcomes of recent policy changes concerns Local Education Authorities, and in Chapters 7 and 8 Monica Taylor, Carl Bagley and Barry Troyna consider key aspects of this. Taylor and Bagley's major survey of English and Welsh LEAs in 1991–92 found that while interest in multicultural education might even have marginally increased, schools' priorities had understandably shifted towards curriculum reform. Revised criteria for the use of 'Section 11' funding have narrowed, not removed opportunities for teachers' in-service support, but cutbacks in expenditure announced for 1994–96 could greatly affect local government services to minority communities. The introduction of ethnic minority grants through Training and Enterprise Councils has been a useful complement, but it has so far provided a great deal less funding and would be a poor substitute for Section 11. Taylor and Bagley also report on Standing Advisory Councils for Religious Education (SACREs), 'one of the most significant innovations of ERA for cultural diversity', and one which has received renewed legislative support with the 1993 Education Act. As they say, SACREs are a consultative mechanism which allows a local voice on the Agreed Syllabus for RE, on collective worship, teaching methods, choice of materials and teacher training, and would appear to be a constructive device with much potential.

In Chapter 8 Barry Troyna notes the 'two distinctive channels'; of government policy in education since the 1980s, *centralization* and *devolution*; the former expressed through a national framework for school curricula and assessment, and prescribed priorities in initial and in-service teacher education, and the latter through local school management, grant maintained schools, open enrolment and city technology colleges. But while seemingly contradictory, these twin initiatives *'coalesce around . . . the weakening, and ultimately dismantling, of LEA influence'*, as Troyna puts it, and he considers the changing role of the LEA as schools begin to determine their own priorities. As noted earlier, schools are now preoccupied with the establishment of the National Curriculum and a complex pattern of national assessment, and in general do not see multicultural education as a salient task. So monocultural schools are unlikely to devote much attention to this and, Troyna argues, will be more interested in'improving their academic performance profiles . . . as a means to . . . attracting students from neighbouring schools, thus ensuring survival if not an increase in their budget'. So, as resources are transferred from LEAs to schools, as Section 11 grants diminish, and as changes in the funding formula for pupil enrolments reduce the importance of inner city location, the outlook both for minority opportunities and for the broader education of all young people seems less than propitious.

On the other hand, the role of school governors has been enlarged under the educational reforms, and particularly in schools with a large ethnic minority enrolment this could be helpful. However, as Troyna (and also Kevin Brehony, in Chapter 9) report, ethnic minority governors are under-represented nationally. In Brehony's study of fifteen school governing bodies in the late 1980s, this was actually not the case; but he found that recruiting and retaining governors in working-class areas could be much more difficult than in middle-class areas, and once recruited, 'certain categories of governors were often silent during the meeting. . . . Typically, it was working class, parent governors who were silent, and women and black and Asian governors who were in a minority on the governing body'. A further issue is governors' access to key committees, finance for example, where day-to-day decisions may be made for later endorsement by the full governing body.

Like the increased authority of school governors, the involvement of parents is a democratic device of great potential value in the education of all children, as was well recognized almost thirty years ago in the 'Plowden Report' (1967) and in many studies of the time. In Chapter 10, Carol Vincent briefly reviews the field and reports her own recent research in multi-ethnic primary schools in working-class areas. The variable sensitivity of teachers to pupils' social/ethnic background has long been an issue, and Vincent describes the alienation felt by many black (*and* white) parents. As has been found elsewhere, for example by Paul Ghuman (1981, 1989), parental perceptions of schooling do not divide neatly on ethnic lines, and are related to a range of factors as Vincent clearly shows. But her threefold typology of parents – 'school supportive', 'detached'; and 'independent' – and the need to develop a fourth 'participant' model which would provide parents with access to a broader policy-making role, offers an analysis of direct relevance to the decline of LEAs, the advent of local school management, and the more complex needs of multi-ethnic schools in the 1990s.

Ultimately, the education system exists to help individual pupils to make the most of the curricula, the machinery and the resources in developing their talents, and Cecile Wright and Heidi Mirza bring us back to this fundamental interface in their respective ethnographic accounts of classroom interaction and pupil learning strategies. In Chapter 3 Wright describes her research in multi-ethnic primary schools where the inability of some teachers to relate effectively to Asian and Afro-Caribbean pupils is of profound concern. She describes a failure to comprehend language difficulties and the significance of cultural taboos, and a tendency to use stereotypes in judging pupil competence and behaviour. The ethnocentrism of some of the young white children she observed is equally depressing. Heidi Mirza's research in south London secondary schools, reported in Chapter 5, studied older pupils, their ambitions and strategies for success. The children of immigrants who possess a strong belief in meritocracy and the value of credentials, these girls pursued educational achievement as a ladder to accessible occupations. Despite what was perceived to be low teacher expectations, they devised a 'strategy of resistance with accommodation', making use of the opportunities and working around difficulties, staying on, taking re-sits.

Gajendra Verma, in Chapter 4, takes up some of these issues in his more extensive review of ethnic relations in secondary schools, and concludes that generalization is difficult: 'The picture that emerged is complex and at times contradictory'. Inter-ethnic relations between pupils and between pupils and teachers, appropriate curricular provision, school policies on race relations, the incidence of prejudice and of racial abuse all appeared to vary. But while the apparent lack of progress in initial teacher education in preparing students for work in a plural society was a depressing finding, the often better ethnic relations in multi-ethnic (compared with bi-ethnic) schools is encouraging and would seem to bode well for the future.

Finally, William Taylor's account in Chapter 6 reminds us that providing an education to broaden the outlook of *majority* culture children and young people is as vital a policy objective for educationalists as providing a full and proper education for those from ethnic minorities, and this volume is devoted to both groups. Presenting a pluralist perspective by permeating the curriculum is not regarded as a high priority in monocultural schools, particularly with all the current changes; and Taylor confirms what other contributors have noted, namely that this will not be helped by the diminishing influence of the LEAs, the loss of in-service funding, and the decline of advisory services – although international pupil exchanges, and development education continue to attract interest and support.

FUTURE DIRECTIONS

The pursuit of a just society is an accepted principle for all people of goodwill, but conviction, rhetoric and commitment require the clothing of policy and implementation. In the light of the major changes in the educational systems of England and Wales, what future directions now seem appropriate for multiculturalism and for schools in an ethnically diverse society? First, in an open, democratic society, continued data collection and dissemination would seem to be essential. The researches reported in this collection illustrate the supreme value of *information* – not least because not all research findings are negative. Ethnic monitoring, for example, has revealed that young people of ethnic minority origin are now well represented in higher education and on a rising gradient (Taylor, 1992, 1993; Modood, 1993). Large-scale surveys produce quantified, generalizable findings, and hopefully funds will continue to be made available to enable us to track the pathways of opportunity and levels of awareness. But they will need to be complemented by the more personal detail provided by interview and ethnography, and these deeper case-studies will continue to be invaluable, always providing that the inherent problems of validity and reliability remain a central concern to researchers so that findings can be widely utilized.

Secondly, and allied to this, we will need an ongoing monitoring of the implementation of the National Curriculum, the decline of the LEAs and the operation of local school management as these affect cultural pluralism in British education. It will be important to have data from rural as well as urban regions, majority as well as minority pupils and parents, staff-room as well as classroom cultures. A structural change yet to come is the introduction of a national Teacher Training Agency in which a central feature will be the much greater involvement of schools in professional preparation. As William Taylor notes in Chapter 6, this could well mean a 'stifling' of teacher educators' current efforts in equal opportunities, at least in all-white schools.

And yet, the single most important conclusion of this volume might well be that the initial training of teachers is now becoming the *main* future avenue for cultural pluralism in education. In Anna King's review of the National Curriculum, it is clear that the educationally most enriching interpretation will depend on classroom pedagogy and the individual teacher's professional judgement. With the transfer of LEA responsibilities to schools, and the loss of LEA initiatives in multi-cultural education described by Monica Taylor, Carl Bagley and Barry Troyna, what teachers have acquired in their initial training may be their only professional resource. Progressive work in monocultural regions, as noted in Chapter 6, is already a function of an individual teacher's interest and skills; and where school governors are unrepresentative or, as Brehony found, diffident, it will again be for teachers to bring forward multicultural issues. Sensitivity to pupils' social/ethnic backgrounds, the skills to relate to parents and to minority pupils, and some competence in dealing with children's racial prejudice, all matters discussed by Vincent, Wright, Mirza and Verma, highlight a long-established concern by many teacher trainers. If such matters are not addressed in initial teacher training they are unlikely in future to be addressed anywhere. So the coming changes in teacher education are quite critical for the education of children and young people in our plural society.

If we are serious in our intent to prepare all young people for life, as equal citizens, in an ethnically diverse society, a combination of political will, expressed through local as well as central government policies, adequate resources, committed schools working with pupils and local communities, and appropriately trained teachers, will all continue to be the necessary conditions fo achieve this goal.

CHAPTER 2

The National Curriculum and Ethnic Relations

Anna King and Peter Mitchell

The introduction of a National Curriculum has fundamental relevance to educational provision for a plural society, and this chapter offers a critical analysis and commentary on its several main dimensions.

THE NATIONAL CURRICULUM AND ITS PURPOSES

In assessing the likely impact of the National Curriculum on ethnic relations, it seems sensible to turn to those educationalists who write on issues of justice and equality in education. Predictably, opinions differ. There are those who are sharply opposed to the whole venture as at present framed, and who characterize the National Curriculum as prescriptive and restrictive. They use words like ethnocentric, nationalistic, Eurocentric, Anglocentric, racist and racialist. Then there are those who claim to discern in the National Curriculum 'windows of opportunity' or 'hooks' upon which to insert good multicultural practice. Others insist that we have the responsibility to *make* the National Curriculum 'work for anti-racism and achievement for all and use every means to adapt it, modify it, exploit it and make it happen' (Eggleston, 1990, p. 11). On the other hand there are those, admittedly fewer in number, who take a much more positive view and who see within the National Curriculum a curriculum for the 1990s in which equal entitlement and a broad and balanced curriculum serve the goals of the future.

So, for example, Gill, Mayor and Blair (1992, p. vii) claim that: 'The Education Reform Act (1988) introduced a National Curriculum rooted in a prescriptive model of national culture, national history, and "the national interest".' Donald and Rattansi (1992) insist that 'one motive behind it [the National Curriculum] was a desire to reassert a largely fictitious national identity – the "imagined community" of nationhood that is supposed to transcend all inequalities, oppressions and exploitation' (p. 5). Hardy and Vieler-Porter (1990) go further and assert that, 'The

Education Reform Act aims to provide a "popular" education within an ideological framework which is individualist, competitive and racist' (p. 106). A Section 11 teacher complains that 'The intention is to pin us down to producing a pliant, technically competent work-force, and give neither us nor the students time and space to think, least of all about issues of justice and equality' (Piper, 1992, p. 8). Yet, if Ron Dearing is to be believed, most teachers now feel comfortable with the idea of the National Curriculum and are prepared to work within it. 'The concept of a National Curriculum has the broad support of the teaching profession' (Dearing, 1993a, p. 18). His explanation of its origin omits all references of an ideological nature. 'The National Curriculum and its assessment arrangements were introduced as the key initiative in the drive to raise standards.'

Reading the text

Post-modernists would see all these different readings of the National Curriculum documents as unsurprising. They would advise us that we are misguided to search for the truth amongst such varying assertions. Documents are capable of many readings and no one interpretation is correct. Derrida would even talk about the instability of meaning in any text. No doubt members of the various subject working parties would encourage us to read their documents as they thought they had designed them to be read, to consider their original intentions as the primary source of meaning and so become their 'model reader'. But the possibility of diverse readings would remain. The radical activist and the government minister or adviser in turn can try to persuade us that their own interpretations were the only ones to have integrity.

Before we roughly brush aside all interpretations but our own, we ought to remind ourselves of the difficulties post-modernists have shown us that are involved in reading any texts, and the National Curriculum and its attendant literature at the very least represents a massive 'text'. Whichever way we choose to read it, we are likely to select information which confirms our own preconceptions and prejudices, to ignore contrary data in order to find a pattern of meaning that most fits our own perspectives. Rorty (1992) urges us to forget the idea of discovering *What the Text is Really Like*, and instead to think of the various descriptions which we find it useful, for our various enterprises, to give. We should simply get on with using texts for our own purposes. If we follow him, the question then becomes changed from 'Does a plausible reading of the curriculum documents allow us to understand them as showing convinced commitment to combating racial inequality in education, and to the goal of a truly pluralistic society?' to 'How can teachers use them to celebrate diversity, promote equality and combat racism?'

This does not mean that any interpretation will do. As Umberto Eco (1992) insists, texts can be 'overinterpreted'. Readings cannot all carry the same weight. But it does follow that what we make of texts will depend very much on the set of values, presuppositions, world view, pragmatic purposes and interests and educational goals that we bring to their reading. This is vividly illustrated by the way that some right-wing MPs have complained that the 'educational establishment' have hi-jacked the present educational reforms. What is at stake here are competing readings of the texts constructed from different ideological and interest bases.

The National Curriculum cannot, however, be understood as a simple straightforward text. It has now become multi-layered, each new layer depending on a particular reading of what has gone before. So at the national level we have the 1988 Act of Parliament, itself shaped by previous legislative practice, followed by further Acts of Parliament, official reports, reviews and statutory orders, National Curriculum Council (NCC) non-statutory guidance and DES/DFE (Department of Education and Science/Department for Education) interpretative circulars. At the local and school level we have LEA and school policy documents, subject department plans and programmes of work, and even individual teachers' lesson notes and the pupils' own records of achievement, all shaped in turn not only by statutory programmes of study, attainment targets, and statements of attainment, but also by the impact of public forms of assessment, prospective league tables and the varied nature and often inequitable allocation of individual schools' teaching resources. And influencing all this are the varying ideological and social commitments of the many participants engaged in the planning and delivery of the National Curriculum, each with their own concerns and interests and exercising very different amounts of power and authority.

We have therefore a situation where certain readings are given priority by, for example, the weight of government administrative decisions, by the allocation of resources, by the relative decline in the authority and powers of LEAs, by the removal of advisory posts, and by changes in inspecting procedures. Possibilities that in theory remain open, in practice become closed; unfavoured avenues of educational change are blocked off. A good illustration of this can be seen in the treatment of religious education. In the 1988 Act, the content of religious education (RE) was for the first time the subject of direct legislation. New Agreed Syllabuses in the subject were to 'reflect the fact that the religious traditions in Great Britain are in the main Christian whilst taking account of the teaching and practices of the other principal religions represented in Great Britain' (Education Reform Act, 1988 Part 1, 8.3). Most practitioners in the field read this in a largely benign way (Hull, 1989; Mitchell, 1993). In spite of its triumphalist flavour no one could quarrel with the facts as stated, and for the first time the law recognized the obligation to teach pupils about the main religions of the world. The recent Circular on religious education, however, reads the Act in a very different way (DFE, 1994). The aim of the government is stated as intending to 'provide pupils with a thorough knowledge of Christianity reflecting the Christian heritage of this country' (para 7). 'The relative content devoted to Christianity in the syllabus should predominate' (para. 350). The question here is not merely the desirability or otherwise of such curriculum developments, although it does seem extraordinarily parochial; but the manner in which the Act is being read. There could many other ways 'to reflect the fact that the religious traditions in Great Britain are in the main Christian'. Ideological and political interests, however, mean that the Government want to point schools in their own direction, and the preferred and reinforced reading of the Act helps to ensure that this occurs.

The experiences of pupils

The most important questions of all – all too easily overlooked – concern the images, attitudes, values and understanding about themselves and their social world that pupils develop through their experiences at school. That is, in this context, how they come to interpret the National Curriculum and what influence it has on them. This will depend not only on the ways their various schools and teachers employ the documents, but also on what different pupils themselves bring to their educational experiences. Pupils are not *tabula rasa*. They are active, even if not always willing, participants in their education. It is what the pupils themselves gain from the National Curriculum that matters most. HMI and OFSTED (Office for Standards in Education) reports (HMI, 1992, 1993, OFSTED, 1993) suggest that since the advent of the National Curriculum standards of achievement have risen, especially in primary schools. Circumstantial and direct evidence reveal marked differences of academic outcomes, even between apparently similar schools (Smith and Tomlinson, 1989; Gillborn and Drew, 1992; Hammersley and Gomm, 1993). Unfortunately, there is as yet no firm empirical evidence to point to the impact of the National Curriculum upon different pupils' attitudes and values.

What is important to recognize is the very diverse nature of the school population. Unless deliberately countered, there is an inevitable tendency in a national curriculum with agreed programmes of study to homogenize pupils, to minimize differences except in terms of predetermined goals and achievements, and to look for agreed outcomes. Yet our pupils come from an ethnically and culturally diverse population, with some majority groups in positions of power and dominance and others experiencing to a lesser or greater extent inequalities and discrimination. It would therefore be very easy for pupils from the majority groups to experience a curriculum that reinforces and celebrates the values, attitudes and goals espoused at home; whilst others, given the same programmes of study, could be made to feel disenfranchised, with their own home cultures belittled or marginalized and their own identities underlined as second-class citizens. And this consequence would be detrimental to the education of the majority groups as well, for it would subtly reinforce those damaging stereotypes of illicit superiority and cultural hegemony which are so destructive of cultural and ethnic harmony based on mutual respect and justice.

HOW COULD THE NATIONAL CURRICULUM HELP FOSTER GOOD ETHNIC RELATIONS?

Is it possible to avoid such dangers? Does our own National Curriculum succeed in doing so? First, it has to be recognized that no national curriculum, even when well-devised and implemented, can by itself ensure the growth of positive and fruitful relationships between the various ethnic groups that go to make up our diverse and pluralist society. This ought not to lead us to underestimate the importance of the National Curriculum. Through its selection of materials and the consequent allocation of time given to its component parts, a compulsory national curriculum must inevitably shape pupils' perceptions of the adult world and have a sometimes decisive influence on their entry into it. And what it omits or ignores will be as important as what it includes. Its silences will speak as loudly as its words. We can, therefore, legitimately ask of the National Curriculum whether its present or potential use is likely to help:

- *Ensure for all pupils whatever their ethnic origin an 'equal entitlement'?*
  This is a foundation for all that follows. By it is meant not merely a legal right to a certain curriculum content. It also implies that forms of assessment, access to materials and methods of teaching ought not to disadvantage pupils because they come from minority groups. Does our present National Curriculum, however conceived, embody in its structures and means of delivery principles of social and educational justice? Does its use offer all pupils, without ethnic or cultural bias, the opportunity to develop their own intellectual and creative potential to the full?

- *Provide pupils with a sufficiently wide world perspective?*
  Will the experience of working within a timetable dominated by the National Curriculum sufficiently enlarge the intellectual, emotional and imaginative horizons of all pupils, so as to help them appreciate the wide range of human diversity and the cultural and intellectual achievements of humankind? And, as well as our sharp and considerable differences, will it enable pupils to understand our mutual interdependence as individuals and as interlocking economic, social and cultural groups, often sharing in different guises some, though not all, of the same norms and life goals?

- *Strengthen pupils' cultural and social identities?*
  This is not easy to delineate. The opposite would be a curriculum that was an instrument of alienation, where pupils did not feel at home, and where their own cultural and social background was depreciated, belittled or ignored. A difficult balance has to be achieved. School studies have to give all pupils a justifiable sense of pride in their own cultural heritage, yet at the same time avoid encouraging in them a closed outlook, insensitive to the dynamic and changing nature of living cultures and contemptuous of the lives and achievements of others. Achieving pupil ownership therefore becomes a pressing imperative for curriculum planners. Pupils have to be convinced that school work is part of their own story and recognizably connected to their own life goals.

- *Increase pupils' powers of critical appraisal?*
  Paul Hirst sharply distinguishes between an education that merely confirms and reinforces the traditions and practices of the past, and one that gives pupils the skills and encouragement to think for themselves, to use evidence and reason to appraise the judgements of others, and to become active agents of their own learning (Hirst,

1985; Pring, 1992)). This is much more than the replacement of what is irrational with what is rational. It involves 'providing them [pupils] with alternative explanatory frameworks' (Troyna, 1993) that are richer, more powerful and more just than those they are intended to replace. Only when the power of past stereotypes is broken and ignorance of past and present oppressions is removed, are pupils likely to progress towards a reciprocal appreciation of each other.

- *Encourage pupils' development as active and responsible citizens in the area of social and cultural relations?*
  Good ethnic relations, whether between individuals or the groups that go to make up our community as a whole, can only be the outcome of positive action. Co-operative and enriching relationships mean much more than the passive acquiescence in each other's existence. And mutual respect and understanding are unlikely to grow where there are unequal and exploitative power relationships. Whilst it would be an illegitimate distortion of the purposes of a curriculum to try to turn it into a vehicle for direct social action by pupils, it ought nevertheless to furnish them with the skills, knowledge and incentives that will enable them at an appropriate time to engage in it. One test, therefore, of the National Curriculum is 'Will its study help foster active and responsible citizenship in the area of ethnic relations?' This goes beyond the giving of information about and practice in the skills of democracy and the mutual recognition of the rights of all to equal and fair treatment. It also requires a curriculum that gives sufficient weight to the exploration of values, that offers insight into the intricacies of corporate action, that does not avoid the study of those felt injustices which can mar our social life, and that encourages a sense of personal and communal responsibility.

ENSURING 'EQUAL ENTITLEMENT'

Ostensibly, as the 1988 Education Act's preamble clearly shows, it has as one of its guiding principles equal opportunities for all. 'The curriculum of a school satisfies the requirement of the Act if it is a balanced and broadly-based curriculum which:

(a) promotes the spiritual, moral, cultural, mental and physical development of pupils at the school and of society; and
(b) prepares such pupils for the opportunities, responsibilities and experiences of adult life.'

Ensuing DES and DFE circulars and guidance documents read this positively as establishing in law the principle that each pupil should have a broad and balanced curriculum which is also relevant to his or her particular needs. They insist that this principle be reflected in the curriculum of every pupil. Moreover, it is not enough for such a curriculum to be offered by the school: if it is to be successful 'it must be fully taken up by each individual pupil' (DES, 1989). This is a theme reiterated in the White Paper *Choice and Diversity: a new framework for schools* (DFE, 1992). 'It is the responsibility of the government and the education service to provide pupils everywhere with the same opportunities.'

This, then, was the overwhelmingly strong educational argument for the National Curriculum – that, in principle, it was inclusive and common to all. Central to the Act were issues of entitlement, of breadth and balance, applicability and coherence. Continuity and progression were to be emphasized, together with the need for positive assessment and parental choice. Ideally, it was to be a curriculum that was transparent. LEAs, governors, teachers, parents and pupils were to be given the kind of detailed curriculum information and guidance that was inaccessible and indeed unachievable before.

Undoubtedly, this represented an advance on what had gone before. Often pupils (particularly black students and those from ethnic minority communities) had widely differing curricular experiences. In primary schools there was often inadequate coverage of subjects such as science, history and geography; and option schemes in secondary schools led to a lack of breadth and balance for many pupils in the 14 to 16 age group (Hargreaves, 1991). The advent of the National Curriculum was intended to ensure that students were no longer able to drop important subjects. Schools could not easily channel those they perceived to be less able towards a primarily non-academic, practical curriculum, an important safeguard for some ethnic minority pupils. This has obvious implications for issues of equality for all pupils. Indeed, a national curriculum not only has the potential to create an entitlement to learning, it could also provide 'the yardstick against which educational inequality can be judged and remedied' (Moon and Mortimore, 1989, p. 7).

In practice this great breadth of curriculum and its complex assessment procedures have been found to be unmanageable. The concept of entitlement was first sacrificed to flexibility and wider choice at Key Stage 4. Against the advice of the National Curriculum Council which wished all ten subjects of the National Curriculum to remain compulsory until 16, only mathematics, English and science remain sacrosanct. The future shape of the curriculum for pupils aged 14 to 16 still remains unclear. This process of attenuation continues. Confronted with the 'flabby Goliath' created by the 1988 Education Act (*The Times*, 3 August 1993), Sir Ron Dearing advised a slimming of both curriculum and national testing. This is intended to oblige schools to teach and test basic skills, but leave them more time to develop subject specializations. The result, it is hoped, will be a better balance of local diversity and nationally approved standards (Dearing, 1994). The intention of these proposals is to reduce the statutory demands of the National Curriculum and to make it less prescriptive, so that it does not occupy almost the entire school timetable. The original subjects – English, mathematics, science, history, geography, art, music, PE, technology, modern language (from 11) and Welsh (in Welsh-speaking schools), will remain compulsory from 5 to 14 as will RE. However, the required content of all but English, mathematics and science will be cut sharply. The effect will be to adopt a two-tier curriculum and testing system concentrating on the basics of English, mathematics and science. From the point of view of teachers, these proposals meet a real need by reducing the time given to the National Curriculum. However, the emphasis on a core curriculum and on the essentials of foundation subjects brings the danger that the curriculum will become even more traditional and safe. That is, unless schools and teachers can be persuaded to use these promised reductions in the compulsory curriculum to pursue multicultural and anti-racist goals. Significantly, the final Dearing report makes no mention of multicultural education at all (Dearing 1994).

The failure to provide guidance
Providing for a commonality of experience through statutory programmes of study and shared forms of assessment is of course one way by which the use of the National Curriculum could help to secure equal entitlement for all pupils. However, this projected commonality of experience has to be enjoyed by an incredibly diverse school population. But, in spite of an avalanche of non-statutory guidance, circulars, handbooks, pamphlets and directives on numerous curriculum matters, no direct and detailed official guidance has yet been issued on *multicultural education*. Even though this was prepared, it was never published. Instead, teachers find references to cultural diversity and educational provision limited to incidental phrases and sections scattered in an almost random way in government and agency publications. This

was no accident. It was the consequence of policy decisions by the highest echelons of the NCC (Tomlinson, 1993), and has inevitably been seen as signalling to teachers the relative unimportance of racial equality and justice in education (Runnymede Trust, 1993, p. 69). Once again, we can see attempts being made to encourage teachers, this time through an engineered silence, to 'read' the National Curriculum in traditionalist ways.

Fortunately, as the Runnymede Trust's own handbook, *Equality Assurance in Schools* (1993) clearly demonstrates, this not an inevitable or even obvious way of approaching the National Curriculum. By carefully analysing government pronouncements and legally binding requirements, and by offering evaluative criteria and examples of good practice for each of the subjects of the National Curriculum, it shows how schools can fulfil their statutory obligations and also provide a just and equitable education for all children growing up in our culturally diverse society. However, it has to be pointed that the 1992–93 Report of HM Chief Inspector of Schools (OFSTED, 1993) indicates that many schools are still failing to provide for the diverse needs of pupils from ethnic minorities. 'Minority ethnic pupils were often insufficiently extended and challenged. In general they were under-represented in top ability sets' (p. 18). The rhetoric of equal entitlement is still far from becoming a reality in too many pupils' lives. All too often many ethnic minority pupils are still deprived of that right.

PROVIDING ALL PUPILS WITH A WIDER WORLD PERSPECTIVE
One of the acknowledged purposes of the National Curriculum continues in official documents to be stated as 'extending pupils' knowledge and understanding of different cultures, languages and faiths' (NCC, 1992). Yet Verma claims that, in practice, 'The dominant culture and ethos which the National Curriculum reflects are those of the white middle class Anglo-Saxon. It excludes the significant input from the so-called Third-World countries. It contains a Eurocentric concept of a static Anglo-Saxon culture which no longer exists. It ignores the contributions by non-western civilisations to literature, maths, science, technology, history, music, geography and art, that have helped to shape today's world' (Verma, 1993, p. 20).

A sweeping statement such as this is obviously as much a rallying cry as a balanced judgement. If correct, it would be a damning indictment of the National Curriculum. To ascertain its truth would require a detailed examination of the many documents that now go to make up the National Curriculum (cf. King and Reiss, 1993; Pumphrey and Verma, 1993). The original working groups drawing up the National Curriculum documentation were asked to address government policy: that ethnic minority pupils should have the same opportunity as all others to profit from what schools can offer, and that schools should preserve and transmit values in a way which accepts Britain's ethnic diversity and promotes tolerance. Some of the members of these groups took this remit very seriously (Semple, 1993, p. 163). For other groups, issues of cultural diversity and the establishment of multicultural education seemed much less relevant. The resulting programmes of study and statements of attainment reflect these divergences. Because of the piecemeal planning inevitable in a curriculum based on sharply separated subjects introduced at different times and reflecting diverse academic traditions, an overall coherent policy was almost impossible to achieve. Even the composition of the different subject groups could have a decisive influence on the final documents (Cox, 1991; Adams, 1993). Matters were made worse by ministerial interventions and amendments to the final statutory orders, almost all of which accentuated a monocultural and traditionalist approach.

Nevertheless, there are places in the National Curriculum literature where achieving a wider global perspective is actively encouraged. For example, a brief article in the NCC *Newsletter* of February 1991 outlines NCC thinking in this area more clearly than almost any other document. Significantly, it is one of the few documents which draw on the previously mentioned unpublished deliverances of the NCC Multicultural Working Party. It stresses that multicultural education is concerned with more than the needs of pupils from ethnic minority backgrounds. 'It seeks to prepare all pupils for life in a world where they will meet, live and work with people of different cultures, religions, languages and ethnic origins.' The article also maintains that the National Curriculum 'contributes to multicultural education by broadening the horizons of all pupils so that they can understand and contribute to a pluralist society' (NCC, 1991, p. 3).

The evidence in support of this that can be gleaned from the National Curriculum Statutory Orders and their accompanying non-statutory guidance is, to say the least, ambiguous. In, for example, geography at Key Stage 2, students have to study in detail a locality in an economically developing country. In Key Stage 3 students are required to undertake a further such study, this time at a national scale. Key Stage 4 involves students in studying the causes of uneven economic development, as well as the causes and geographical consequences of the distribution of ethnic, religious or linguistic groups in particular areas. Ostensibly, such study ought progressively to broaden the horizons of pupils by helping them to appreciate how others live. But this brings us to the heart of one of the fundamental controversies surrounding this aspect of education. On the one side, it can be argued that this apparent stress on the economic aspects of life is a way of minimizing the importance of cultural diversity, and so of avoiding the challenge of different value systems. Even more detrimentally, if the economic perspectives being employed in such study are to a large extent shaped by Western conceptions of life, it can lead to a serious underestimation of the actual achievements of the culture being studied. Horizons can be enlarged without their essentially parochial nature being challenged. Yet, on the other hand, as Gill and others have pointed out when discussing the teaching of geography, 'A focus on cultural pluralism may divert attention from issues of economic inequality and power' (Gill, 1993, p. 148). Obviously, though difficult, it is not impossible to achieve a balance between these two themes. Their treatments are not necessarily as incompatible as is sometimes supposed (Rattansi, 1993; Fyfe, 1993; cf Troyna, 1993). Much depends, as always, on the detailed way geographical topics are approached in the classroom. As Walford has strongly argued, 'The critical factor in exploiting their possibilities will be the pedagogy used in the classroom' (Walford, 1993, p. 105).

In spite of an often-present bias towards Western culture, music, art, foreign languages and physical education and dance all offer opportunities to widen the cultural perspectives of pupils (King and Reiss, 1993). A much more pessimistic judgement has to be made about mathematics, one of the core subjects, scarcely reduced by the recent pruning of the National Curriculum. Alan Bishop (1993) asserts that from a cultural perspective, the current national mathematics curriculum is a disaster. He points out that some mathematicians and mathematics teachers still firmly believe that mathematics has *nothing* to do with society, and that mathematics education *should* have nothing to do with societal issues. The report of the working group reflects such views:

Many of those who argue for a multicultural approach to the mathematics curriculum do so on the basis that such an approach is necessary to raise the self-esteem of ethnic minority cultures and to improve mutual understanding and respect between races. We believe that this attitude is misconceived and patronising.

The kind of criticism Bishop and others have levied at the mathematics national curriculum is that pupils are not shown that mathematics is the product of many cultures. Little or no attention is given to people, and the few mathematicians mentioned by name are Europeans. It treats mathematics as value neutral, and its aesthetic aspects are largely unnoticed. The emphasis is entirely on conceptual understanding, algorithmic performance and problem-solving processes. According to Bishop, affective and attitudinal aspects are ignored, and the aesthetic appeal of, for example, geometrical design is never mentioned. Motivationally, there is no appeal to imagination, feeling, stimulating interest, fascination, awe or wonder. The mathematics curriculum is culturally cold, barren and dead. There is no attention given to issues in society. Society is an unproblematic context to be drawn on as a source for examples on which to practise benign mathematical procedures. Such a minimalist approach fails to convey the power of mathematics to reveal inequalities, differences, discriminations and orders in society which ought to be addressed. Yet Bishop is able to give examples of how teachers have been able, whilst working within the National Curriculum, to introduce different cultural ideas into the classroom, to humanize the process of doing and inventing mathematics, and to focus on the issues of the pluralistic society.

Similarly confused messages can be found in the regulations and guidance governing science. During the 1980s it was increasingly recognized that science education in schools was frequently narrow, male and Western in character, and efforts, often local in nature, were made to remedy this (Ditchfield, 1987). Yet as Reiss (1993a) points out, 'The story of science in the National Curriculum has been one of a successive diminution of the centrality of multicultural and anti-racist science in official publications' (p. 68). So, for example, the reduction in the number of attainment targets from 17 to 4 in 1991 led to the disappearance of Attainment Target 17 on 'The Nature of Science' which many had seen as a powerful vehicle for multicultural and science teaching (Watts, 1993). Nevertheless, there are numerous places where programmes of study in science can be explored in ways that will expand pupils' horizons beyond that of a monocultural white, male, Western-dominated understanding of the subject (Reiss, 1993b). Everything will depend on the ability and enthusiasm of teachers to exploit such opportunities. It is for this reason that the public forms of assessment now being devised will be of crucial importance. For if, as seems likely, teaching becomes increasingly assessment driven, the nature and scope of the latter will have a decisive effect on the way subjects are approached in the classroom. Once more, a particular reading of the National Curriculum will be forced on teachers. The parameters of pupils' horizons will be substantially set by the cultural assumptions embodied in the modes of assessment.

STRENGTHENING PUPILS' CULTURAL AND SOCIAL IDENTITIES

Will the experience of being educated largely through the National Curriculum help to develop individual pupils' sense of cultural and social identity in a way that also makes them sensitive and appreciative of others? The 1988 Act certainly includes amongst its main aims the cultural and social development of pupils. But increasingly this seems to be interpreted in a narrow way. The development and revision of English as a core subject clearly illustrates this tendency. The original orders and non-statutory guidance were less prescriptive than for many other subjects. Admittedly, there were defects. Insufficient attention was given to the needs of pupils whose home language was not English (Savva, 1990). Nevertheless, teachers could use the essentially permissive Statements of Attainment in ways that responded to the diverse needs of their pupils. Indeed, they felt encouraged to use texts from a wide range of cultures (Marland, 1993). Yet the publications which followed indicated that the Government's intentions were not so liberally inclined. The literature anthology on which assessment was to be based showed a distinct narrowing of the field to largely Anglo-Saxon texts. This tendency has continued to characterize the consequent planned revisions of the orders. So, for example, the new draft English National Curriculum Orders insist on a more rigid enforcement of spoken standard English, something which is likely to undermine students' confidence in their home language when this is not standard English (Parrinder, 1993). Indeed, Foster goes so far as to claim that 'The draft orders appear to be part of a government attempt to reassert a narrowly English national identity through the National Curriculum' (Foster, 1993).

A similar critique can be made about history, a subject in the national

Curriculum which has aroused some of the fiercest controversies and the widest debate (Booth, 1993; Figueroa, 1993; Fines, 1993). It is not hard to see why. Our understanding of the past is at the heart of our understanding of our personal and national identity. It is not surprising, therefore, given our present political situation, that British history remains the core of the curriculum, though there are at various points some supplementary units provided where the history of a non-European society can be studied. The fact that history can now be given up at the end of Stage 3 also puts a great deal of further pressure on the construction of the history curriculum. But though the curriculum as it is now framed has as its core British history, the situation is ameliorated by the way the syllabus is framed. The three Attainment Targets as at present constituted, 'knowledge and understanding of history', 'interpretations of history' and especially 'the use of historical sources', emphasize the importance of methodology. They encapsulate an approach which ought to enable pupils to come to terms with the essentially contestable and debatable nature of historical knowledge, that it is never neutral, but is always a story told from a particular point of view (cf. Kernaghan, 1993).

The question can be put in a multicultural context as, 'Whose history?' and 'whose past?' How are we to relate National Curriculum history to pupils who come to schools from diverse backgrounds? In what sense does a British Gujarati Hindu pupil feel the present curriculum is her story? Do we stress the continuing development of a society within the British Isles, or do we take the diversity of the inhabitants in terms of ethnicity, gender, class, origin, as a starting point for plural histories? Unfortunately, the proposed assessment procedures based on short, sharp national tests (SEAC, 1992), with an emphasis on the mastery of historical knowledge, seem likely to vitiate any such discussion. In spite of recent research evidence which points to the inadequacy of this approach to assessment (Booth and Husbands, 1993), it will once again encourage teaching to become assessment driven, and primarily concerned with outcomes rather than those processes and input which are essential if the strengthening and development of cultural and social identity is to be one of goals of studying history. A recent example shows just how invasive of values, assessment procedures can be. It is taken from the national reading and spelling test set in 1992 for Key Stage 1 (DES, 1992). The pupils' spelling test booklet that, at the beginning of the test, all children must have unopened in front of them, had on it a full page picture of a mixed bathing scene with adults as well as children present. The message given to many of the young Muslim pupils taking the test must have been one of alienation or perplexity, since here was something contrary to the moral and religious teaching of many Muslim homes, yet presented to them with all the weight of an official test. Similar serious insensitivities have occurred in GCSE questions (Mathematical Association, 1992; Richardson, 1993).

INCREASING PUPILS' POWERS OF CRITICAL APPRAISAL

Undoubtedly, one of the marks of a successful education is its power to help pupils to think for themselves. We have already seen that, in spite of brave beginnings, the National Curriculum has in too many cases been increasingly directed towards the achievement of ideological ends. This need not stop education provided under its umbrella from being open and critical. Even the obstacles to this presented by over-prescriptive assessment procedures can sometimes be circumvented by enlightened teaching. But a subject-based National Curriculum with a built-in hierarchy which elevates some subjects and by exclusion marginalizes others, inevitably lays down parameters within which such thinking is to be encouraged. From the start, competence in language, numeracy and scientific method was given priority within the structures of the National Curriculum. Critics saw this as a powerful form of indirect indoctrination.

> Indoctrination is basically to do with preventing reflection. Directly inculcating doctrines is only one way of doing this . . . A most powerful way of indoctrinating pupils is by so organising their studies that certain kinds of reflection – about political matters, for instance – are off the agenda. (White, 1988, p. 121)

It is this element that has caused most alarm to supporters of multi-cultural and anti-racist education. Unless pupils are given sufficient and appropriate opportunities to reflect critically about the multifaceted causes of racism and about ethnic and cultural relationships, their thinking in such areas will become attenuated, and their ability to make informed judgements about such matters lessened. Even if we accept Halstead's (1992) view that 'racism is at root a moral issue' and that 'any attempt to eradicate it through education belongs to the domain of moral education rather than political education' (p. 44), we are still pointing to one of the weaknesses rather than strengths of the National Curriculum.

The development of critical thinking poses further problems for those concerned with the fostering of good ethnic relations. One aspect of the National Curriculum that causes concern to many leaders of ethnic minority communities in this country is what they see as the tacit assumption of Western secular values embedded in it (Ashraf, 1988; Islamic Academy, 1991; Mabud, 1992). For them, the critical thinking so prized by educationalists too easily degenerates into sceptical relativism; an apparently innocuous cognitive process leading to an unacceptable ideological stance. This clash of value systems is not easily resolved (Halstead, 1988; 1992) and there seems little doubt that the National Curriculum as at present constituted is likely to accentuate rather than lessen the gulf between them.

ENCOURAGING PUPILS' DEVELOPMENT AS ACTIVE AND RESPONSIBLE CITIZENS IN THE AREA OF SOCIAL AND CULTURAL RELATIONS

It is here that the paradoxical nature of so much of the National Curriculum becomes most apparent. As was mentioned earlier, the 1988 Education Act clearly states that one of its educational objectives is to prepare pupils for 'the opportunities, responsibilities and experiences of adult life'. 'Education for Citizenship' was chosen by the NCC as one of five cross-curricular themes. The NCC *Curriculum Guidance on Education for Citizenship* (1990) also accepted that such an education would help increase 'awareness of and work towards resolving some of the tensions and conflicts that occur between groups which perceive each other to be socially, racially, ethnically or culturally different' (p. 6). The problems arise once we ask how this is to be achieved. Even the advice given at Stage 4 seems to emphasize the passive role of citizens learning how the system works (Webster and Adelman, 1993). The emphasis seems very much on maintaining the status quo. Once again, the lack of any sustained attention to subjects such as social studies reveals the paucity of what is likely to be achieved in this area, given the immense pressures under which schools are now labouring to excel in the core subjects.

CONCLUSION

We began with the idea of different readings of the National Curriculum. Politicians and educationalists alike read the National Curriculum according to their own ideologies. We have argued that in crucial respects, and in spite of fair words of overall policy, the National Curriculum in its detailed unfolding has involved too many concessions to a narrow interpretation of our cultural heritage and what it means to be a British citizen. And these failings have been reinforced by assessment procedures frequently driven by utilitarian considerations and market forces. This is not to deny that there are many places where enterprising teachers are using the National curriculum to help pupils explore the riches and deficiencies of our complex social world, and to increase the life-chances of all their pupils. Yet there is a fundamental difference between what is mandatory and obligatory and what is permissive and optional.

It would be misleading to end on such a pessimistic note. It is too easy to neglect or ignore the exemplary work being in done say, in Year 1 in a village school in Hampshire, in favour of the larger picture, and so miss the living reality of children whose imaginations at the end of the twentieth century are being nourished with the art, literature and poetry of the world. It is important, therefore,not to accept as inevitable a 'given' traditionalist monocultural reading of the various texts involved in our present curriculum constructions, and to recognize that they necessarily remain open for much more progressive interpretations. The aim is not to replace one 'given' reading with another more politically correct 'given' reading. A more democratic objective is to provide space for a diversity of readings so that teachers and pupils alike can come to appreciate other and richer ways of seeing their social world and their potential roles in it. A curriculum so used would be both enlightening and empowering; a powerful instrument in our battle to create a more just and equal society for all our citizens.

CHAPTER 3

Ethnic Relations in the Primary Classroom

Cecile Wright

The perceptions of Asian and Afro-Caribbean nursery/infant and middle school children held by their white teachers and classmates, are considered in this ethnographic study of multi-ethnic classrooms.

INTRODUCTION

The last two decades have witnessed a great deal of both academic and popular interest in questions concerning the academic achievement of children from a variety of ethnic minority groups within the British educational system. Although parental aspirations and support for their children have always been high (e.g. Tomlinson, 1984; Brah and Minhas, 1988), over the years the enormous amount of literature in this area points to an apparently poor performance of black[1] pupils (especially those of Afro-Caribbean origin) at all levels of their school career.

Current patterns of performance are extremely difficult to discern, although the indications are that many ethnic minority children continue to under-perform. Nuttall and Goldstein (1990), for instance, in their analysis of 1990 GCSE examination results from six London Boroughs (based on a cohort of 5,500 pupils), found that Asian children's performance was as good as that of white children, and both achieved higher than pupils of Afro-Caribbean origin. Massey (1991), however, points to evidence that Asian children achieve at the same level as whites only because they stay in education longer; and she also noted that some Asians, notably Bangladeshis, performed well below all other groups.

Over the last twenty years, there have also been questions concerning the reasons for the poor educational achievement of black pupils and the means by which this situation can be remedied. During the 1970s and 1980s a range of explanations were advanced regarding black children's under-performance, but the most influential by far was the culturalist argument. Essentially, this viewpoint raised questions concerning the educability of black pupils. It saw black pupils' educational achievement in terms of 'cultural deficit'. That is to say, that black pupils' adaptation to school was considered to be hindered by features in their own culture (e.g. Driver, 1977; Banks and Lynch, 1986).

The late 1980s and the 1990s saw a shift in the research agenda and a move away from seeing black pupils as the problem within the education system, to concerns with the process of schooling itself and the practices which place black children at a disadvantage within the education system. In this respect, there is now a small but growing number of detailed ethnographic studies concerned specifically with the analysis of black children's experience of schooling (Fuller, 1980; Carrington, 1983; Furlong, 1984; Green, 1985; Wright, 1987; Foster, 1990) which inevitably brings into focus the breadth and diversity both of their school experience (as mediated via their ethnic origin, gender and to a less extent social class), and their response to this experience (e.g. Mac an Ghaill, 1988; 1992; Gillborn, 1990). These important ethnographies have helped produce a clearer picture of the processes and structures which disadvantage black children within the education system. Leaman and Carrington (1985), for instance, point to the ways in which black children are channelled from the academic curriculum into a sports one. Fuller (1980) and Wright (1987) indicate that black pupils are not achieving their full academic potential because of teachers' racism, low expectations, institutional practice and procedure, and so on.

Inevitably within such a relatively new research area, there is much work to be done, for example, in relation to black children's primary schooling, where there is a noticeable lack of research. Although a few studies have examined specific aspects of this area, such as teaching styles in multiracial classrooms (Green, 1985), racist incidents between children (Troyna and Hatcher, 1992), and multicultural policy initiatives (Grugeon and Woods, 1990; Carrington and Short, 1989), there would appear to be relatively little by way of substantive studies of black children's experiences within the primary school setting. This chapter seeks to address the latter. The central focus will be on relationships within the classroom. Of particular interest is an examination of the process and practices which combine to disadvantage black children within the classroom setting.

The data on black children's day-to-day classroom experiences reported below form part of a much broader ethnographic study of four multi-ethnic, urban primary schools, in one Local Education

Authority, where I spent two full academic years (1988–90) focusing on black children's all-round school experience.[2]

The four schools were: Adelle School, Bridgeway School, Castle School and Dewry School.[3] The first three schools are nursery/infant schools for 3–8-year-olds. The latter is a middle school for 8–13-year-olds. At these schools, 970 pupils and 57 staff were observed in the classroom. The observations involved classroom settings and non-classroom settings in the schools. Almost all staff and pupils who were observed were formally and informally interviewed. A number of sets of parents were also interviewed. The application of an ethnographic methodology, with its emphasis on intensive observation and interviews is able to capture sensitively the school experience in its entirety.

TEACHER–PUPIL RELATIONS

British primary education is generally assumed to be rooted in a child-centred ideology (Alexander, 1984). The quality of interpersonal relationships and experiences offered to the child at the school level is fundamental to such an approach. Regardless of whether the primary ideology is as widespread as claimed, the first impression of the schools in the study was that a pleasant atmosphere and a constructive relationship existed between teachers and children. There was an emphasis on providing caring support and a friendly and encouraging environment for all children. This approach was also reflected in the schools' pedagogy. There was a degree of sensitivity to the needs of the different groups of children as shown by some use of multicultural material and images. The vast majority of the staff (e.g. teachers and support staff in the classroom) seemed genuinely committed to ideals of equality of educational opportunity.

However, classroom observation revealed subtle differences in the way white teachers treated black children. Differences in teachers' treatment of these children were observed both within the nursery and junior classrooms. In the nursery units,[4] children came together as a group each day for 'story time' and (English) language work. Through effective discussion and questioning, the teacher encouraged the children to extend their spoken English, through talking about stories, songs, objects and so on. In these formal sessions, the Asian children were generally observed to be excluded from the discussions, on the assumption that they could not understand or speak English. On the occasions when the Asian children were encouraged to participate in a group discussion, teachers often communicated with them using basic telegraphic language. When this strategy failed to get any response, the teachers would quickly lose patience with the children and would then ignore them. This was also the observation of the black nursery nurses working in the nursery units, as the following comment from Bridgway School reveals:

> They [white teachers] have got this way of talking to them [Asian children] in a really simple way . . . cutting half the sentences, 'Me no do that' sort of thing . . . and that is not standard English. And they've [teachers] got this way of saying words 'That naughty' and they miss words out and it really does seem stupid. . . . I feel that it's not my place to say 'Well that's a silly way to speak to children'. I worry about what it tells the white children who think that Asian children are odd anyway.

Teachers often expressed open irritation or frustration when they believed that the Asian children's poor English language skills interfered with their teaching. The scenario below illustrates experiences common to the schools observed.

In a classroom in Adelle School, 5–6-year-olds are working on a number of activities. The class teacher calls children out individually to listen to them read. She asks an Asian girl, recently arrived from Pakistan and in the school for less than a term to come to her desk.

TEACHER: *(to Asian girl)* Right, let's see what you can do. *(Teacher opens book, pointing to a picture.)* This is a flower, say flower.
Rehana nods nervously, appears a little confused.
TEACHER: This is a flower. After me, FLOWER.
Pupil doesn't respond.
TEACHER: *(Calls for assistance from one of the Asian pupils.)* Zareeda, would you come here a minute. *(Zareeda walks over to the teacher's desk.)* What is the Urdu word for 'flower'? *(Zareeda fidgets nervously.)* Tell her in Urdu that this is a flower.
Zareeda looks very embarrassed, refuses to speak. A few children gather around the teacher's desk. Zareeda hides her face from the children who have gathered around the teacher's desk.
TEACHER: Come on Zareeda, what is the Urdu word?
Zareeda refuses to co-operate with the teacher, stands at the teacher's desk with head lowered, looking quite distraught.

TEACHER: Zareeda, if you're embarrassed, whisper the word to me.
Zareeda does not respond.
TEACHER: *(Visibly irritated)* Well, Zareeda, you're supposed to be helping, that's not the attitude in this school, we help our friends. You're supposed to be helping me teach Rehana English. . . . *(To the Asian girls)* Go and sit down, both of you . . . I'll go next door and see if one of those other Asian children can help me. *(Teacher leaves the room.)*
The incident has attracted the attention of the whole class. Whilst the teacher is interacting with the Asian girls, the white children are overheard making despairing remarks about 'Pakis'.

In the classroom, many of the Asian children displayed a quiet and controlled demeanour; in comparison with other children they appeared subdued. There was a sense in which the Asian girls seemed invisible to the teachers. They were rarely invited to answer questions and take a lead in activities in the classroom. Interestingly for children of this age group, greater classroom co-operation was observed between Asian boys and girls than was the case for other pupil groups. In the classroom, these children operated as a closed group. Initially, such a reaction to their classroom experience was in itself perceived to be a problem by some teachers, as reflected in this comment from a teacher at Bridgeway School:

> The Asian children tend to be self-isolating. I have to deliberately separate that group. They tend to ignore all other children – are not too happy sitting next to anybody else and see themselves as their own little group. Now they tend to converse in their own language. I'm afraid I have to say, 'Now come on, stop.'

When asked to explain why Asian children conversing in their mother tongue in the classroom was a concern, she pointed out:

> Because I don't know what is being said. It could be something against one of the other children in the class. I mean, I've no idea what is going on. Often one [Asian child] will come up to me and say 'Miss he's swearing', that kind of thing. They always tell on each other of course. But no, I don't encourage that, at least not in the normal classroom situation. They [Asian children] do go as a special group to Mrs Reeves [English as a second language support teacher] and she does special stories in Urdu with them.

Among the negative responses to Asian children expressed by teachers was also open disapproval of the customs and traditions, often considered to pose problems for classroom management. Such disapproval added to the negative experiences of school for some of these children, precisely because of the contradictory expectations of home and school. Preparing for physical education lessons, for example, posed some difficulties for the Asian girls because pupils were required, particularly at the nursery school, to undress in the classroom. The girls employed a number of creative measures to acquire some privacy, such as hiding behind chairs or under desks. The teachers often showed total disregard for the feelings of these children, openly disapproving of what they considered was over-sensitive, modest behaviour on the part of the Asian girls. At the end of the PE lesson the Asian girls were the recipients of teachers' sarcasm – 'Well, don't you wish you were all as quick getting undressed?'

The anguish experienced by the Asian girls was expressed by these 7-and 8-year-olds at Adelle School:

PARVIN:	We don't like PE. I get a headache when we do PE.
RASHIDA:	I don't like it because we are not allowed to do it.
CW:	Why?
PARVIN:	Because it's like my mum and dad said, her mum and dad, if you do PE you get Gonah.[5]
RASHIDA:	We go to mosque and if you do PE and you just go to mosque like that, you get smacked from that lady. That's why we don't like to do PE. We don't want trouble from God for doing PE.
PARVIN:	Because we don't allow other people to see our pants, so we hide behind the table when we get changed for PE.
CW:	What does the teacher say when you hide behind the table?
PARVIN:	Sometimes she shouts.
CW:	Have you told the teacher about your feelings?
PARVIN & RASHIDA:	No, no.
CW:	Why?
RASHIDA:	Because we're scared.
PARVIN:	Because we don't like to, she would shout.

The girls are expressing a fundamental conflict between the perceived expectations of their background and the requirements of the school. However, they were reluctant to share their feelings with the class teacher, because of the fear of being reprimanded. Thus, the teacher was perceived as being unsupportive.

Another example of teacher insensitivity in dealing with Asian pupils is illustrated by the following scenario at Dewry School. The teacher was distributing letters to the class to take home to parents to elicit their permission for a forthcoming school trip. The teacher commented to the Asian girls in the class, 'I suppose we'll have problems with you girls. Is it worth me giving you a letter, because your parents don't allow you to be away from home overnight?'

The cumulative effects of teachers' attitudes towards Asian children was to create a sense of insecurity for these children in the classroom. Moreover, the attitudes of the teachers influenced the Asian children's social disposition among their classroom peers. They were extremely unpopular, especially among their white peers. Indeed, children of other groups would refer to the very same features of the Asian children's perceived character deficiencies (which the class teacher had previously drawn attention to in the classroom) to tease and harass them. Such responses tended to counteract the positive attempts by teachers to address multicultural issues, and led to an ambivalence from Asian children on curriculum topics or school celebrations focusing on aspects of their traditions or customs. On the one hand, they expressed some pride in having aspects of these acknowledged by the school. Yet on the other, they were concerned that this often exacerbated the teasing, ridicule and harassment which they felt they received daily, particularly from the white children.

THE AFRO-CARIBBEAN CHILD IN THE CLASSROOM

As with the Asian child, the Afro-Caribbean child attracts a range of teacher expectations of behaviour and educational potential, right from the nursery class. While the Asian child may experience a pattern made up of assumed poor language skills and negative attitudes towards their cultural background alongside expectation of educational attainment, the Afro-Caribbean child's experience is often largely composed of expectations of bad behaviour, along with disapproval, punishment, and teacher insensitivity to the experience of racism. Some Afro-Caribbean children of Rastafarian origin also experience a cultural disapproval. An example of such assumptions revealed at a very early stage took place in a nursery group of 4-year-olds in Castle School:

TEACHER: Let's do one song before home time.

PETER: *(White boy)* Humpty Dumpty.

TEACHER: No, I'm choosing today. Let's do something we have
             not done for a while. I know, we'll do the Autumn song.
             What about the Autumn song we sing? Don't shout out,
             put your hand up nicely.

MANDY: *(Shouting out)* Two little leaves on a tree.

TEACHER: She's nearly right.

MARCUS: *(Afro-Caribbean boy with his hand up)* I know.

TEACHER: *(Talking to the group)* Is she right when she says 'two
             little leaves on a tree'?

WHOLE GROUP: No.

TEACHER: What is it, Peter?

PETER: Four.

TEACHER: Nearly right.

MARCUS: *(Waving his hand for attention)* Five.

TEACHER: Don't shout out Marcus, do you know, Susan *(white
             girl)*?

SUSAN: Five.

TEACHER: *(Holding up one hand)* Good, five, because we have got
             how many fingers on this hand?

WHOLE GROUP: Five.

TEACHER: OK, let's only have one hand because we've only got five
             leaves. How many would we have if we had too many?
             Don't shout, hands up.

MANDY: *(Shouting out)* One, two, three, four, five, six, seven,
             eight, nine, ten.

TEACHER: Good, OK how many fingers have we got?

MARCUS: Five.

TEACHER: Don't shout out Marcus, put your hand up. Deane,
             how many?

DEANE: Five.

TEACHER: That's right, we're going to use five today. What makes
             them dance about, these leaves?

PETER: *(Shouting out)* The wind.

TEACHER: That's right. Ready here we go.

Teacher and children sing: 'Five little leaves so bright and gay,
dancing about on a tree one day. The wind came blowing through
the town, whoooo, whoooo, one leaf came tumbling down.'

TEACHER: How many have we got left?

DEANE: *(Shouting out)* One.

MARCUS: *(Raising his hand enthusiastically)* Four.
TEACHER: *(To Marcus)* Shush. Let's count, one two, three, four.
TEACHER: How many, Deane?
DEANE: Four.
TEACHER: Good, right, let's do the next bit.
Teacher and children sing the next two verses.
TEACHER: How many have we got left, Peter?
PETER: Don't know.
MANDY: Two.
TEACHER: I know that you know, Mandy.
MARCUS: Two.
TEACHER: *(Stern voice)* I'm not asking you, I'm asking Peter, don't
            shout out. We'll help Peter, shall we? Look at my fingers,
            how many? One, two. How many, Peter?
PETER: Two.
TEACHER: Very good. Let's do the next bit.
Teacher and children sing the next verse. At the end of the verse:
TEACHER: How many have we got left, Susan?
SUSAN: One.
TEACHER: Good, let's all count, one. Let's do the last bit.
Teacher and children sing the last verse. At the end of the verse:
TEACHER: How many have we got left?
ALL CHILDREN: None.
TEACHER: That's right, there are no leaves left. Marcus, will you
            stop fidgeting and sit nicely.

Marcus was frequently the recipient of teacher control and criticism. He was often singled out for criticism, even though several pupils of different ethnic origins were engaged in the same behaviour. In a conversation about the above observation, the Afro-Caribbean nursery nurse attached to the unit commented:

> Marcus really likes answering questions about things. I can imagine he's quite good at that because he's always got plenty to say . . . but they [white teachers] see the black children as a problem here.

Black nursery nurses in another nursery unit of Bridgeway School also expressed concern about the attitudes of white colleagues towards Afro-Caribbean boys in particular. One of them pointed out:

> The Head of the Nursery is forever saying how difficult it is to control the black children in the nursery, because they only responded to being hit . . . there is an attitude that they all get beaten up at home

and they're all used to getting a good slap or good punch. There are one or two [black children] that they are quite positive about . . . they happen to be girls. I think it is a very sexist nursery. That black girls, they are positive about, are thought to be clean, well spoken, lovely personalities. As for the boys, I think boys like Joshua [Rastafarian] and Calvin who have recently moved into the reception class, they were labelled disruptive. When Fay [Afro-Caribbean nursery nurse] was there she really got these two children to settle, because they had somebody to relate to, that understood them, realized that they weren't troublemakers. They just needed some body to settle them, especially Calvin, he related to her really well. Then just when he was settling down they upped and took him [transferred to the reception class] . . . He went right back to stage one, he sat outside the classroom for the first few months of school apparently . . . all he used to do was sit outside the classroom. I used to go over to speak to him, I'd ask him what had happened. He used to say 'The teacher said, I've been naughty, so she's put me outside.'

In contrast to the lack of attention which the Asian children often faced, Afro-Caribbean boys received a disproportionate amount of teachers' negative attentions. For example, there was a tendency for Afro-Caribbean and white boys to engage in task avoidance behaviour, to fool around when they should be working and be generally disobedient. Teachers were observed to be more inclined to turn a blind eye to flagrant breaches of normal classroom standards when committed by white boys, or to be lenient in their disapproval. By contrast, similar conduct on the part of Afro-Caribbean boys was rarely overlooked by the teachers. Furthermore, Afro-Caribbean boys were sometimes exclusively criticised even more when peers of other ethnic origins shared in the offence. Such experiences led Afro-Caribbean boys to identify their relationship with teacher as a special difficulty. Samuel, a 7-year-old Afro-Caribbean child at Bridgeway School, talked of what he perceived to be the teacher unfair treatment of other Afro-Caribbean pupils:

SAMUEL: I always get done and always get picked on . . . I want to go to a black school with all black teachers, it's better. I want to go to a school with just black people.

CW: Why?

SAMUEL: Because when you go to a school with white people they give you horrible food and you're always picked on when you don't do nothing. When it's white people, they just say stop doing that and stop doing this.

CW: Are you saying that you would like some black teachers here (in the school).

SAMUEL: Yes.

CW: Have you ever told anybody this, have you ever told the teachers?

SAMUEL: I haven't said that to any of the teachers . . . because they'll be cross and say the white people just treat black people the same as other people. And one time someone hit Sandra [Afro-Caribbean child] and she was crying and if it was a white person and I said 'Miss she's crying', she would have went there straight away but when it was Sandra, she [the teacher] just ignored me. And she said 'Get in the line' [join the queue] and I said 'You only think about white people'. Then she told Mrs Johnson [headteacher] and Mrs Johnson started shouting her head off at me.

CW: So you felt that the teacher didn't do anything because Sandra was black?

SAMUEL: Yes, because it was a white person, she would say 'What's the matter', and then she would have said it didn't hurt, she just say 'Stand against the wall.'

CW: Do you think that the teacher treats black children differently to white children?

SAMUEL: Yes.

CW: In what ways?

SAMUEL: Because when it's black people, and they just run down the stairs. I mean when Martin [white boy], he ran off, she said 'Come back, stop at the door' and Martin didn't hear, Martin ran off. And then Richard told me that the teacher want us to come back to the classroom, so I walked back. Then I told on Martin, and Miss just told me to shut up, she said, 'Be quiet'.

CW: What about the Asian children, the Pakistani children, how do the teachers treat them?

SAMUEL: Treat them same as the black people.

CW: In what way?

SAMUEL: It's just that they treat Pakistani people a little better than black people.

CW: Can you just tell me why you say that?

SAMUEL: Because every time everything goes wrong in the class, and everyone's messing about around the carpet, they call out me, Rick and Delroy [both Afro-Caribbean] and that. But they don't call the white people and the Pakistani.

CW: How does this make you feel?

SAMUEL: *(Long thoughtful pause)* Sad.

This view was also echoed by older children. Benjamin, an 11-year-old Afro-Caribbean child at Dewry School, said:

BENJAMIN: My teacher can be all right, but other teachers irritates me a lot. This teacher called Mrs Lucas irritates me. When everybody's making a row in the hall, they call my name, instead of other people's . . . they don't like black people.

CW: What makes you say that your teachers don't like black people?

BENJAMIN: They don't, because there's a girl in my class, Raquel. There is only me and her in the class that's black. Miss Smith, she's always involving Mr Jones [the headmaster] a lot. Always going to see Mr Jones. It's alway's black children getting done. You know Raquel's brother, he was in trouble a lot, and it was always because of other kids, white kids . . . This white pushed Raquel down the stairs. Now if it was me, I would have got detention. That boy never got detention. He went in the head's room for about three minutes and came back out. The girl [Raquel] was curled up on the floor in pain. You should have seen all her legs, cut up. And there's this prejudiced dinner lady that don't like blacks.

In addition to their perceived regular experience or reprimands, children felt that the other teachers discriminated against them in the allocation of responsibility and rewards. A 9-year-old Afro-Caribbean child at Dewry School said:

In the first school the teachers were really prejudiced. There was quite a lot of coloured people in the class and Miss Butler . . . she'd never picked any coloured people to do a job and nearly all the white people got a biscuit, but the coloured people never. Like if a white person wanted to go to the toilet, she'd say yeah, but if a coloured person wanted to go to the toilet, she'd say no.

A teacher at Dewry School expressed her objection to being accused by the older Afro-Caribbean children of being prejudiced:

> I was accused of doing several things last year. 'I didn't like black.'
> 'You are only saying that because I'm black.' 'You wouldn't be
> picking on anyone else' – this came particularly from Delroy who
> has got a big chip on his shoulder. I think it's because his dad left
> and there is a lot of emotional instability there. But I objected to that
> . . . I am not saying that I am not *me*, I am sure that I respond to things
> in a very unfavourable way, but I am fighting it. I am not saying I
> am pristine and my halo is glowing, but at least I am aware of my
> own shortcomings and I do make positive steps to overcome what
> has been instilled in me for years. Whether or not things come out
> sort of unconsciously without me knowing. I am sure that if I knew
> things were coming out, then I would take positive steps.

THE RASTAFARIAN EXPERIENCE

One group who seemed to be particularly prone to experiencing prejudice were the Rastafarian children. Here too, expectations seem to have
emerged even in the nursery class. For example, an Afro-Caribbean
carer at Castle School expressed her considerable distress at the
responses of white colleagues to Levi, a 3-year-old Rastafarian child
who was having difficulty adjusting to the nursery environment. Levi,
on occasion, would lash out in frustration. She felt that her white
colleagues were reluctant to accommodate his needs as they would
normally do for a white child in a similar situation. As she states:

> When Levi first came in [to the nursery], he did things. I got the
> feeling that Maureen [white teacher] resented him, because he took
> up too much time. He had only just turned 3. She used to say 'Well,
> I'm not going to waste my time like that.' If Levi messes about, I
> think sometimes the way she handled him, made him do things. If
> a child is going to bite you or scratch you, you'd make sure they
> didn't. You'd hold their hand or you would stop them. She didn't,
> she just let him do it, then she'd flare up and walk across [to the
> school] and tell the head. In the end the head said, 'We've got to
> keep a record of his behaviour, write down the incidents.' I just didn't
> write anything down. He's lashed out at me . . . he's come back to
> me the next day and said sorry about what he's done. And I think,
> 'Fair enough. he's only a child.' I just think Maureen blows it up. I
> don't see him as a problem. Confidential notes are kept on him. . . .
> I don't think his mother knows. What upsets me about it is that when
> this first happened, the reason why the head said that she wanted to

keep records on things that he'd ever done was in case he ever needs statementing.[6] She would have the evidence. I was really upset, he's 3. I'm really glad that Levi behaves the way he does, he says sorry whenever he does things. . . . Only bad things go in this book. I never write in this book. I don't agree with them [colleagues] because you don't know who's going to see it or where it's going to go.

By the time they were older, Rastafarian children were seen by some teachers as a particular threat to classroom management:

I would say that probably the black children, particularly the Rastafarian children, are taking the lead in quite a lot, they are making the running quite often, but not in all cases. Those children I'm sure are being made particularly aware by their parents as regards racism. And there is a problem of a small child trying to negotiate a world which they have been made aware is a racist one. You know, they've got to watch out – and actually finding out that their teacher is one. A teacher faced with such children is quite vulnerable. I think it is very complex, because they're sort of getting their own back in a racist white world.

An example of this was given by the headteacher of Castle School, recounting her experience with a 4-year-old Rastafarian boy. As with the teacher quoted above, she expresses a sensitivity to the child's experience of racism, but an apparent incomprehension in knowing how to tackle this.

He was in his first term in school so he was under 5, and he was vulgar in class. He had this habit of running wild and hurting other children, and we actually removed him from the class before he actually hurt other children. So he had been removed and he came into my room where he didn't want to be, and he was angry and he just screwed up his face and said, 'I hate you, I hate you, you are white . . . and you're not a Rasta'. He felt that I was getting at him because he was black. I think it was the first time I had actually confronted the issues, and that's what I feel with several of the Rastafarian children in particular, that's what they see. So there is this enormous barrier because of who we are.

MULTICULTURALISM IN THE CLASSROOM

In all the schools, individual teachers were observed to be genuinely trying to take the multicultural nature of the classroom into account in curriculum application. A common practice was to draw on the resources provided by the children themselves. Unfortunately, the teachers' efforts were not always immediately recognized, and their sincerity was often questioned by the ethnic minority children concerned. The teachers' efforts often only served to make the ethnic minority children feel awkward and embarrassed.

This situation was observed to occur for two fundamental reasons. First, the teachers often appeared to lack confidence, basic factual knowledge and understanding of the areas or the topic they were addressing. More significantly, the teacher also clearly communicated this lack of competence to the class. For instance, teachers frequently mispronounced words or names relevant to the appropriate area or topic. This frequently got laughter from white children, but floods of embarrassed giggles from the black children. This situation unintentionally served to make topics or areas of knowledge associated with ethnic minority values and cultures appear exotic, novel and unimportant, esoteric or difficult. Moreover, the intended message of the teacher's approach was often at variance with the black children's experience of racial intolerance in the school. The black children's responses to the sincere intentions of individual teachers to use them as a resource were essentially to refuse publicly to co-operate with the teacher, dissolve into giggles or lower their heads with embarrassment, deny or conceal skills or knowledge. The white children, on the other hand, often laughed, ridiculed, taunted or looked on passively.

The lesson reported here, in a class of 10-year-olds in Dewry School, highlights aspects of this observation. As part of its language work, the class was looking at the linguistic composition of the school. The teacher was using a text printed in two languages – Urdu and English – as a resource.

TEACHER: Last time we talked a little about the different languages we speak at home and in school, and we made a list on the board, and I said that we would talk about this book that I found in the library *(holds the book up to the class)*. Rehana and Aftab might be able to help me. It is an unusual book. Can you tell me why? *(Holds book up for class to inspect.)*

WHITE GIRL: It's got funny writing.

TEACHER: It's written in two languages. English and . . . can you tell me Rehana?

WHITE BOY: Jamaican.

REHANA: *(Shyly)* Urdu.

TEACHER: Is that how you say it? Urdeo?

Rehana laughs, embarrassed. White pupils snigger.

TEACHER: *(To Rehana)* Say it again.

REHANA: Urdu.

TEACHER: Urdeo.

Asian pupils laugh, embarrassed.

TEACHER: Say it again.

REHANA   Urdu.

TEACHER: Urdeo.

Asian pupils laugh, embarrassed.

TEACHER: Say it again.

REHANA   Urdu.

TEACHER: *(Mimicking Rehana but showing signs of defect in the pronunciation, laughs)* Urdeo.

TEACHER: *(Laughingly)* How do you say it, Aftab?

Aftab holds his head down, refuses to respond.

WHITE BOY: It's Pakistani language.

TEACHER: Can we write it on the board? *(Teacher writes the word 'Urdu' on the board.)* Because you see what we've been saying. We pronounce things differently. But not just to lots of other countries. We pronounce things a bit differently than everywhere else apart from 'Hometown'. Paula (white girl), where do you come from?

PAULA: Portsmouth.

TEACHER: How long have you been living in 'Hometown'?

PAULA: Don't know.

TEACHER: Since you were little. So Paula has lived most of her life in 'Hometown', but Paula's dad has lived most of his life in Portsmouth and all over the place. And he doesn't talk like me. He doesn't talk like Paula. He's got what we would call an accent. A quite different accent. He pronounces lots of things quite differently. You are fortunate really, because lots of your teachers come from different parts of the country. I come from 'Hometown'. I've lived in 'Hometown' all my life. Mrs Mason comes from 'Hometown', Miss Robinson comes from 'Hometown'. I think that's it ... I don't think any of the other teachers do. They come from all over the place, all over the country. When you live in a different part, not just the world, but in England, you pick up different accents. Now an accent is when you pronounce words

differently. One word that I would pronounce differently
is 'Urdeo'. I know that 'Urdeo' is completely wrong,
(looks over to the Asian pupils). Is it spelt like that
in Pakistan *(pointing to word 'Urdu' written of the
board)?*

REHANA: *(Shyly)* No.

TEACHER: No, it's not spelt at all like that because that is not
'Urdeo' writing or *(with a grin)* 'Urdoo'. A lot of things
in 'Urdeo', as we found a lot of things in Ancient Egypt,
cannot be translated exactly, because there are some
words that come in Egyptian, that we haven't got in
English, some words in English that we haven't got in
Egyptian, and there are some words in English that we
haven't got in Arabic. That's why I told you that some
parts of the Bible are quite difficult to translate because
they were not written in English but . . .?

AFRO-CARIBBEAN
BOY: African.

WHITE BOY: Welsh.

TEACHER: *(Laughing)* No, not Welsh.

WHITE GIRL: Jewish.

TEACHER: Arabic, originally written in Arabic. It can't be directly
translated. It's the same with the book. This can't be
directly translated. *(To Asian boy)* Can you read that?
(Boy bows his head). I think he's shy, that's fair
enough. Well, I can't read it, I might even have it
upside down, I don't know. *(To Asian girl)* Can you
tell us about 'Urdeo', is it written like that *(pointing left
to right)* or written like that *(pointing right to left)*?

REHANA: No, that way *(pointing right to left)*.

WHITE PUPIL: Backwards.

TEACHER: It's written from right to left?

REHANA: Yes.

TEACHER: No, it's not backwards. It's English that's written backwards.

WHITE PUPIL: *(Exasperated)* Is it?

TEACHER: Don't forget that when the Ancient Egyptians and lots of
Eastern countries were writing, we were still swinging in
trees and living in holes in the ground.

Pupils laugh.

TEACHER: And living in caves. We couldn't write, and they could write in hieroglyphics. The Egyptians wrote downwards. The Chinese write down from top to bottom. I'm not sure where, but I think there's somewhere which actually writes upwards, is it the Japanese? Bottom of the page to the top of the page. We wouldn't get Aftab to read this book because he's a little bit shy. I know he can read it . . .

TEACHERS' VIEWS

So far, I have concentrated on both Afro-Caribbean and Asian pupils' relationships with teachers from the nursery to the infant classroom. I have focused on the pattern of classroom interaction, and in particular, on how this is mediated by the children's ethnicity. In both cases, pupils' ethnicity was shown to adversely influence their relationships with teachers. Classroom observation indicated that teachers tended to treat Afro-Caribbean children (especially boys) in a more restrictive way than other pupil groups. For instance, issuing orders rather than encouraging them to express their ideas. Asian children, on the other hand, received less individual attention; they tended to be overlooked or underestimated by teachers. These children were also frequently the recipients of teachers' expressed annoyance and frustration. Reflected in these patterns of classroom interaction would appear to be teachers' expectations and 'typing' of these pupil groups. In order to explore this further, it is necessary to examine teachers' expressed views or adopted perspectives of both Afro-Caribbean and Asian pupils.

Classroom observation studies in a variety of settings suggest that, on the whole, teachers categorize or develop typifications of the children they teach (see, for example, Rist, 1970; Leiter, 1974; Hargreaves *et al.*, 1975; Sharp and Green, 1975). It is recognized that the use of typifications is a normal part of interaction in many social situations (Burrell and Morgan, 1979). However, the classroom context is a particularly significant one in which the teacher has to face and cope with a relatively large number of children. Given the teacher's occupational reality, typing is a means of reducing the complexity or, as Schutz (1970) states, 'making the world of everyday life "cognitively manageable"'. Thus, the teacher simplifies by classifying. Related to the typification that teachers develop of pupils is the 'ideal pupil' model. The notion of the ideal pupil is a construction which derives primarily from the lifestyle and culture of the teacher concerned.

The ideal for teachers is likely to be a child who acts in ways which are supportive of teachers' interest-at-hand, who enables them to cope and so on. Work by Becker (1952) and, more recently, Sharp and Green (1975) has suggested that teachers differentiate between pupils according to how closely they meet the ideal pupil criteria. Children, therefore, tend to be classified and typed by the ways in which they vary from the ideal. For instance, social class factors have been found to be reflected in teachers' 'specifications' of the ideal pupil. The classroom observations reported above suggest that ethnic differences also influenced the way in which teachers viewed their pupils. Teachers' views in relation to their experience of the classroom were concerned with the children's motivation and adjustment to the learning situation. Their views of the children's educability revealed extremely complex feelings. Often these revealed an ambivalence about their working conditions. Yet they generally exhibited personal and professional concern for their children.

The teachers' main concerns about classroom life related, first, to the perceptions of the children's competence and, secondly, to their behaviour in the classroom. The levels of competence across all groups of children were considered by the majority of the teachers to be relatively poor. But certain skills were recognized to be poorer in the white children, as this teacher from Castle School explained:

> In all groups, the speech, language, listening, the concentration, are low, generally at lack of competence levels. There is also low energy levels, tiredness, lassitude . . . poor responses to requests and a lack of compliance that goes across the board. If I were referring children for special needs, they would be more likely to be white. In fact, for language development they would be more likely to be white than Asian, because relatively speaking the Asians are making progress given that you take into account that English is a second language. These children are more competent in English than the children who had been exposed to English . . . from English parents. That is when you really get worried, because you realise that the level of competence is deteriorating.

However, the majority of teachers, such as this one from Adelle School, considered all the children positively disposed to most aspects of classwork:

> Generally speaking the children do have, within limitations, a good attitude to work. They have limited concentration skills, but within those parameters they do actually do their best. The attitude to work

is one of 'I will do my best to do this'. I would say a child who doesn't try is fairly rarer than the ones who do. I think most of them have a strong desire to please and are also proud to please . . . They like the idea of doing their best, and if you say, 'Would you like to try again?' if you don't make an issue of it, they will do it again.

Further probing showed that children were differentially categorized on the basis of their orientation to work. For instance, white girls and Asian children, particularly boys, were considered to be the most motivated groups. On the other hand, Afro-Caribbean children were often considered to reveal the lowest motivation, a view expressed by the teacher below:

I would say that the Asian boys, in general, are the most individually motivated in that it seems to come from within, from whatever input they have had at home, but they are much more determined to succeed, they know their work and they listen, they have the greatest listening skills in my class and this is a very generalised overall. The difference between white boys and Afro-Caribbean children is that there is no difference. If they have been to bed early, then they might do well that day. If something happened in the playground, they are not going to. They don't seem to have any incentive or deep urge to want to succeed in that educational way that the Asian boys do. I do sometimes feel though, especially last year, that some of the children, Afro-Caribbean, felt like they were under-achieving and consequently because of that they wouldn't try. They would get to a point where if they reached a problem like in a stage in maths which they hadn't come across and they were stumped, they would get upset about it, over the top, dramatic, upset about it, rather than just, 'I can't do this, how do you do it?' It was like 'I can't do it, because I am hopeless'. I had two children in particular last year who reacted in this way.

Teachers regularly reported the prevalence of problem behaviour in the classroom and around the school. The problems commonly referred to by teachers were aggressiveness, disobedience, distractibility, overactive behaviour, teasing, quarrelsome attitude, children being over-demanding, conflict with peers, having temper tantrums and emotional problems. Boys were considered to be more of a problem than girls, and Afro-Caribbean children were seen as being a greater problem than white. Asian children were less associated with behaviour problems. On the other hand, Afro-Caribbean boys were generally associated with aggressive, disobedient and distractible behaviour. Teachers frequently talked about feeling worn down by the sheer number of teacher–pupil interactions which involved some element of control or response to acts of indiscipline, particularly on the part of the Afro-Caribbean children. Furthermore, teachers felt that a succession of disruptive behaviour moments in the classroom often led to a change in the nature of their interaction with the children. Thus, a point articulated by a teacher:

> I would say some days I fulfil virtually nothing. Quite seriously, some days it's a battle. Some days you are quite happy at the end of the day, I feel I have achieved quite a lot, it all depends really on the temperament of the children. And I mean the powerful children in the class, their temperaments really do dictate the mood of the class, which is quite sad in a school like this, because it means that the new children and the quiet children get swallowed up, that worries me. They don't get the attention at the time they should have. These quiet children are likely to be girls, more girls than boys, but I do have some boys who will just get on with what they have to do and don't hassle me at all. I have one little Asian girl who I would like to spend more time with, because she has got a lot to offer, she just sits there and gets on with what she has to do and doesn't bother me at all. I think that it is how they are brought up, don't you? To be quiet and get on with it, and they are not troublemakers at all, they are very nice children. They are swallowed up definitely, which is sad. Delroy and Vincent [two Afro-Caribbean boys] are the trouble, very disruptive. I have to admit I like Delroy, I don't think I would have survived if I hadn't liked him. I mean quite seriously as well, there is something very appealing about him. At times I could strangle him, he's a very nice boy, he's got a very nice nature, he's very kind. You get him on your own, you know, in the right place at the right time, he can be very kind. Vincent, I have to be careful with because I find him very difficult to relate to. I mean possibly I could spend more time with them all, but at the moment I can't. I am afraid my attitude tends to be negative and I have to think 'Come on now, be positive.'

An examination of teachers' classroom logs, where daily experiences were recorded, showed a tendency for some teacher to direct their frustration at the Afro-Caribbean children.[7] This was reflected through the nature of the teachers' written comments, which often ranged from negative stereotyping to insults. For example, this recording on Justin (aged 6), an Afro-Caribbean boy:

> I think Robert [fellow pupil] may be in little pieces by the morning. He had an argument with Justin today and I've seldom seen a face like it on a little child. The temper, rage and marked aggression was quite frightening to see. I wouldn't be surprised in years to come if Justin wasn't capable of actually killing someone. When he smiles he could charm the birds off trees, but when he's in a temper he is incapable of controlling himself. He has an extremely short fuse, is a real chauvinist and to cap it all he's got a persecution complex. He has to be handled with kid gloves.

A comment on the behaviour of Ruth (6 years old), an Afro-Caribbean girl, was in a similar vein:

> What a thoroughly objectionable little bitch, she's intelligent enough to egg others on and seem totally innocent herself. She pinches, nips and uses her brain to impose her will on others. She's one of those children who can't bear others to have friends – she likes to break up friendships (and is very good at it). If she were to use her brain in the way a normal child would, she would be bright by any standards.

Not all the teachers' comments recorded in their classroom logs relating to Afro-Caribbean children were harsh and intemperate in tone. None theless, the illustrations presented were symptomatic of the feeling of some of the teachers. Overall, the teachers' views showed a general tendency to associate Afro-Caribbean children (particularly boys) with behavioural problems. In contrast, in their general conversation, as well as in their interviews with me, teachers often cited Asian children as a group being a 'pleasure to teach'. However, classroom logs revealed certain contradictions in their attitudes. Some teachers were less favourably disposed to those Asian children who were perceived as having learning problems arising out of language difficulties; those who were perceived as operating as an exclusive group; and those who tended to converse in their 'mother tongue' in the classroom. In general, teachers showed greater approval of those Asian children who were perceived to be socially integrated in the classroom and proficient in the English language.

PEER RELATIONS

An aspect of the 'primary ideology' is a form of pedagogic folklore which, *inter alia*, views childhood as an age of innocence. Regarding issues of 'race' and ethnicity, the popular belief still exists among teachers that young children are 'colour blind'. Moreover, primary teachers assume that young children, whilst capable of unacceptable behaviour, remain free from the malign influences of individual racism.

In the nursery classroom, children reflected their awareness of racial and ethnic differences in conversation with both teachers/carers and peers, and attributed value to these differences. A dialogue between Charlene, a 3-year-old Afro-Caribbean girl and Tina, a 4-year-old white girl during creative play in Castle School illustrates this perfectly.

CHARLENE: *(Cuddling a black doll)* This is my baby.

TINA: I don't like it, it's funny. I like this one *(holding a white doll)* it's my favourite. I don't like this one *(pointing to a black doll)*. Because you see I like Sarah, and I like white. You're my best friend though, you're brown.

CHARLENE: I don't like that one *(pointing to the white doll)*.

TINA: You're brown aren't you?

CHARLENE: I'm not brown, I'm black.

TINA: You're brown, but I'm white.

CHARLENE: No I'm not, I'm black and baby's black.

TINA: They call us white, my mummy calls me white, and you know my mummy calls you brown. When you come to visit if you want . . . She'll say 'hello brown person. . .' I like brown, not black. Michael Jackson was brown, he went a bit white.

Observations also suggest that children at this early age were showing a preference for members of their own racial/ethnic group and a desire to mix and play with them rather than with others. This 'own-group' preference did on occasion reflect antipathy towards children of other skin colour or cultural groups. The children's preference of members of their own racial/ethnic group is corroborated by an Afro-Caribbean Child Care Assistant at Bridgeway School:

The white children, particularly a set of white children, even though they related to me and Tazeem [Asian carer] all right, they won't play with anybody else,when I say with anybody else I mean black or Asian children. There are a couple of black children that won't play with Asian children but they won't play with white children either. I've noticed that the Asian children play very well and they play well amongst themselves and alongside each other, but they don't mix themselves as well . . . But I think there is an attitude in the school that makes the Asian children feel negative about themselves as well.

Even at this early age, white children tended to be extremely negative towards the Asian children in both their attitudes and behaviour. They often refused to play with them and frequently subjected them to threatening behaviour, name-calling and hitting. An example of this is shown in the following incident at Bridgeway School. A group of four white boys (aged 3–4) were collaboratively building a tower block out of the building blocks. An Asian boy walked over with the thought of participating. Two of the boys were heard to say vehemently. 'No, Paki, no, Paki'. Another boy pushed the Asian boy aggressively. The Asian boy wandered off looking quite dejected.

The nursery teachers/carers were also aware of similar incidents of this nature. As an Afro-Caribbean carer at Bridgeway School points out:

> Peter . . . [the] blond headed boy, I notice that he used to go up to the Asian children in a really threatening way, just threatening behaviour. He wouldn't say anything. If the Asian children had anything he would take it off them. The Asian girls, they'd leave things, by just the way he looked at them. They'd leave something if they were playing with it. He would look at them and they would drop it.

In the classroom, white children engaged in persistent racist name-calling, teasing, jostling, intimidation, rejection and the occasional physical assault on black and ethnic minority children. Aspects of this behaviour are illustrated in the following incident from Adelle School. I was in a classroom observing and working with a group of six white 6-year-olds on English language and number tasks. Taseem (an Asian girl) came over to the group, and with a rather desperate look on her face asked me to help her.

TASEEM: Miss Cecile, can you help me do times by?
(Taseem was working on a multiplication exercise which she did not fully understand. The ten sums she had completed for this exercise had been marked as incorrect by the teacher and she had been asked to do the exercise again. I spent some minutes explaining the exercise to Taseem. The children in the group were very resentful of the fact that I had switched my attention from them to Taseem and also that she had joined the group.)
CW: *(After having finished explaining the exercise)* Taseem,

    do you understand how 'times by' works?

JANE

(a white girl): No, she won't understand, she's a Paki.

Taseem is very upset by this comment and is on the verge of tears.

CW: *(To Jane)* What do you mean?

JANE: Because she's a Paki.

The other children in the group are sniggering.

CW: And why should she not understand multiplications because she is a Pakistani?

JANE: Because she's not over us and she's not in our culture.

MICHAEL

(a white boy): She's Paki! *(Laughs)*

CW: What is our culture?

JANE: England.

CW: She is in England, she lives in England.

JANE: Yeah, but she comes from Pakistani.

ALICE

(a white girl): Yeah, Pakistani, she was born in Pakistan she means.

TASEEM: *(Dejected but in protestation)* I wasn't. I was born here.

JANE: She couldn't understand, that's what I think because she speaks Paki.

OTHER CHILDREN: *(To Taseem)* Where were you born?

CW: Yes, just because she speaks 'Pakistani' it does not mean that she can't understand how to multiply.

JANE: Because when I say something, she doesn't know what I say. And when it were assembly they were doing a Paki dance.

CW: Taseem was born in England, her parents are from Pakistan, but she was born in England.

TASEEM: My parents are here.

The researcher continues to assist Taseem with her number work. The other children become increasingly resentful.

JANE: *(Sharply)* Will you help me now?

Some of the children take to taunting and name-calling Taseem. However, sensing my disapproval of their behaviour, they adopt a strategy of name-calling by sounding out the letters.

JANE: P-A-K-E, P-A-K-E!

ALICE: *(Quietly spoken, but so I would hear)* She's a Paki!

CW: What does P-A-K-E mean?

JANE: *(With a mischievous grin, whispering)* She's a Paki!

TASEEM: *(Visibly distraught)* Miss, I want to go out to play.

Echoing of P-A-K-E from the other children.
ALICE: She's a Paki, that's what it means.

This encounter not only highlights the existence of racism in the very young, but it also shows that the children are well aware of its taboo status. On recognizing my displeasure with their remarks, they endeavoured to disguise their intent. The teachers, with only a few exceptions, mentioned that racial intolerance was prevalent among the children. Indeed, the white children's attitude and behaviour towards the Asian children was a concern for the majority of teachers. A teacher at Adelle School explains:

> The Asian children are getting so picked on, it's awful. In the playground the Asian girls never leave the teacher's side. One little girl last week, they [white children] never left her alone, she was really frightened. I mean she really did need protection . . . but we can't stand next to her all the time. Every time I looked, somebody was at her.

One strategy for avoiding expressions of racial intolerance was to separate children of different ethnic groups. The following teacher's comment was typical of many that were expressed to me:

> I have to think very carefully when I select children to work together because, more often than not, white children will refuse to sit next to or work with a Pakistani. You have to bear this in mind so as to avoid any nastiness.

In their view on aspects of school, many of the white children volunteered particularly vehement feelings towards the Asian children. Some also expressed a certain abhorrence at the prospect of being taught by a black teacher. The example below from Dewry School pointedly illustrates these views:

JASON
(white boy, 12): I don't like the Pakistani children. I call them Pakis. Mostly Zahid, he's about the best one in the school.
CW: Why do you not like the Pakistani children?
JASON: Don't know. Like blacks because I've got a lot of black friends. Most of me friends are black anyway. I've got more black friends than I have white.
CW: What have the Asian children done for you to dislike them?

JASON:	Got me in trouble with the police, and that . . . They blame me for going in houses . . . Saying that I've been smashing the windows and that.
CW:	Did you?
JASON:	*(Long pause, smirk)* No.
CW:	Do you think that it is really right for you to dislike people for no reasons?
JASON:	*(Defiantly)* Yes.
CW:	What's right about it?
JASON:	They're buying all shops and all that . . . There's only one shop what isn't a Paki shop round our way. And they're not going to let Pakis take it. Mr Smith round our way, he's white.
CW:	How do you know he's not going to let this happen?
JASON:	Because he's told me mum and that the rest of the shops been taken over by Pakis. It's not right for white people. Every time they walk into a shop they see a Paki.
CW:	What's not right about it?
JASON:	Don't know, I don't like it.
CW:	Providing there are the things in the shop that you wish to buy, does it matter who owns it?
JASON:	*(Angry)* I don't go to Paki shops.
CW:	It could be said that you're racially prejudiced?
JASON:	If I'm prejudiced I wouldn't like blacks at all, but I do like blacks. Some of me friends are black . . . there's no black shop owner on our road, they're all Pakis except for one.

It is interesting to note the complex nature of Jason's reasoning. On the one hand, he expresses hostile attitudes towards Asians. At the same time he hastens to add that he cannot be considered 'racially prejudiced' because he has black friends.

Many of the white children expressed a definite view against being taught by black teachers. My discussion with two young children in Bridgeway School, Samantha (aged 7) and Claire (aged 6), encapsulates this view:

SAMANTHA:	Ranjit is the best behaved [in the class].
CW:	Why is she the best behaved?
SAMANTHA:	Because she helps – she works here.
CW:	Who is Ranjit?
CLAIRE:	She's that lady.

SAMANTHA:	She's that lady.
CW:	Can you describe her to me?
SAMANTHA:	She's got long black hair, she's got a striped jumper on and she's got black eyes . . .
CW:	And is she a teacher?
SAMANTHA:	No, she helps Mrs Moore [class teacher], helps us.
CW:	How do you know she's not a teacher?
SAMANTHA:	Because she's not here all the time – she only comes Wednesday, Thursday and Friday mornings . . .
CLAIRE:	. . . and a little bit . . .
SAMANTHA:	She's brown.
CLAIRE:	She's yellower than Zahra (an Asian girl in the class).
CW:	Have you ever been taught by a brown teacher?
SAMANTHA:	No.
CW:	Would you like to be taught by a brown teacher?
SAMANTHA:	*(Aghast)* No.
CW:	No? Why?
CLAIRE:	I don't like it.
CW:	Why don't you like it?
CLAIRE:	I just like talking with . . . I like talking with white teachers and *(under her breath)* I don't like talking in Paki's language . . .
SAMANTHA:	In Urdu.
CW:	Why don't you want to be taught by a brown teacher?
SAMANTHA:	Because we don't like her because . . . she speaks Urdu.
CW:	Why don't you like people speaking in Urdu?
SAMANTHA:	Because Urdu people are from Pakistan and nobody knows what they're talking about.
CLAIRE:	. . . and we don't want to learn Urdu . . .
CW:	So you don't want a brown teacher?
CLAIRE AND SAMANTHA:	*(Together)* No!
SAMANTHA:	I'd like a French teacher . . .
CW:	You'd like a French teacher? Why would you like a French teacher?
SAMANTHA:	So I could go to France when I grow up and I'd know the language . . .
CW:	But wouldn't you like to go to Pakistan when you grow up?
CLAIRE AND SAMANTHA:	*(Together – aghast)* No way!

CW:	No way? Why?
SAMANTHA:	Because it's too far and I might get sunburnt because it's always sunny there and *(under her breath)* the people . . . and sometimes it doesn't sunshine . . .
CW:	You don't like the sun?
SAMANTHA:	Sometimes I do.
CW:	So you wouldn't like to have a brown teacher then?
CLAIRE AND SAMANTHA:	No.
CW:	Don't you think a brown teacher would be a good teacher?
SAMANTHA:	No.
CW:	No? Why?
SAMANTHA:	She is sometimes, but sometimes she'd speak in Urdu to the other children because some children like the Urdu and don't understand English and she'd speak in Urdu.
CW:	And wouldn't you like her to do that?
SAMANTHA:	No. Because we'd think she wasn't listening to us because she wasn't . . .
CLAIRE:	Because we'd think she's playing [not being serious with them].

CONCLUSION

The classroom is regarded as an essential aspect within the education system. Indeed, it is a commonly held view that teachers have a significant influence on the extent to which any legislation or policy is translated into effective classroom practice. With regard to race equality within education, there is a sense, then, in which the classroom has a crucial role to play in the promotion of 'good race relations'. In this chapter, I have drawn on my ethnographic study of multi-ethnic primary classrooms. Of particular importance was the examination of classroom processes and their effects. This chapter explained teacher and pupil interaction, and peer relations. Essentially, subtle differences are reported in the way white teachers treated black children. Asian children were sometimes excluded from discussion, or dealt with in a way insensitive to their cultural background. In this respect, even where teachers wished to treat children fairly and create equality of opportunity for all their pupils, it would appear that this conflicted with the routine processes in the schools, such as dress codes for physical education.

Concerning Afro-Caribbean children, the chapter provides extracts from classroom interaction and suggests that teachers appeared to expect bad behaviour from the pupils. Moreover, Afro-Caribbean children were inclined to be selected for criticism even though white pupils were indulging in similar behaviour. Rastafarian children were particularly subjected to teachers' adverse attitudes. In this regard, teachers held generalized images of pupils; for example, the view that Afro-Caribbean children are less motivated towards school and more likely to display 'behaviour problems'.

Among the pupils themselves, racial harassment featured prominently in their interaction. Asian pupils, in particular, were frequently victimized. However, there was no official school policy addressed to this problem. Finally, with respect to the pedagogical orientation featured within the classroom, teachers tried to take the multicultural nature of classrooms into account. But their lack of knowledge and confidence hampered their efforts, and led to embarassment and awkwardness.

Overall, the detailed extracts of classroom interaction have illuminated the breadth of black children's experiences within multicultural/ethnic classrooms. They highlight the processes and practices which combine to disadvantage black children within the education system. In terms of remedying this situation, there is a complex array of issues to be addressed. Among these, in this post-Swann period, are questions concerning educational policy, recent legislation, teacher education, provision for ethnic minority pupils and adequate resources to meet the needs of teachers working with ethnic minority pupils. At the level of the school and questions relating to school policy, there are the issues of school and classroom management, the profile of the staff and the pedagogical and administrative orientation of the school.

CHAPTER 4

Ethnic Relations in Secondary Schools

Gajendra Verma[1]

This chapter reports a wide-ranging study of ethnic relations in nine secondary schools, and discusses the variations in inter-ethnic perception, process and behaviour of both pupils and teachers.

CONTEXT

There has hardly been a time when British society was not to some degree multicultural or multi-ethnic. Celts, Angles, Saxons, Scandinavians, Normans, all found a home here and contributed to the development of a nation. Later on came Jews, Huguenots and other refugees from Europe, Asia and Africa. Parekh (1990) has argued that the nature of this historic diversity differs in both degree and nature from Britain's present plural society. Nonetheless, it provides an important backcloth to twentieth-century developments, and undermines the myths that issues of race and culture have only arisen because of post-war immigration.

The concept of ethnic diversity has gained considerable currency since the 1950s, and has generated much discussion about the nature of British society. It has also become an area of acute controversy within the context of education. The context in which the debates and discussions have evolved could be seen under four overlapping dimensions: socio-economic and political, educational, national, and international. The range of situations and problems examined within these dimensions is wide. Collectively, such analyses have important implications for the ways in which society regulates itself – through legislation, social policy, educational provision and so on. Several studies and reports published so far have implications for the ways in which we perceive our society (DES, 1985). They have contributed to the debate about the way society and its educational system are organized, the common values that should be upheld, and the ways in which the past, present and future should be projected. In a plural society such a debate inevitably involves contentious issues of culture, language and ethnic relations. These issues have long been the source of considerable controversy in education, for the British have traditionally regarded formal schooling as the major institution for the transmission of society's core values and beliefs. Therefore, whenever disagreements over these values and beliefs have arisen, they have been reflected in the schools. Their impact over the last two decades has increased.

Many misconceptions exist concerning the size, growth and composition of ethnic minority groups living in the UK. It is often overlooked that half of the ethnic minority population was born in Britain and nearly three-quarters are British citizens. While many schools have responded to the changing social patterns, there is still much ignorance and misunderstanding among young people. A study of inter-ethnic relations in schools carried out by Verma (1992) showed that schools containing considerable numbers of pupils from ethnic minority groups were much more advanced in developing school policies on ethnic relations than schools with few such pupils. This study also found that 'few teachers were at all knowledgeable about the religions, cultures, values and customs of the ethnic minority groups of their pupils. Often this was attributed to the fact that, with very few exceptions, issues of ethnicity and culture formed no part of their initial training.'

Britain's minority communities are diverse and complex. There are religious communities (for example, Muslims) which cut across cultural and racial groupings. There are communities which share a common linguistic or geographical heritage which may unite beyond religious or other differences. One example of this is Britain's Gujerati community which consists of orthodox Muslims and associated sects (Ismailis, Bhoras, and Ishnasheris), a range of Hindu groups and a small number of Jains and Parsees.

Some communities, including the Chinese and certain European groups, are dispersed throughout almost every town and village of Britain and until recently have had a relatively limited corporate voice. Others are more closely identified with specific towns or districts (like the Jews in London, Leeds and Manchester). Many black communities are found almost entirely in the inner city areas, forming what has been described as an 'underclass' of modern society (Rex and Tomlinson, 1979).

The pattern is further complicated by the varying degrees of separatism or integration within communities; the tension between orthodoxy and radicalism within religious groups; and the search for and rediscovery of linguistic, religious or racial roots of second and third generation immigrants, who might otherwise have been largely assimilated into mainstream British culture. The pattern is dynamic. It is influenced by the attitudes and power of the dominant cultural groups, as well as by the developing (or ossifying) cultures within minority groups. It is clearly important to avoid simplistic descriptions of ethnicity.

Over the last ten years or so, concerns have been expressed about the nature and quality of inter-ethnic relationships among pupils in multi-ethnic schools, and the impact school policies and practices may have on them. However, it would seem impossible to understand such relationships without some reference to the broader issues of interaction between communities in British society at large. The pattern of relationships between dominant and minority communities in society can be complex. The Swann Report (DES, 1985) speaks of two polar positions which the relationship might take: assimilation, in which minority groups lose all distinctive characteristics; and separatism, in which minority communities exist in the same society but with the absolute minimum of contact in order to coexist.

Today, race relations in Britain form part of the complex pattern of urban living, impinging upon a wide range of social issues and provision including housing, employment, policing, social services, and youth work as well as education. In these and other areas of life, ethnic minority groups continue to experience the impact of racism, not least in the lack of access to resources. While national and local government legislation has gone some way to working towards equality of opportunity, stimulated in part by the fear of urban unrest in the late 1970s and 1980s, there is still no wholehearted commitment to total reform. Tomlinson (1990) concludes her review of policies and practices influencing minority communities in urban Britain by suggesting that it will be a long time before policies and practices produce a positive impact on the lives of ethnic minorities.

By the late 1980s, preoccupation with the demands of the Education Reform Act, 1988 and the National Curriculum had diverted much attention and energy away from programmes of multicultural or anti-racist education. As we will see later in this chapter, the present study shows that teachers' answers to questions about developing multicultural policies or curriculum responses frequently refer to the pressures of the National Curriculum or other recent educational innovations, preventing them giving such matters the attention they deserve (Verma, Zec and Skinner, 1994). An in-depth analysis of the National Curriculum suggests that minority cultures have been neglected in the development of the core and foundation subjects. Many minority children and young people are presented with an Anglocentric curriculum which is not only alien and exclusive, but obliterates the realities of their own identities and experiences (Verma, 1992).

A review of various studies and reports shows the range of complex factors which impinge directly or indirectly on the lives and education of all pupils in British schools. Evidence about the quality of inter-ethnic relationships in schools is scarce and inconclusive. School responses have been diverse and inconsistent, and often dependent on local (or even individual) initiatives rather than central government guidelines and support.

The Swann Report (DES, 1985) found much evidence to suggest that many obstacles lay in the path of children from certain ethnic minority groups (e.g. West Indian and Bangladeshi), which lessened their chances of fulfilling their educational potential. Among those obstacles, it was argued in the report, were those created by poor inter-ethnic relationships – both inside schools and in the wider society; by prevalence – again, inside and outside schools – of low levels of inter-ethnic knowledge and understanding; and by the relative failure of schools to prepare *all* pupils, of whatever origin, for life in a multi-ethnic and multicultural society. One of Swann's main recommendations was to conduct research aimed (*inter alia*) at discovering more about factors internal to schools and inter-ethnic understanding, and the development of attitudes appropriate to life in a plural society.

THE STUDY

It was in this context that the study on which this chapter is based was conceived and conducted. Five basic assumptions underpinned the study: These were:

(a) that the state of inter-ethnic relations in the UK continues to be a matter of concern;

(b) that inter-ethnic tension and conflict are correlated with racial prejudice and discrimination;

(c) that the educational system constitutes an important focus for consideration of the connected phenomena of inter-ethnic conflict and racial discrimination

(d) that there is a clear connection between inter-ethnic relationships on the one hand, and educational opportunities and attainments of pupils of ethnic minority origin on the other;

(e) that 'good inter-ethnic relationships' means more than the mere absence of overt hostility or conflict between persons or groups. The phrase suggests, *inter alia*: substantial and reciprocal knowledge and understanding of ways of life between pupil groups of different ethnicity, and between teachers and pupils; substantially shared values concerning, for example, respect for persons, tolerance, rights and duties, together with public commitment to such values throughout a school; and a considerable degree of positive interaction between persons and groups of different ethnicity.

It was our intention that the research should enable us to discern factors in the schools which tend to promote good inter-ethnic relationships. Specifically, as a result of this study, and through the dissemination of its findings, it was hoped that those involved in the shaping or execution of policy in schools would have access to:

(a) a better understanding of the issues, problems and opportunities associated with inter-ethnic relationships;
(b) a clearer grasp as to which of those issues, etc., are capable of being addressed by the school;
(c) a sharper awareness of the factors which promote good inter-ethnic relationships; and
(d) a basis for a more systematic and proactive approach to the practicalities of inter-ethnic relationships, in such contexts as formal and 'hidden' curricula, staff development, pastoral regimes, cultural life in the school, school–community relationships and communication with parents.

Within the limits of time available, and in order to allow for a reasonable depth of study in each school, it was decided to aim for a sample of 10 schools. Constraints on time and access reduced the final sample size to 9 schools. The nature of the research required that all schools in the sample should include among their students some from ethnic minority backgrounds; and to ensure a reasonable degree of ethnic mix, only those with a minimum of 25 per cent ethnic minority students were considered. In addition, all schools chosen had comprehensive intakes and were mixed by gender. The final sample of 9 schools (4 from the south and 5 from the north-west) was drawn from six Local Authorities, 2 in the south of England and 4 in the north-west. The proportion of students from ethnic minority backgrounds varied from 25 per cent to 75 per cent.

In order to provide a reasonable range of ages, it was decided to focus on second-year (year 8) and fourth-year (year 10) students. A sample of one in twelve was used. Students were chosen from the year lists by starting with a random number between one and twelve, and then including every twelfth student. Limitations on time meant that not all teachers in each school could be interviewed, and the following teachers were identified as key members for the study: *(a)* all senior staff: they would have the ultimate responsibility for the implementation of the school's policy and practice, and would have the widest overall perception of inter-ethnic relationships in school (for example, through dealing with discipline matters); *(b)* any teacher supervising the school's multicultural/anti-racist education policy; *(c)* all ethnic minority teachers (if at all possible), especially those teachers from black or Asian backgrounds; *(d)* as many heads of faculties (or departments) as possible, as this would provide useful data about the function of the curriculum in influencing inter-ethnic relationships.

The research was essentially ethnographic. However, it is important that ethnographic researchers are also open to other methodologies, and questionnaires and surveys also have their use in ethnography. Hence, a questionnaire was designed to collect a large quantity of data from students in order to provide a broader backcloth to the research findings. All second- and fourth-year students completed the questionnaire, which consisted mainly of multiple-choice questions with a four- or five-point scale. Where appropriate, open-ended questions or options were included. Students were asked to identify communities, religious and language groups to which they felt they belonged, and to indicate their experience of positive and negative relationships in school, including experience of bullying and name-calling. The study consisted of a series of detailed case studies, and its potential value was dependent on the use of research instruments which were compatible with the ethnographic approach. However, the fact that as many as nine schools have been studied in this way, together with the administration of a questionnaire to a large number of pupils across the nine schools, does inject a *quantitative* dimension to the data which proved helpful as a backcloth against which to place the ethnographic data. Furthermore, the researchers' own observations (in formal and informal situations) were seen as a necessary additional dimension.

Four main perspectives on inter-ethnic relationships shaped the study of each school: the experiences and perceptions of staff; the experiences and perceptions of students; the formal position of the school as represented by official documents; and the observations of the researcher while in school. Research instruments were designed to gather data in all these areas. It was clear from the outset that the perceptions and experiences of staff would be central to any understanding of the state of inter-ethnic relationships in the schools and the procedures being adopted to promote good relationships.

Gathering data from students about their experiences of inter-ethnic relationships and their views about school policy and practice proved more complex. Researchers have often reported the reluctance of pupils to respond in asymmetrical interview situations, and a tendency to resort to defensive, monosyllabic responses. However, for the reasons outlined above, it was felt that a semi-structured interview approach, supplemented with informal conversations and small group discussions, would produce the most accurate and revealing data. The schedule was designed to gather specific data about experiences and attitudes, while allowing freedom to explore issues seen as important by the interviewee. The areas covered were similar to those developed for the teachers, so that comparisons could be made between the perceptions of teachers and students.

Using the instruments outlined above, a large quantity of rich data was obtained. Detailed semi-structured interviews were conducted with almost 200 teachers and nearly 300 students. Several hundred hours were spent in observation and informal conversations. Questionnaires were completed by more than 2,300 students. A wide range of documentary evidence was collected from schools and Local Education Authorities (LEAs). Drawing on the various kinds of data generated by the research instruments, a portrait of each school was produced. The key areas, and the various perceptions of these, which emerged may be illustrated in the form of a matrix (see Figure 4.1).

PATTERNS ARISING FROM THE STUDY

The picture that emerged is complex and at times contradictory. We are cautious about making even tentative generalizations about (for example) the quality of relationships in one school or in all of them; or about teachers' views as compared with pupils', or about regional differences. This reflects not only the great variety of *perceptions* of the quality of relationships within as well as between schools, but also the various messages which arose from the different methods of enquiry adopted. Nevertheless, the questionnaire data

Figure 4.1

Views and experiences of					
	Heads	Teachers	Pupils	Researchers	Others
The state of race relations					
Impact of policy					
Influence of teachers					
Impact of the curriculum					
Equipping of teachers					
Effect of special provision					

proved useful in eliciting from a large sample a broad pattern of student responses on a number of key issues, and some patterns of significant difference between schools and between different ethnic groups. Interviews and discussions with students and teachers revealed more of the texture of those differences than could have been expected from the quantitative data alone. However, the quantitative data was valuable in providing a background of suggestive patterning (see Verma, Zec and Skinner, 1994, for a detailed school-wise analysis).

The questionnaire and interview evidence, which were on the whole well-aligned, suggested that ethnic minority students had a less positive view of inter-ethnic relationships than others; that this was particularly true of Bangladeshi pupils (and, not surprisingly, of others from newly or recently arrived families, such as refugees); that Afro-Caribbean students felt, if anything, more positively than students in general (although the feeling was not always reciprocated), and that membership of a religious minority *as such* did not materially affect the picture.

What did seem to affect the picture, however, was the degree of ethnic diversity in each of the nine schools. In the questionnaire, four schools received the lowest scores for the response: 'they get on very well'. Of those four schools, three had a substantial Bangladeshi community and one an equally substantial Gujerati community; in all cases the other large element was white 'Anglo-Saxon'. The fact that three of the schools were in the northern sample is much less significant than the fact that three of the five northern schools were mainly 'bi-ethnic' rather than multi-ethnic, and only one of the four southern schools. That demographic difference between the two groups of schools may, indeed, reflect differential settlement patterns in the UK; but, with only nine schools involved in the research it is impossible to make such a generalization.

A typical picture of a multi-ethnic school, as reported by most students and teachers, was one in which observed classroom grouping tended to be determined far more by gender than by ethnicity. Very few examples were observed in lessons of blacks sitting next to blacks or Asians sitting next to Asians, and there seemed to be nothing unspontaneous about the cross-ethnic groupings. Observed groupings away from the classroom exhibited the same tendency. Students in the more ethnically diverse schools often expressed the view that it was impossible not to mix, both inside and outside the classroom. Patterns of stronger intra-ethnic preference tended to emerge in the bi-ethnic schools. On the whole, the most likely context for strongly stated intra-ethnic preference was found with Muslim student groups in bi-ethnic schools, where security, mutual support and gender were the most commonly expressed criteria for choice of friends.

It may seem obvious that the degree of mixing between students of different ethnicities in a school is positively connected with the quality of inter-ethnic relationships; but that was not the unanimous view of the teachers. A teacher at one school accepted intra-ethnic grouping 'because of their common ground. People should be proud of their heritage'. At another school, a teacher said 'We all find our own friends. Why should we force things?' Such remarks typify the attitude of a number of teachers in schools where intra-ethnic grouping was more common than cross-ethnic mixing. In the two schools in which there was a numerical (and increasing) majority of Bengali Muslim students, some teachers expressed strong concern at that numerical dominance. In one of the schools, several teachers saw the growing proportion of (mainly) Bengali students as the main cause of a decrease in cross-ethnic mixing. Another teacher saw it as posing a threat to inter-ethnic harmony. At both of these schools, a considerable number of teachers expressed unease about the perceived degree of demographic polarity along ethnic, and in some cases linguistic, lines, and saw it as causing polarization in inter-ethnic relationships:

If we had a better balance in each class, [mixing] would tend to happen more naturally. In a way, it can be quite unhelpful because if you take certain classes, some of the local grown products are two or three in maybe twenty-five, so they probably feel they've been taken over. . . . So in a way I think it can be quite unhelpful having so many kids of a particular ethnic origin in a group.

The other behaviour which also seemed to vary in a proportion to a school's ethnic diversity was inter-ethnic abuse on 'racial' or religious lines. Briefly, students in the four bi-ethnic schools reported higher levels of name-calling on the whole than in the more diverse schools. In the questionnaire, a significantly higher proportion of Muslim students than others reported experiencing name-calling fairly or very often, and Muslim students were, of course, to be found in higher proportions in the bi-ethnic schools.

In sum, the quantitative data, interviews and discussions with students and teachers and our own observations convinced us that inter-ethnic relationships were better in the five relatively multi-ethnic, than in the bi-ethnic, schools. By 'better', we mean 'more harmonious, mutually tolerant, interactive, collaborative and friendly'. We do not necessarily mean that they were more free from any kind of conflict – though this was probably true of some of the schools as compared with some others.

It is noteworthy that hardly any of the schools in the research were in a position to provide a definitive picture of the make-up of the school by ethnic group. There was evidence of uncertainty about aims and methods of generating information on the ethnic make-up of the school. In fact, none of the schools in the south kept records of the ethnicity of students. Despite the lack of accurate statistical information, there were many examples of practical measures taken by schools to acknowledge the presence of ethnic minorities; there were also many cases of failure to do so. However, schools should – indeed, must – know their students; this is the first prerequisite for providing an appropriate educational – and, as far as possible, social – environment for all of them.

In general, it appeared that the more ethnically diverse a school was, the less sustained and proactive it seemed to be in its communication with ethnic minority parents as ethnic minority parents. This state of affairs could be explained by a lower sense of urgency about the matter in schools where the pattern of ethnicity was comparatively fragmented and varied, compared with schools where there was a large constituency to consult. Another overlapping explanation might be that the highly diverse schools tended to be located in areas of longer-established multi-ethnic settlement, where minority communities were less self-contained. But neither of these explanations justifies the failure of a school to be an effective communicator with all of its parents and the communities they represent. However, we did encounter numerous particular examples of good communication with parents at the highly diverse schools – in many instances more successful than at the others.

Turning to the ethnic profiles of teaching staff, there was a major difference between the northern and southern schools which is difficult to explain. The fact that most of the southern schools were also more ethnically diverse in their student composition than their northern counterparts is not necessarily relevant. In any case, one school, with its 17 ethnic minority teachers and an absolute majority of Bangladeshi students, was a notable exception to that pattern. Three interconnected factors are likely to have been relevant. First, the fact that all the southern schools were in Greater London and benefited from the mobility and cosmopolitanism that this implied. Second, the southern schools had a much longer track record of comprehensivization and multi-ethnic intakes than all, except perhaps one, of the northern schools. Thirdly, the relatively high staff turnover in the south compared with the northern schools (the average age and length of service of staff in the former were considerably lower than in the latter), meant that there must have been more opportunities for teachers from ethnic minority communities in the London schools.

If ethnic minorities are under-represented on a school's staff, the school should do everything short of illegal reverse discrimination to redress that imbalance. (By 'under-representation' I simply mean a lower level of representation than the proportion of ethnic minorities in the population as a whole.) This is nothing more than a policy of promoting equal opportunity in a society whose ethnic minorities have been the disproportionate victims of inequality, and it is to be justified in terms of that general principle. But there is also a specific justification – at once social and educational – for such a policy: that a school should exemplify, not just deliver, a multicultural education.

The research schools differed markedly in the extent to which they were in a position to control their ethnic and other kinds of intake profile. Government policy on the organization of secondary education, especially the injection of 'market forces' and the assault on LEAs, is likely to exacerbate that Darwinistic tendency. If the likeliest candidate for good inter-ethnic relationships is a school with a thorough pupil mix of ethnicity, ability and socio-economic backgrounds, together with a cosmopolitan staffroom, there is clearly no point in just calling on schools to acquire those characteristics. But it would seem reasonable to expect schools to know and understand as much as possible about their intakes, and to do everything in their power to make themselves a welcoming environment to all students and to attract and cherish teachers from ethnic minority backgrounds.

The six LEAs in which the research schools were situated were all committed, at least on paper, to equal opportunities and the promotion of intercultural understanding. However, there were wide differences between and within schools in teachers' evaluation of the LEA policies. The majority thought that the policy statements in themselves were satisfactory or good (as far as they felt able to judge); a minority felt that they were vague and platitudinous. One teacher wondered whether it might not be 'overstated' and might cause alienation. A very common criticism was that the policy statements contained no suggested strategies for implementation; another was that LEA support for implementation at school level was inadequate. Teachers were much more aware of the existence and detailed contents of their own school policies than those of the LEAs. The composite view expressed to us by many teachers was that the key to effective policies comprises ownership, implementation and monitoring. There was no consistency across the sample schools in these attributes, although clearly some schools were taking them very seriously.

In all the schools, the majority of teachers interviewed said that their initial teacher training (ITT) had done almost nothing to prepare them to teach in multi-ethnic schools. The majority of these teachers had received their training more than twenty years ago, when issues of race and culture were on the whole not seriously addressed in training institutions. But interviews with more recently trained teachers provided very little evidence to suggest that ITT was responding to cultural diversity in any substantial or consistent way. Often there was little difference in perception of the value of their initial training course in preparing teachers for multi-ethnic schools, between those trained very recently and those trained in the 1970s. But recently trained teachers were more likely than older colleagues to comment on having gained some insights into this area, particularly if they had chosen a college or university in a multi-ethnic area.

The evidence from the teacher sample supports the conclusion of the

Swann Report (DES, 1985) that initial teacher training had on the whole failed to prepare teachers adequately for teaching in plural Britain. All current ITT programmes are required to demonstrate that they include a multicultural and equal-opportunities dimension; it may thus be assumed that all recently trained teachers will have received some preparation for teaching in multi-ethnic schools. But the introduction by the Government of largely school-based initial training raises the question of whether and how student (or apprentice) teachers will in the future gain knowledge, critical understanding and experience in the areas of equal opportunities, ethnic diversity and multicultural education. The pattern for the schools and LEAs in the present study showed some increase in the number of teachers who had received relevant *in-service* teacher education (INSET), compared with the picture presented by the Swann Report (DES, 1985). However, the report's expressed hope for the permeation of all INSET with multicultural sensitivity had yet to be realized for most teachers in this sample.

There were noticeable variations in students' perceptions of intercultural knowledge and understanding between different ethnic groups: more ethnic and/or religious minority students than all other students claimed to know 'quite a bit' or 'a lot' about others' cultures. There was considerable variation in students' perceptions between schools: more students in the northern schools felt they knew 'quite a bit' about others' cultures than those in the southern schools. There was also a strong tendency for northern students to report more positively than those in the south on the extent to which teachers helped them to understand other students' cultures. It is interesting to note, however, from the analysis of questionnaire responses that these apparent regional variations did not correlate well with the overall quality of inter-ethnic relationships as perceived by students. For this and other reasons it is at least clear that levels of intercultural knowledge alone cannot determine the quality of inter-ethnic relationships.

Teachers who were optimistic about the potential benefits of increased intercultural knowledge tended to base their view on intuition more than on specific examples. Our view, based on what we saw, is that some teachers are too close to their subject-matter and to their students to see the benefits actually taking place. It is, perhaps, worth reflecting that not the least of the possible advantages of the 'action research' model of teachers' professional development is that it does challenge them to analyse practices – perhaps very good practices – which they otherwise either take for granted, or consciously relate only to externally imposed instrumental goals. A considerable proportion of teachers interviewed put more emphasis on the limitations of planned transmission of intercultural knowledge and appropriate values by the school when set against the influences of home and the wider community:

> We can give them a sense of equal value, but translating it into the playground is another matter. Children suffer prejudice everywhere in society. It's a slow process to change the school so much.

Other teachers emphasized the importance of parental influence, and of the state of community relations in the school's catchment area. Their awareness of those influences was sometimes reinforced by our own perceptions. However, both in interviews with students and teachers and through our own observations, we have been made aware of how powerful community factors can be in shaping relationships in school. On a number of occasions, particular problems in the local community which had a 'racial' dimension seemed to be having a considerable, if short-term, impact on the quality of inter-ethnic life in the schools.

Correlated with the fact that students tended to see planned provision by the school as a limited source of knowledge and understanding of others' cultures, were teachers' own confessions of ignorance in this area. There was considerable variation between schools in the amount and quality of information provided on cultural diversity (for example, through displays, multilingual information and resources, material on religions, resources supplied by local communities reflecting students' cultures, relevant publications in the staffroom and library, etc.). Interviews with teachers revealed that, while many of them were knowledgeable, experienced and sensitive in one relevant way or another, this was due much more to long experience of working in inner-city multi-ethnic and multi-faith situations, or to other relevant life experience, than to specific and substantial professional development in which learning more about students' cultural backgrounds was a major element. Overall, many teachers expressed a lack of sufficient knowledge of their students' cultural backgrounds. It is, therefore, not surprising that on the whole students tended to see their own intercultural knowledge as arising more from life than from planned school provision.

Teachers' perceptions of the curriculum as part of a school's response to cultural diversity were undoubtedly affected by the impact of National Curriculum requirements, which at the time of the research were engaging teachers in new, time-consuming and often bureaucratic tasks. An additional factor shaping approaches to a curriculum sensitive to cultural diversity was the particular situation of certain schools at the time; for example, reorganization involving the introduction of ethnic minority students in sizeable numbers; and newness, and transfer from the Inner London Education Authority (ILEA) to a new Borough Authority. A third factor which seemed relevant to many aspects of inter-ethnic relationships was the ethnic make-up of the schools studied. Some of the teachers in schools which in the main had a large proportion of one ethnic minority group talked about the undesirability of a merely 'bi-ethnic' curriculum, and stressed the importance of a global perspective. That view highlights the issue of whether a curriculum for cultural diversity should be based on the rationale of reflecting the ethnic composition of a school and neighbourhood; or whether the rationale should be independent of local demography.

In all schools, the majority of students said that they learnt very little in lessons about how different groups of people in Britain lived. A somewhat higher proportion, though still a minority, said that they learnt something in lessons about the world outside Britain. Most students seemed not to be conscious of curricular aims of imparting world perspectives or awareness of cultural diversity in Britain. The extent to which development of knowledge and values appropriate to good relationships is addressed across the faculties and departments of a school, and not only in isolated areas and by enthusiastic individual teachers, at least reflects the extent to which there is a whole-school approach to the issue of relationships. In some of the nine schools studied there seemed to be a high level of consciousness of the importance of inter-ethnic relationships and equal opportunities in general, and this was reflected across the curriculum. In others, the picture was much more fragmented, and curriculum responses to cultural diversity were relatively dependent on individual initiative.

Overall, ethnic minority students were under-represented in extra-curricular participation, with Muslim girls the most likely not to take part. If such involvement and informal contact with other students and staff is as effective as many teachers argued in promoting good inter-ethnic understanding and relationships, then the low level of participation by Asian students is likely to lessen the impact of attempts to develop a whole-school response to cultural diversity. Unfortunately, evidence presented by most teachers indicated that the number and scope of extra-curricular activities in schools are in decline.

The degree to which schools responded to minority needs varied across the sample. In all but one school, where most teachers felt that the school had made slow progress in responding to minority needs, teachers reported that their schools were taking such needs seriously and developing appropriate responses. However, in all schools, the philosophical and practical problems associated with such responses were often raised.

The main 'special' provision mentioned by teachers in all schools was ESL/E2L. The range of provision varied. Most schools provided some language support for parents at parents' evenings, or used translating services from time to time for letters or newsletters. However, often schools depended on the goodwill of teachers or others who spoke minority languages rather than an LEA support service.

The second most frequent area of response to minority students was towards religious needs, particularly of Muslim students. Teachers from all schools spoke about the importance of respecting religious beliefs and practices. However, the nature and range of practical responses to minority religious needs varied substantially. In most schools, assemblies tended to be broadly Christian with some recognition of other faiths, particularly at festival times. Teachers were asked if they were aware of any particular requests made by minority communities. All the schools which reported such requests argued that they tried to respond, usually successfully. Most issues were to do with dress, translation of documents, and matters to do with games and PE. In some schools it was reported that there were few such requests. Although most teachers were in favour of their school responsibility to the felt or perceived needs of minority students, there was also a degree of ambivalence. The tensions mentioned by many teachers were often alluded to in one way or another.

The effective implementation of school policies (or principles) depends to some degree on the quality of interpersonal relationships – between the headteachers and their staff, between senior management and other teachers, and between teachers and students. In the absence of any specific questions in the research instruments, it would be unwise to make generalizations about how students viewed the attitudes of teachers towards race or the responses of teachers to minority students. However, it was clear that a small proportion of students interviewed (both black and white) felt that some teachers were racially prejudiced in their treatment of ethnic minority pupils. In most schools, this perception was supported by one or more of the teachers interviewed. There was also evidence of ethnic minority students believing that their teachers had low expectations of them.

The frequency of reported (abusive) name-calling varied considerably between students. Students in the schools with a high proportion of one ethnic minority (bi-ethnic schools) reported higher levels of name-calling on the whole than students in the more truly multi-ethnic schools. In this sample, name-calling to do with race was reported most frequently, although among ethnic minority students, religion was also often mentioned. A significantly higher proportion of Muslim students compared with others reported experiencing name-calling fairly or very often. Evidence obtained in this research supports the view reported by other researchers that name-calling, even if it is not intended to be offensive, leads to a progressive breakdown in relationships between students, resulting in increased inter-ethnic tension and hostility.

The question may well be asked whether a school which had a well-defined and published set of guidelines on dealing with 'racial' incidents was likely to deal with them more effectively than a school which did not. In those schools where systematic attempts appeared to be made to deal with 'racial' incidents procedures varied, but all involved some sort of documentary recording. More striking was the variety of perceptions even within schools as to what the recording procedure actually was, and whose responsibility it was. In at least one school staff opinion seemed to differ on whether the senior teacher who kept a log of incidents should do so, because of the contestability of the concept of racism. It is difficult to resist the judgement that there was more evidence of schools' earnestness of intention about dealing with racism than there was of consistency, consensus and confidence within the schools in identifying and confronting it.

It would be easy to over-react to the tendency of some students in some schools to group. After all, most students in most schools spend their time in all-white groups. Small groups are constantly forming and reforming around friendships, social background, gender and common interests. In multi-racial schools, grouping on shared ethnic, linguistic or religious interests become that much more obvious. We agree with the teacher in a northern school who commented, 'They do tend to stay in groups but it doesn't matter. We all find our own friends. Why should we force things?' However, it would be naive to suggest that such grouping never resulted from a sense of alienation or fear on the one hand, or aggressiveness and intimidation on the other. Schools need to be sensitive to the causes of grouping. Except in situations where a grouping of students was perceived as a threat (to other students or even teachers), there was no unanimous view about its impact on the quality of inter-ethnic relationships.

CONCLUSION

It has not been possible within the confines of this chapter to explore fully the data gathered, and how our thinking was influenced by the conduct of the investigation. However, it is hoped that it will nonetheless offer some insights into the complex of interacting factors and processes that bear on ethnic relations in secondary schools. This chapter concludes, again drawing on the study, by outlining what one might expect to see in a school seeking to promote good ethnic relationships:

- It should seek to get to know its students very well.
- It should be concerned that its teachers become interculturally literate. This will have clear implications for professional development programmes; and, in the content of devolved budgets and scarce resources, opportunities should be seized where possible to use resources exemplified by staff and others in the schools.
- It should be tireless and constant in its determination to inform, consult, explain and persuade in implementing policy and practice in the areas of inter-ethnic relationships and equality of opportunity in general.
- It should seek to recruit, retain and promote minority teachers. That need not entail positive discrimination of the sort that would be illegal; it would entail a legally and morally legitimate policy of affirmative action. Ethnic minority teachers should never be marginalized, whatever the official reason for their appointment.
- A school and its curriculum managers should be clear that (even) within the National Curriculum, the opportunities for routinizing a multicultural curriculum, in all subjects, *on good educational grounds*, are plentiful. That should be a priority. There is no excuse – or need – for an ethnocentric curriculum (see Pumfrey and Verma, 1992; 1993; Verma and Pumfrey, 1992; 1994).
- It should seek to maximize the opportunities available for extra-curricular activities, especially those in which ethnic minority students can realistically participate.
- A school mainly containing a polarity of two ethnic groups – say, white Anglo-Saxon and Bengali – should do all it can to prevent polarity turning into polarization.

- It should build a clear, democratically formulated and pervasive framework of democratic values, and should locate its determination to confront the repertoire of inter-ethnic abuse within that framework. Senior managers should consistently manifest their commitment to it; whether or not that code of values takes the form of a written constitution is, perhaps, less important. The code should be accompanied by clear procedures, which involve class and year teachers, parents and the community, and which are publicly known.

- A school should not hesitate to repudiate any tendency of members of its staff (academic, administrative or ancillary) to manifest racist attitudes or behaviour. A culture of prejudice or stereotyping among staff should be unequivocally rejected.

CHAPTER 5

The Schooling of Young Black Women
Heidi Mirza

Chapter 5 describes the meritocratic perspective of second generation Afro-Caribbean young women and their negotiation of educational pathways, in the context of parental aspirations and egalitarian female role perceptions.

It is now established that significant numbers of young black women do relatively well at school.[1] However, understanding relative black female success is an aspect of social enquiry that has vexed educational researchers and policy-makers for many years. An examination of contemporary educational discourse over the last three decades reveals an interesting paradox of exclusion and inclusion with regard to young black women in educational research. The former, the *exclusion* of young black women in race and education studies appears to be fuelled by political undercurrents which, since the 1960s, have sought to maintain the myth of black underachievement (Mirza, 1992). On the other hand, when young black women were *included* in educational research in the 1980s and early 1990s,[2] their relative success was explained within the problematic context of 'the strong black female' (Mirza, 1993). With its reification of motherhood and marginalization of the black male, this popular theoretical construction appears to be the outcome of an attempt to explain achievement within a discourse whose underlying premise maintains the 'idea' of underachievement.

If the contemporary discourse on race and education renders black female success invisible and the myth of the 'strong black mother' appears to be the outcome of inappropriate, ethnocentric theories of female oppression that dominate educational research, then how do we attempt to theorize the black female positive orientation to education? In a critical evaluation of these existing explanations, I argue that young black women engage in a dynamic rationalization of the education system. My findings show that young black women, who identify with the notion of credentialism, meritocracy and female autonomy, strategically employ every means at their disposal in the educational system and classroom to achieve a modicum of mobility in a world of limited opportunities: an aspect of enquiry that is often either ignored or misunderstood by policy-makers and educational researchers, for whom black women still remain invisible.

THE STUDY[3]

For the purpose of rethinking black female academic achievement, I examine the experiences of second-generation African Caribbean women living in Britain. These young women are the British-born daughters of migrants who came to Britain in the 1950s. Encouraged by the British government's recruitment drive for cheap skilled and semi-skilled labour, these West Indians came from their newly emerging post-colonial countries to work mainly in the hotel and catering, transport and hospital services. The recipients of crude anti-immigrant hostility, and, later, the more subtle workings of institutional racism, these black migrants and their descendants have experienced many obstacles to their social, economic and political advancement.[4]

The overall aim of the project was to investigate the complex influences that affect the career aspirations and expectations of young black women. The 62 young black women in this study, who were aged between 15 and 19 years, attended two average-sized secondary schools in two of the most disadvantaged inner city Boroughs of south London. Comparative data was collected on the aspirations and expectations of young white working-class women and men as well as young black men. This data, which acted as a 'control', is not reported here in detail as the findings discussed relate to only one aspect of this research project; that is, the educational orientation of young women of African Caribbean descent.

In each school, a random sample was drawn from pupils in the fifth and sixth years. All pupils and schools were given fictitious names. At St Hilda's, a co-educational Catholic school, a sample of 128 (65 per cent) black and white male and female pupils was taken, whereas 70 (35 per cent) were taken from St Theresa's, a single-sex, Church of England school.

The study combined a longitudinal survey approach with a school-based ethnographic study. The young black women and their black and white male and female peers, who numbered 198 in all, and who could be objectively identified as coming from working-class homes, answered questionnaires, and were interviewed and observed in their homes and classrooms over a period of 18 months. Of these, 62 (31 per cent) were African Caribbean young women; 13 (7 per cent) were African Caribbean young men; 77 (39 per cent) were young women from other (mainly white) backgrounds; 46 (23 per cent) were young men from other (mainly white) backgrounds.[5] Several parents and teachers of these pupils also participated in the study.

The data reported here highlighted three influences on black female educational motivation. First, the cultural orientation of working-class migrants toward meritocracy and credentialism. Second, the strategic rationalization of post-sixteen education and careers. And third, the expectation of economic independence and the prevalence of relative autonomy between the sexes. Each of these three factors is explored below.

MIGRATION AND MERITOCRACY: THE ORIGINS OF A NEW SOCIAL MOVEMENT?

Gilroy (1987) argues that the struggle for educational opportunities among Britain's black communities merits recognition as a new social movement. Such 'fragile collectivities', he explains, are characterized by their mobilization around the collective consumption of services, develop a distinct cultural identity, and operate by means of a self-managed political autonomy. Indeed, among the West Indians' collective but autonomous political struggle for better educational conditions, a distinct community identity did evolve (Pearson, 1981). Gilroy suggests that while these collectivities or movements are not necessarily agents for social change, they are nevertheless symptoms of 'resistance to domination'. It could be argued, as indeed I wish to suggest here, that the extent, direction and intensity of the black female positive orientation to education is significant enough to qualify their collective action as an educational movement. An investigation into the rationale and internal dynamics of such a movement offers a new direction in the investigation of black female achievement.

My research findings show that the first-generation West Indian migrant identification with the ideology of meritocracy is important in shaping the characteristics of a second-generation black females' educational movement. Positive attitudes to education, and the lack of restrictions on female labour-market participation within West Indian families, were major factors in accounting for the high educational aspirations of the young women in the study. A detailed consideration of West Indian, working-class, migrant cultural characteristics, which I undertake here, revealed that in fact young black women were strongly influenced by their parents. The explanation for young black womens' positive orientation seemed to lie within an understanding of the transmission of the West Indian migrant working-class ethos, the values of which had filtered down to the girls from their parents, and had subsequently been modified.

It is often the case that people migrate for 'a better life'. This is as true of the West Indians who came to the UK as of any other group of people. West Indians came to Britain in the 1950s in what can be argued as both a male and female headed migration, in search of better opportunities for themselves and their children. While objectively, occupational opportunities for migrants are restricted by specific constraints with regard to their disadvantaged labour-market position, there is another dimension to migrant life: that of their own subjective occupational orientation. This internal cultural dynamic of migrants, what I call the 'migrant effect', refers to the degree to which migrants themselves pursue the goal of upward occupa-tional mobility, particularly for the next generation, by striving for educational achievement and qualifications. The influence of this 'migrant effect' on educational outcomes may vary according to the culture of the migrant group, the country of settlement, and economic and social conditions (especially significant is the extent of racial exclusion and discrimination); but it nevertheless remains a characteristic feature among many migrant groups (Alba, 1985).

Glazer and Moynihan (1963), in their study of American migrant society, *Beyond the Melting Pot*, discuss the drive for educational credentials among the many migrant groups in the US. They describe the Jews' 'passion' for education; the Italian concept of (family) social status through the professional occupations of their children; the Puerto Rican capacity for hard work and the value they place on schooling. Of the West Indian migrants who came to the USA in 1920–25, Glazer and Moynihan write, 'The ethos of the West Indians . . . emphasised saving, hard work, investment and education . . . buying homes and in general advancing themselves' (p. 35). They remark that West Indians such as Marcus Garvey, 'furious' at the prejudice they encountered in America (which they felt was far greater than that among the whites in their home islands), turned to radical politics. Bettelheim and Janowitz (1977) support this thesis of political involvement, claiming that blacks, having the lowest ethnic status have therefore the highest level of class consciousness.

Indeed, a degree of political consciousness among early black migrants to the UK has been demonstrated by the 'Black Education movement' set up by this generation of migrants (Chevannes, 1979; Pearson, 1981; Tomlinson, 1985). The struggle for basic educational rights has been a political focal point for the 'black community' since the 1960s. However, as Tomlinson observes, it is not so much a radical movement but one that seeks to ensure equality of opportunity for migrant children within the education system. Confirming that migrant parents have strong educational aspirations for their children, Tomlinson (1982) writes, 'The parents, very much aware of the discrimination their children could face in seeking employment after school, placed great faith in the acquisition of educational qualifications to help overcome this' (p. 34).

Parental recognition that the British education system discriminates against the black child has resulted in the establishment of black supplementary schools, spearheaded by the action, in particular, of black women. These separate black schools embody the belief that education will ultimately help black children to succeed in an 'English' system, by providing them with the credentials necessary for employment or further education and training in the majority society.

It was found in the study that black parents wanted improved educational standards for their children, and despite the general feeling of disillusionment and mistrust towards the schools their daughters attended, still retained their faith in the meritocratic ideal. Among the parents interviewed it was clear that securing educational opportunities for their children was of central importance. As one father explained:

> We work to give our children opportunity. We earn to pay rent, buy a little food. Man, there was no time for bettering ourself. Our children, they now have the benefits to better theyself, education and so on. We didn't have these opportunities, our childrens now have these opportunities and we's work hard for them. [sic] (Mr Burgess, London Transport maintenance)

Clark (1983) puts forward a thesis as to why poor black families succeed in education. He argues that too often studies emphasize family composition (i.e. single parent families, etc.), and not family disposition (i.e. beliefs and values). This is an important point. Black girls in the study did seem to derive much of their determination for 'getting on' from their parental orientation, and both the passive and active support this engendered. It was apparent that West Indian parents did encourage their daughters and were proud of their successes in many different ways. Many of the young women in the study described how their parents had an important role to play in influencing not only their cultural identity, but also in shaping their specific educational outlooks, both of which combined to make them what they were today:

> Both my parents brought me up in the West Indian way. They brought me and are still bringing me up in the way their parents brought them up. I would like to pass this West Indian tradition down to my children so that this tradition lives on and never dies. (Karen, mother: nurse; father: London Transport maintenance)

Nancy Foner (1979) in the late 1970s makes the following observation about the orientation of West Indian migrants' children towards education in the years to come. She writes, 'The struggle to get a good education may, however, become a central focus in their lives; the second generation set their goals higher than their parents have, and measure their achievements and prospects by English rather than Jamaican standards' (p. 217). Indeed, as Foner predicted, the second-generation West Indian girls in this study did show a strong commitment to education, and in particular identified with the meritocratic ideal as a means of 'getting on'. This was clearly illustrated in the girls' optimistic statements. For example:

> Black people work hard and want to really make something of themselves. I want to get on in my life. (Maureen: aspiration social work; mother: office worker; father: carpenter)

> I believe you can really change things for yourself, it is up to you but you really can. (Laurie: aspiration sports woman; mother: secretary; father: BT engineer).

A fundamental belief that these young black women share is that no matter who you are, if you work hard and do well at school you will be rewarded in the world of work. The goal of 'equality of opportunity' that it encompasses suggests that the occupational outcomes of pupils should be a reflection of their educational achievements, regardless of class, race or gender. It is ironic that such an outwardly individualistic ideology which centres around the notion of credentialism and meritocracy, expressed in the desire for personal academic qualifications, should engender a collective social movement. It is equally ironic that this 'meritocratic' ideal, while a fundamental pillar of liberal democratic society and hence enshrined in the British educational system, should also be a central ideology of a black female educational movement: a movement whose motivation appears to be a strategic rationalization of the very system that oppresses them. Whatever the ideological orientation of such a movement, it nevertheless enables young black women to 'resist domination' and to achieve social change in a world of limited opportunities.

'STRATEGIC RATIONALIZATION': THE CHALLENGE TO SUBCULTURAL THEORY

In the 1980s, the notion of 'subcultures of resistance' became the perceived wisdom for not only explaining the persistence of working-class inequality, but also sexual and racial inequality. This notion of subcultures of resistance was developed from the influential work of the cultural reproductionists who, in the late 1970s, dominated the analysis of social inequality in Britain.[6] This theory, which suggests that through their own activity and ideological development, young working-class men and women reproduce themselves as a working class, appeared to offer the ideal framework for developing an understanding of positive black female orientation to education. The preoccupation with subculture which dominates the small but distinct body of scholarship on young black women in Britain, has had far reaching consequences for our understanding of black female academic motivation. Today, romantic, celebratory notions of black female 'subcultures of resistance' prevail in both our commonsense and academic discussions. The notion of subculture appears to have been employed, firstly because it offers an imaginative and interpretive account of the girls' 'lived out experiences' of racism in the classroom. And secondly, it offers an understanding of creativity, activity and resistance, while leaving intact the pervasive myth of black underachievement. Emphasizing the subcultural features of youth remains descriptive, diverting our attention away from the structural issues which determine the quality of the experience of those being studied; issues such as unemployment, compulsory miseducation, the prospect of low pay and dead-end jobs.

Challenging the existing and popular explanation of positive motivation, that is subcultural identity, I argue instead that young black women engage in a dynamic rationalization of the education system. My findings show that young black women strategically employ every means at their disposal in the educational system and classroom in order to negotiate the institutional practices, and overcome the limited resources that shape their educational opportunities. An examination of the schooling of young black women revealed a challenge to the central

characteristic of black female subcultures; that is, the strategy of resistance within accommodation, or the anti-school/pro-educational position.
Often the young women would sit at the back of the classroom and carry
on with 'prep' or homework, neither being disruptive nor participating.
Fuller (1982) suggests that the negative classroom stance which she
also observed among the girls in her study, was a manifestation of the
'subcultural' resistance to the negative connotations that arose from
being black (in school) and female (at home). She suggests the forms
of action by the black girls in her study were strategies for trying
to effect some control over their present and future lives by publicly
proving their own worth through their academic success. Ten years on,
Mac an Ghaill (1993), employing a more celebratory account, suggests
that the mixture of rebellion and acceptance displayed by the 'black
sisters' in his study was an extension of the historical survival strategies
found among the oppressed. In Gillborn's (1990) interpretation of the
female subculture in his study, he asserts that the strategy of resistance
and accommodation revolved around protecting younger pupils from
experiences of sexual harassment and racism suffered at the hands of the
teachers, together with a solidarity borne from the common experience
of future domestic roles.

However, there was little evidence to support any of these views
of the often obvious classroom dissent among young black women.
The girls simply appeared to be getting on with their own work as
a means of rationalizing what they considered to be unproductive and
wasteful lesson time. It was clear that the young women had developed
a strategy by which they gauged those lessons and teachers that were
worth listening to. Their response to certain reachers was the result
of the girls' particular and unique orientation to education, which was
clearly the outcome of their identification with meritocratic ideals, a
product of their West Indian migrant social class background. Clearly,
the young women held similar expectations about education and success
as their parents. This accounted for their often-stated preference for
strong discipline in the classroom which they identified as 'control', and
organized, structured lessons which they regarded as 'good teaching'.

It was a fact that, in many cases, the girls' academic energies
were often diverted to strategies aimed at avoiding unpleasant sce-
narios within the school environment, rather than in the activity of
learning. It was not uncommon to find teachers expressing openly
their misgivings about the intellectual capabilities of the black girls
in their care. During informal conversation and formal interviews

that I had with them, 75 per cent of the teachers in the study made at least one negative comment about the black girls they taught. I was told by one fifth-year teacher and careers mistress that:

> Most of these girls will never succeed . . . they are just unable to remember, the girls just can't make it at this level ('O' level and CSE), never mind what is demanded in higher education. There is what I call 'brain death' among them . . . unable to think for themselves.

All too often the recognition of these negative assessments led the girls to look for alternative strategies with which to 'get by'. These strategies, such as not taking up a specific subject or not asking for help, were employed by the girls as the only means of challenging their teachers' expectations of them, and as such were ultimately detrimental to the education of the pupils concerned.[7]

If the overall effect of the young black womens' schooling was to restrict opportunity rather than facilitate it, then the strategy of 'staying on' in pursuit of educational qualifications can be seen not as a subcultural stance but a rational response to their impoverished secondary school experience. In her study, Fuller (1982) observed the girls' commitment and resoluteness in their efforts to achieve their goals. While she was right to do so, she was in my view less correct in describing this positive orientation as a 'subculture of resistance', the outcome of a reaction to negative parental and societal pressures towards them as being black and female. In my study, 'staying on' was the way many working-class black women expressed their aspirations for 'getting on' in life, when clearly their educational experience had restricted them.

Literature examining the educational characteristics of young black women suggests that they, more than any other group, and in particular in contrast to their white female counterparts, endeavour to pursue their education beyond the statutory minimum requirements.[8] My study upheld these findings, demonstrating that 80 per cent of black female pupils wished to continue in full-time education after the age of sixteen. These findings contrasted with the responses of the white girls, only 65 per cent of whom stated their preference for staying on. It was also found that the majority of young black women in the sixth forms were doing GCSE and 'O' level resits rather than 'A' levels, in order to get the grades and subjects they had previously been unable to attain.

The motivation for achievement through educational qualifications is, for young black women, reflected in their choice of social work jobs. The occupations they chose always required a course or several courses of rigorous professional training. Thus, when we consider the reasons why the girls aspired to high-status, caring jobs, they were in effect expressing their meritocratic orientation within the constraints of a racially and sexually divisive educational economic system. In the example of Dianne, it becomes clear as to what is the nature of and mechanism by which this 'rationale' operates. She explains:

> I have chosen to go to college at the end of the year because the job I want to do only happens at college and not at school. The course I want to do is social care and lasts up to 2 years. At my age now I would not go into a job because the payment at 16 is disgraceful, so if I go to college for 2 years then I would leave and get a job after I know that I am qualified. (Dianne, aged 17; father: welder; mother: cook; ability range, high)

Dianne's statement clearly shows that her decision to do social care is based largely on the fact that for her it offers the opportunity to go on and enhance her financial status by virtue of increasing her occupational mobility. Educational qualifications are seen as part of that process, and for black women social work is a known and safe option in which to strive for such a goal.

Similarly, office jobs were regarded as upwardly mobile choices for young women whose migrant parents had been, or still were, located in the often unpleasant, badly paid sector of unskilled/semi-skilled manual labour in the UK. These jobs were pragmatic choices, for not only did they present attractive prospects to the girls as far as pay and conditions were concerned, but they were also attainable in terms of the necessary qualifications.

While the majority of black women do opt for what can be described as the more traditional 'gendered' black women's careers, there was some evidence that black girls were far more likely than their white peers to move willingly into traditionally male occupational preserves. Their desire for woodwork and other conventionally defined 'male' subjects at school is often cited as evidence of this uniquely black female tendency (Griffin, 1985; Riley, 1985). Their relatively higher uptake and enrolment on 'trade' and access courses, leading to plumbing, electrical and carpentry training, is also used to indicate this trend. Why should this be so? To date, the explanation for this 'phenomenon' has centred around an argument which suggests that this willingness is a form of resistance; a conscious statement of 'blackwomanhood'. However, in my opinion, the willingness of young black women to undertake traditionally male work is the outcome of two aspects that are related to their orientation to education and work.

Firstly, all the evidence so far suggests that young black women are primarily motivated in their career aspirations by the prospect of upward mobility. A job, therefore, is an expression of the desire to move ahead by means of the educational process. The belief in the promise of a meritocracy and the rewards of credentalism spur black women on to take up whatever opportunities that may become available and accessible to them, especially opportunities that entail a chance to increase their further educational qualifications. Secondly, there was no evidence of any cultural constraint that inhibited a woman from aspiring to any occupation that she felt competent to train for and undertake, an aspect of enquiry to which I now turn.

THE SOCIAL CONSTRUCTION OF BLACKWOMANHOOD: CHALLENGING THE MYTH OF THE SUPERWOMAN

Within the subcultural model, the central dynamic for black female motivation is the strong role model of the mother figure, and in particular the 'unique' orientation to motherhood. However, in an assessment of the cultural construction of gender among young African Caribbean women which I undertake here, there was little evidence to support the notion of the 'strong black mother'.

'The strong black mother', as constructed in educational research, is not unlike its better known counterpart, the 'black superwoman'; a popular image with the press.[9] Despite its dubious merits, the media myth of the dynamic black superwoman, busy outstripping her male partner in terms of achievements in education and work, has been uncritically adopted as a social reality in the public mind. Employing a similar rationale, the academic notion of the 'strong black mother' suggests that black women possess internal and natural strengths that account for their endurance and ability to overcome the structural racism and sexism they face in the workplace and in the home.

Though on the surface the notion of intergenerational maternal support appears a logical and positive interpretation of black female motivation, it nevertheless presents many problems for the development of educational and social policy with regard to black women. Because black women are seen able to motivate themselves by drawing on their inner strengths and cultural resources, it engenders a complacency towards them. Young black women, who are seen as the beneficiaries of special maternal encouragement, and enjoy the advantage of positive role models, are considered part of a privileged and select club. In contrast, young black men, whom it is deemed are marginal within the family structure,and therefore do not receive any special maternal support, remain subject to the injustices of racism and discrimination. It is clear however, that the positive intention of this account of differential achievement has conservative implications. Our attention is subtly turned away from the importance of racial and sexual discrimination, highlighting instead cultural determinants to economic success or failure.[10]

There is little evidence to suggest that black women succeed at the expense of their male partners. The asymmetrical pattern of attainment in education and the labour market is not a reflection of cultural favouritism within the family. The findings of this study suggest that among young black men and women a situation of relative autonomy between the sexes prevailed. Within this particular definition of masculinity and femininity, few distinctions were made between male and female abilities and attributes with regard to work and the labour market. It was this, and not the positive role model of the strong black mother, that has resulted in the positive female orientation to work and education.

In the interview data provided by the young black women, strong feelings about the need to work was evident. In their expression of this desire, these women located the essential role of their mothers (or female guardian or relative) as an important inspiration, as the following statements show:

> I want to be like my mother, well-liked, sociable, outgoing and most of all successful. (Joanna, aspiration: teacher; mother: secretary)

> My mother has had to work hard to bring us up, and she brings us up in the West Indian ways. She's had to take shit at work, but I think she's brave (Anita, aspiration: social work; mother: cook).

However, the young women also stated that while they wanted to work, they did not wish for a repetition of their mothers' experiences. They often spoke of their mothers' work, which was discussed invariably in terms of hardship and sacrifice. They always gave a unanimous 'no' to the question, 'Would you like to be like your mum and do the same sort of work?' The key to why this situation of positive orientation and commitment to work should prevail was provided by the girls themselves. While the statements they made showed that they expected to work, just as their sisters, mothers, aunts and grandmothers had done for generations before them, they (and this is the important point) expected to do to without the encumbrance of male dissent. This meant the young women did not regard their male relationships, whether within the institution of marriage, or not, as inhibiting their right to work in any way.

Studies have persistently attributed the relatively high proportion of black women in the economy to the absence of a male provider or his inability to fulfil his role.[11] This pathological explanation of the black family (that has come about from the belief that it is 'culturally stripped', essentially a hybrid of Western culture) has failed to acknowledge that in the Caribbean what has evolved is an essentially egalitarian ideology with regard to work. An ideology that, as Sutton and Makiesky-Barrow (1977:323) observe, 'emphasizes the effectiveness of the individual regardless of gender'.

The study revealed a notable lack of sexual distinctions about work among second-generation West Indian youth. Many girls said that they did not see any difference between themselves and their male counterparts in terms of their capacity to work and the type of work they were capable of.

> I think men and women have the same opportunities, it is just up to you to take it.

> Men should do the jobs women do and women the jobs that men do. There's nothing wrong with men midwives, I think all men should find out what it is like to have a child, its the nearest they can get to it.

Similarly, the West Indian boys in the study had no objections to their future partners working.[12] They were in full support of their womenfolk being gainfully employed, as the following statements illustrate:

> My mum, she's a cook and she looks after me and my brother . . . I think if I got married, I don't see no difference, I don't see it any other way really. (Davis, aged 16, aspiration: armed forces)

Ironically, the dynamic that has produced this equality between the sexes within the Caribbean social structure has been the external imposition of oppression and brutality. Davis (1982) documents the evolution of this egalitarian ideology. She argues that under the conditions of slavery, egalitarianism characterized the social relations between male and female slaves in their domestic quarters. Here, the sexual division of labour did not appear to be hierarchically organized. Both male and female tasks, whether cooking or hunting, were deemed equally necessary and therefore considered neither inferior nor superior to each other. Sutton and Makiesky-Barrow (1977), in their study of Barbadian society, make this comment about the West Indian female orientation to work. They write,

> Women are expected not only to contribute to their own and their children's support, but also to acquire and build separate economic resources, control their own earnings and use them as they see fit. Men readily accept the idea of their wives working; in fact a man might boast of his wife's position and earnings. (p. 307)

This attitude to work, marriage, and motherhood among black women has been misinterpreted by white socialist feminists. While they have argued that for white women, marriage is a 'psychologically and materially oppressive institution' (Barrett and McIntosh, 1982), they state that for the West Indian, marriage is 'no more than a prestige conferring act' (Phizacklea, 1982:100; see also Sharpe, 1987:234).
This suggestion appears to imply that black people 'mimic' the social institutions of the dominant white society. The effect of this 'commonsense' assumption has been that marriage, the family, and male relationships in the West Indian context are dismissed as unimportant in the lives of black women.

However, Caribbean feminists provide evidence to the contrary. For example, Powell (1986) suggests that West Indian women are strongly marriage-orientated, though there seems to be little urgency regarding its timing. While conjugal relationships, motherhood and childrearing were important dimensions in the lives of black women, they did not perceive their unions as presenting barriers to the things they wished to do. In support of Powell's findings, it was not uncommon to find among the young women in the study statements such as this:

> Work is as equally important in marriage, or your relationship. I don't care if its marriage or not, whatever, I think it's important. (Floya, aged 16, aspiration: data processor)

This did not mean, as Riley (1985:69) seems to suggest in her analysis of similar types of statements, that young black girls were pursuing a course of aggressive assertion of their femininity (which in the case of black girls is interpreted as female dominance) at the expense of all else, especially permanent male relationships. Nor, as Fuller (1982:96) suggests was this the manifestation of a 'going it alone' strategy. In my opinion what the young women were articulating was a much more subtle ideological orientation than either of these two authors suggest. Unlike their white peers who appear to have absorbed the dominant ideology that women only take on major economic roles when circumstances prevent their menfolk from doing so, the black girls held no such belief about the marginality of their economic participation and commitment to the family. Providing for the children and the household was regarded as a joint responsibility, as the following statement illustrates:

> I think it is important for a woman and man to work; to both provide for your family is an important thing to do. (Karen, aged 16, aspiration: computer programmer)

The existence of joint responsibility is more widespread than most sociological commentators of both radical and conservative ideological persuasions care to acknowledge. Providing evidence of joint economic responsibility, there are high proportions black women in the labour market relative to black men. While 80 per cent of black men in Britain work, so do 75 per cent of black women (T. Jones, 1993; *Employment Gazette*, 1993).

The issue of relative economic and social autonomy between the sexes should not be confused with the matter of the sharing of domestic labour or the permanency of male/female relationships, as is so often the case. That West Indian men do not equally participate in household tasks is well documented, as is the tendency towards instability of consensual relationships, (Justus, 1985; Moses, 1985; Powell, 1986; Besson, 1993). These facts, however, do not impair the matter of joint responsibility towards consanguineal offspring or children within a consensual relationship. Relationships with joint responsibility towards the household, within the context of relative autonomy between the sexes, are a common feature of West Indian life.

Clearly the evidence does suggest that West Indian women do have different relationships within their families and, in particular, with the males in these families, that contribute to a unique orientation to work. Explanations as to why this may be so point to the central concept of an ideology of meritocracy in West Indian working-class life, in which both men and women appear to participate equally. As Sutton and Makiesky-Barrow (1977) observe,

> The position a woman acquires often results from her own achieve-
> ments rather than her spouse, and women tend to be individually
> ranked even if they are married. . . . Women as well as men are
> preoccupied with finding a way of 'rising' a notch above within the
> social hierarchy, and both look to the occupational system of doing
> so (p. 302).

Lee (1982) makes the following interesting observation with regard to
the ideology of meritocracy and its effects on the equality of opportunity
between the sexes. He writes with regard to the Irish situation:

> The less a culture emphasises merit, the more resistant to equality
> are the males likely to be . . . if only because the supremacy of
> the dominant males does not depend on superior merit. They are
> therefore likely to feel vulnerable to what they perceive as a threat
> posed not so much by women, as by ability in women. (p. 10)

In a culture that places a value on merit, such as the West Indian
working-class culture in Britain, the syndrome that Lee describes in
the Irish situation does not appear to arise in the black British context.
It would seem from the evidence given by the males in the study that
female labour-market participation is not perceived as a threat to their
own economic and social status.

Acknowledging that there is a specific form of black femininity
among young black women, characterized by an egalitarian ideology
with regard to appropriate male and female roles, allows us to move
towards a more satisfactory understanding of the persistence of young
black women's pursuit of educational qualifications than that provided
by the idealized notion of the 'strong black female'.

CONCLUSION: POSITIVE STRATEGIES IN A NEGATIVE CLIMATE

As a theoretical tool for analysing black female educational experience,
the subcultural model obscures our understanding of the black female
positive orientation to education. With its emphasis on 'cultures of
resistance', subcultural analysis has romanticized the classroom experience, suggesting that young black women overcome disadvantage
through their identification with their 'strong black mothers'. As British
black women themselves, Bryan, Dadzie and Scafe (1985) explain that
such well-intentioned accounts by social scientists,

> . . . portray black women in a somewhat romantic light, emphasising

our innate capacity to cope with brutality and deprivation, and perpetuating the myth that we are somehow better equipped than others for suffering. While the patient, long-suffering victim of triple oppression may have some heroic appeal, she does not convey our collective experience. (pp. 1–2)

Revealing the true, rather than the assumed nature of the black female 'collective experience' has been my concern here. My findings show that black women engage in a dynamic rationalization of the education system. They strategically employ every means at their disposal in the educational system and classroom in order to negotiate the institutional practices and impoverished resources that limit their educational opportunities. This was clearly illustrated by their desire to stay on into post-compulsory schooling, and also through the career choices they made. Many young women stayed on longer in order to redress the unsatisfactory outcome of their schooling in terms of educational qualifications. Similarly, the black girls chose caring or office occupations, not so much because of the nature of the job, but they used the stated educational requirements as a vehicle for obtaining more or better qualifications. This they did in order to enhance their career prospects and satisfy their desire for credentials often denied them at the secondary level.

Thus, young black women 'resist domination', not by way of their subcultural stance at the classroom level, but through the influence of the West Indian working-class migrant orientation toward the meritocratic ideal. This they expressed through their overwhelming desire for personal academic qualifications. Such a desire was reflected not only among the young black women in my study, but is mirrored on a national level. The Labour Force Survey indicates that 77 per cent of young black women aged 16–24 have achieved a recognized qualification at GCE 'A' level or equivalent, or lower (*Employment Gazette*, 1993). It could be argued that this quiet but persistent 'collective action', aimed at obtaining social mobility through credentials, takes the form of a contemporary social movement, the ultimate outcome of which is the subtle 'resistance to domination.'

In the recent climate of educational reform, the creative and dynamic rationalization strategies of black, working-class young women are now being tested to their limits. There has never been any pretence that educational reform has been for the benefit of the ethnic minorities. In fact, as Gilroy (1990) makes quite clear, the reverse is true. The attack on the anti-racist/multicultural classroom is central to the ideology of the New Right. Anti-racism and multiculturalism, identified as an assault on traditional 'good old-fashioned British education', has been seen as responsible for the decline in educational standards (Palmer, 1987). Tomlinson (1993) provides further evidence of the lack of commitment to issues of equity in recent educational reform. In the political struggle over the National Curriculum, she reveals, first hand, the process which led to the official disbanding of the Multicultural Task Group.

Radical ideological education reform in Britain, with its opposing twin planks of strong centralization and more parental choice, was popularized on the premise of the decline in standards (Lawton, 1992). In 1988, with the inception of the Education Reform Act, it was predicted that without any significant financial investment, far from raising standards, these reforms will herald 'a new Victorian era in education' (Ainley, 1988). In the mid-1990s this has already begun to happen. A recent disturbing report on the effect of educational reform on urban schools[13] concludes, 'The rising tide of educational change is not lifting these boats' (OFSTED, 1993:45). The report found that their achievements were significantly below the national average in attainment and entrance at GCE level. Schools were immersed in day-to-day crises, leaving no time for strategic planning or good management. Standards of work were appallingly inadequate, and the quality of teaching was superficial and unchallenging to the pupils.

Most significantly for the young black women who have been discussed here, the report found post-sixteen opportunities were seriously limited for young people who did not perform well in GCSE examinations. The extent of breakdown in co-ordination and information in adult and post-sixteen education services, effectively boycotts the systems these young women have evolved in their struggle to strategically overcome the odds of their already impoverished educational careers; odds which are now increasing with intensity.

CHAPTER 6

Ethnic Relations in All-White Schools
William H. Taylor

This chapter considers a generally neglected aspect of education in a plural society, the educaton of majority culture pupils, and critically reviews the impact of current changes in national policy.

INTRODUCTION

England[1] can be divided into two ethnic contexts: those densely populated conurbations where most of the country's black immigrants have settled since the 1950s, and the sparsely populated counties which have only very small numbers of black residents. However, there is a slow migration between town and county (*Social Trends*, 1993), and it is not unusual for villages to have one or two black residents. This chapter concentrates on the rural shires and considers how, despite widespread indifference among their adult population, schools are preparing pupils for their likely future mobility in a multi-ethnic nation.

Despite a mass of post-1988 Education Reform Act (ERA) exhortation and the potential to permeate the National Curriculum with the values of equal opportunities, ethnicity does not figure in any continuous or explicit way in the daily work or the staff development of schools where there are no or few black pupils, since other priorities dictate the direction of curriculum development. Confronting what the seminal Swann Report (1985) described as the 'pernicious evil' of racism is taken by some as a legitimate focus in every young person's education, though many in the shires dither about appropriate responses to this, and the term 'anti-racist education' is usually perceived as threatening (McCarthy, 1990). They prefer to believe that there is no serious racism in their region, and feel that schools could be creating rather than reducing intercultural trouble (ethnicity being only one of many cultural categories in our complex society) by giving curriculum space to any form of multicultural education.

Writers like Anderson (1989) and Klein (1989) take heart from the National Curriculum and its 'entitlement' element, but entitlement can be a pious hope rather than a practised reality, and its detail may be interpreted in many ways and operationalized within a particular context. Nor is Lawlor (1994) alone in arguing that 'entitlement' is a form of paternalism and dictation which disregards the possibility in a democracy of being entitled *not* to learn something; and some teachers are still heard to argue in the 'white highlands' that multicultural education is not an automatic entitlement. The core values of an entitlement curriculum ought to include interpersonal and inter-community respect in a multi-ethnic Britain which is part of a multinational European Community and a wider world. Constructive participation in reciprocally appreciative intersecting communities should be a *sine qua non* of all citizenship education (Taylor, 1993a). Good education develops the whole person, the social and emotional aspects of the human condition being as important as the intellectual, physical, moral and aesthetic. These considerations should be central to multicultural education, in rural as well as in urban schools. It would be foolish to pretend that, in the context of multicultural education in the shires, there is a 'typical' school, or that, within any school, there is a linear progression in its work in this sphere, as the evidence supports the view that the range and nature of response is considerable.

Although there are few overt expressions of the ugliest forms of racism in rural regions, circumstantial evidence suggests that latent racism is extensive. Both the synagogue and the mosque in Exeter have been vandalized from time to time, and 'monkey chants' from the stadium's terraces have accompanied the appearance of Exeter FC's black player, despite the club's public statement decrying all forms of racism. Popple (1990) gives accounts of racial abuse in south Devon, reporting that welfare agencies are not prepared to take racism seriously. Based on rather selective evidence, Jay (1992) presented a deeply disturbing picture of racial harassment being experienced by some local black residents in the south-west of England. Some local black residents (not interviewed by Jay!) however deny having been at the receiving end of racial discrimination, so it would be wrong to assume that his is the complete picture. Although they make good journalism, anecdotes prove nothing, though they indicate both positive and negative dynamics in the shires. Many churches, charities and community action groups in small towns exist to fight racism, and they greatly outnumber the handful of people who vote for the rare neo-nazi candidate at a local election.

Table 6.1   *Ethnic minority population in the south-west of England*

County	Region with highest number of non-white inhabitants (%)		Region with lowest number of non-white inhabitants (%)	
Avon	Bristol	5.1	Wansdyke	0.6
Cornwall	Penwith	0.7	Caradon	0.5
Isles of Scilly		0.0		0.0
Devon	Exeter	1.3	Torridge	0.4
Dorset	Bournemouth	1.6	Purbeck	0.5
Somerset	Taunton	0.7	Mendip	0.5

Table 6.2   *Ethnic majority population in the NW, NE, SE and SW corners of England*

	Maximum (%)	Minimum (%)
Cumbria (NW)	99.8	99.1
Kent (SE)	99.6	98.5
Northumberland (NE)	99.0	92
Tyne (NE)	99.2	98.2
Surrey (SE)	98.7	94.3
Cornwall (SW)	99.5	99.3
Devon (SW)	99.6	98.7

A DEMOGRAPHIC NOTE

There may be no typical mono-ethnic location, but, by including for the first time a question about ethnic origin, the 1991 Census provides a numerically authoritative demographic picture of the country's ethnic minority population. There are no equally authoritative measures of ethnic minority school populations, but it can be safely assumed that these reflect the demographic pattern of the wider community. Britain's black population is expected to rise from the current 4.5 per cent to about 7 per cent, where it should stabilize (Diamond and Clarke, 1989). At present, the black population is younger than is the white population, and this has implications for the school population. Britain has a net population loss from emigration/immigration (*Population Trends*, 1991). Table J of the 1991 Census describes the ethnic minority population, and it shows the geographical peripheries of England having many districts with no or almost no ethnic minority inhabitants. For the purposes of this chapter, the five south-western counties are taken to typify the peripheries. Tables 6.1 and 6.2 offer a demographic summary on the basis of the Census's Table J.

Apart from the large city of Bristol, the numbers of ethnic minority citizens are low, even in large towns such as Swindon, Bournemouth, Exeter and Taunton. These numbers include people whose origins are Caribbean, Indian, Chinese, African and 'European' (e.g. Cypriot).

The 'white highlands' are clearly white, at least numerically. The south-west includes many elderly white people who retire to the region, attracted by its tranquillity and 'Englishness' (which might be a euphemism for absence of black neighbours). The region has high unemployment and is low-waged, and this may aggravate the long-established suspicion of newcomers. 'Grockels', an ancient pejorative Devon word for non-Devonians, and 'Emmetts', the equivalent in Cornwall, long pre-date a black British citizenry. The non-white populations in these counties are concentrated in the conurbations. The south-west is a major tourist region, and its non-white population is significantly increased during the summer months. Its educational institutions attract substantial numbers of overseas students. For decades, many black immigrants arrived in the UK at West Country ports, usually to pass quickly through the region on their way to the Midlands or London, though the story of Equiano (McKeith, 1988) demonstrates how dangerous it is to assume that black people never settled or prospered in the region. Despite this, ethnicity is not on the ordinary person's agenda, nor indeed on the agenda of many of the region's schools. When it is, it is in response to some specific incident which has attracted media attention, but an ephemeral interest is not sustained for long.

Five years ago, the DES (DES, 1989a) requested details from every LEA about pupil ethnicity in their statistical returns. This was the first such request and it ought to have provided comprehensive data. Data for Devon (DCC, 1992), based on returns from schools, are set out in Tables 6.3a and 6.3b, but not every school made a return and replies were not checked. Repeated requests by the author to the other Local Education Authorities (LEAs) in the region were required before data were supplied. One LEA replied that it was 'a waste of time to collect such insignificant numbers'. The picture is replicated throughout the region, the exception being the city of Bristol.

PRIORITIES IN THE RURAL SHIRES

Within a national consensus of broad aims, the latest version of which underpins the National Curriculum, teaching priorities are determined by individual schools in order to address local concerns. The Parents

Table 6.3a   *Numbers of pupils in Devon schools*

	Total	Black	Chinese	Indian Subcontinent	Unclassified	White
Primary						
Yr1	11,663	20	17	20	2,877	8,729
Yr2	11,142	17	10	12	2,654	8,449
Secondary						
Yr7	10,806	8	9	6	3,347	7,436
Yr8	10,633	8	5	6	3,353	7,261

Table 6.3b   *Numbers of pupils in Devon schools: non-European 'mother tongue' usage*

	Cantonese	Gujarati	Hindi	Panjabi	Turkish	Urdu
Primary						
Yr1	11	1	2	0	3	6
Yr2	4	0	1	3	1	2
Secondary						
Yr7	3	1	0	0	0	4
Yr8	3	0	0	2	0	2
There are no Bengali speakers.						

Charter (1991) and parent school governors (since accumulative legislation of the 1980s) oblige headteachers to heed consumers' wishes. Multi-ethnic schools and their communities are likely to arrange their priorities differently from virtually mono-ethnic neighbourhoods. A 'national' curriculum is 'nation-wide' in that every school has to work to attain similar scholastic targets; but the hidden curriculum is less prescriptive, and a school's rules and ethos are likely to reflect local community values and beliefs. What is self-evidently a priority in one school because of the daily reality of its pupils and their parents may be a low priority in another, and transferring practices that are successful in one particular cultural context will not automatically succeed elsewhere.

In all schools the needs of all pupils are paramount, but in multi-ethnic schools the needs of ethnic minority children have a special importance. The following are likely to be among the school's daily priorities:

1. Raising the academic attainment of Afro-Caribbean and Bangla-deshi pupils (HMI *Annual Reports*, 1990–1);
2. Examining why so many Afro-Caribbean pupils are excluded from school;
3. Ensuring that school meals reflect religious values;
4. Supporting English-language acquisition;
5. Addressing racially linked harassment and violence;
6. Facilitating school–home links by using community languages and appropriate liaison staff.

Schools in the rural regions will inevitably focus on the needs of the ethnic majority. Their priorities will include:

1. Providing accurate information about Britain's ethnic minorities;
2. Developing reciprocal respect for others in culturally pluralist Britain;
3. Permeating the whole curriculum with multi-ethnic concerns and avoiding tokenist 'bolting-on';
4. Getting ethnic majority pupils to recognize and challenge racism;
5. Preparing ethnic majority pupils for an adult life outside their natal neighbourhood;
6. Convincing school governors that Britain's cultural diversity is an educational issue for their school.

HMI (1992) found an unacceptably wide gap between policy and practice in the context of equal opportunities in many schools; but their criteria for inspection focused on how a particular school addresses the needs of its on-roll pupils, thus effectively ignoring concerns about racism from their reviews of mono-ethnic schools where there are virtually no 'on-roll' black pupils.

Learning to combat racism may be an ideal objective in the long term, but learning about cultures may be the only feasible learning for some individuals and schools in the immediate term. Eliminating racism may be the ultimate aim, but knowledge of customs or festivals will constitute appropriate learning for some individuals and schools. Context rather than dogma should shape teacher expectations of pupil learning – of attitudes as well as skills and knowledge. Pupils' positive learning needs to be positively rewarded, even if the learning falls short of some notional ideal.

FINDING SPACE FOR MULTICULTURAL EDUCATION IN MONOCULTURAL SCHOOLS

Every day the mass media enter our homes. Hall (1981) has argued that the media play a significant role in perpetuating racism, yet media values are seldom discussed in the average home. Schools would seem to be appropriate places for doing so, as there is an ongoing need for individuals to re-examine their social construction of reality. Opportunities within the school's curriculum need to be found in order to encourage students to examine the validity of generalizations and assertions made about the interests and aptitudes of individual members of ethnic minorities, which are used – by school teachers as well as by the media – to explain why some pupils are more active or successful in one subject rather than another. If schools do not provide this opportunity, students (and their teachers?) may never learn to recognize how myth and prejudice can feed each other. The justification for every British schoolchild to get some kind of multicultural education was argued convincingly in the Swann Report. Yet there is little in the 1988 ERA or its serendipity that is obligatory in this field. There is plenty of exhortation, plenty of 'shoulds' but virtually no 'musts'. This creates possibilities, but it also legitimizes inaction or procrastination. Though many all-white schools include it in their priorities, it seldom becomes a top priority. Someone on the school staff may be given a specific brief for it, but that in itself does not necessarily guarantee action. In a climate in which standard assessment tests and local management of schools (SAT-LMS) are important, a school's management is dominated by issues that are immediate, and the reality of far-off multi-ethnic cities can all too easily be forgotten in the rural regions.

Multiculturalism is a National Curriculum 'dimension' (NCC, 1989), which means that every subject 'should [sic] reflect the culturally diverse society to which pupils belong' (DES, 1989b). But which 'society' is being referred to, local or national or international? Non-statutory guidelines indicate that *every* school is expected to promote 'positive attitudes to cultural diversity' (DES, 1989b), in order to give children a number of starting points from which to consider prejudice and help them come to terms with both cultural diversity and racism as societal realities. Little of this rhetoric is new.

The National Curriculum Council (NCC) has so far failed to offer guidelines for multicultural education. The Runnymede Trust has felt obliged to do so, and has produced an excellent booklet (1993) which has been well received by schools. It is based on the conviction that every school in the country should *(a)* provide high quality schooling for every pupil, *(b)* actively address multicultural perspectives in its routine curricula, and *(c)* prepare its school-leavers for purposeful participation in the post-school, adult multi-cultured world. It locates a study of race equality and cultural diversity within the National Curriculum. The rural county of Somerset has provided each of its schools with a copy of this publication in order to encourage them to address racial prejudice, cultural identity and citizenship in multi-ethnic Britain.

THE MIXED BLESSING OF OFFICIAL POLICIES

It became fashionable in the 1980s for LEAs and schools to develop official policies about their work in multicultural education. At best these offered a framework, a checklist, an ethos; at worst, they collected dust on a forgotten shelf. Without effective monitoring and evaluation, policies have little value. Without funds to pay for detailed inspections, monitoring can lack credibility. Few LEAs have funded effective management of the implementation of these policies. Sometimes this has been tagged on to the responsibilities of the special educational needs adviser! Even as part of the equal opportunities adviser's brief, little is guaranteed, as gender usually dominates this domain in most schools.

Ideally, each school ought to have a formal multicultural/anti-racist policy in order to address recruitment and development of staff (not just teaching staff), all interpersonal relationships in the school community, course content and resourcing, and parental and governor involvement. This could defend a school from accusations of being tokenistic, if it were to ask its solitary black father or an unwilling traveller mother to become school governors. Policies, like creeds, are statements of the ideal, but they need to be realistic since too remote a vision can be demoralizing. Without official policies, much depends on the charismatic personal attributes of individuals. Policies do not in themselves guarantee change, but they can justify action, such as appointing school–community officers in order to educate parents to understand why ethnicity is relevant to their children's educational needs. However, financially hard-pressed schools are unlikely to find the salary for such a post. Local inspection schedules in rural areas which include this concern tend to centre on international and intercultural aspects rather than racism awareness, and even these can be pushed off an already crowded inspection agenda.

Devon's 1989 policy contained reference to policy implementation, but this had little impact as there was no obligation on schools, and no school was censured for inaction. Inaction can all too easily be rationalized and defended. The draft of the latest Devon policy on equal opportunities contains more specific requirements of schools in the multicultural field, and draws attention to the potential of the National Curriculum's cross-curricular themes. However, undergraduate student teachers working in schools on cross-curriculum implementation in east Devon have found that schools are sticking closely to the five named 'themes', and are not using the 'dimensions' as foci for specific lessons. A Local Education Authority (LEA) may have a policy but it no longer has a budget, and it will have to rely on persuasion to get individual schools to use their LMS budgets to develop curricula in accordance with LEA guidelines.

In 1987, every LEA was written to (Macfarlan, 1993) in order to get copies of their multicultural policies. By 1993 all had replied. Some denied having any, some sent only brief statements, and detailed materials invariably came from areas which had large ethnic minority populations. This collection demonstrates the size, nature and time-scale of post-Swann activity in creating policies. It confirms the view that response in the shires has been uncertain, slow and concerned more with cultural diversity than racism. However, the patchiness revealed in these official guidelines disguises the continued commitment of small numbers of individual teachers and support networks scattered throughout the nation.

Devon's well-developed international education policy stresses links between schools in various countries and arranges many exchange visits across national frontiers. Schools in north Devon, for example, have regular visits from both teachers and pupils from eastern Europe, especially from Hungary. It seems illogical that headteachers can – and do – easily defend 'European awareness' on the grounds of Britain's membership of the European Community, and almost with the same breath defend ignoring 'multicultural awareness' on the grounds of there being no black local residents. This is an oft-repeated scenario in rural schools, and development education, concerned with societal development on a global scale, is more likely to be found, particularly in primary schools, than is any course or lesson on Britain's ethnic composition. Development education, international education and multicultural education all seek to reduce pupil insularity, an objective which can be accommodated into every National Curriculum subject as well as into the general ethos of the school. In many schools in the shires these subjects are allies. Their essence can be part of both the explicit and the implicit curriculum; they have both cognitive and affective aspects.

The ESG (Educational Support Grants) policy (DES, 1987), which greatly boosted LEA efforts to develop their multicultural resources, has been examined by Tomlinson (1990). This programme has now all but disappeared, and few schools in the shires are using their in-service budgets to sustain its gains. Over thirty secondary schools in the south-west were recently asked[2] if any of their compulsory staff development days had been used for this purpose. Only one said that this had happened, a few had included it in wider issues such as cross-curricular themes, some were thinking about it; but most stated in a matter-of-fact manner that there was not enough time or cash even to address other issues considered to be more pressing.

In Somerset and Cornwall, ESG funds supported clusters of schools in developing specific curricular themes. Themes included 'India' and 'Caribbean literature'. Somerset produced and circulated bulky typescript accounts of these, the kind that county councillors like to see. Wiltshire and Devon have also organized whole-school events: African arts having been especially popular (Smith,1987). It is realistic to expect this kind of focused work to continue in the foreseeable future. The fine eighteenth-century painting of the black gentleman Olaudah Equiano in Exeter Museum has inspired local schools not only to research Igbo culture, but also to challenge stereotypes about the lifestyles of black British citizens. Schools have benefited from using important resources in the south-west such as Plymouth's large Chinese Cultural Centre and Bristol's Multicultural Education Centre. The educational needs of travellers' children are supported by nationally funded advisory teachers and mobile units. Travellers constitute a small but regular minority in the south-west, and many of the specialist advisory staff work not only with travelling families and the schools which their children attend, but also make contributions to school courses on Personal and Social Education (PSE) when questions of equality, prejudice and stereotyping are considered in a context of which the pupils have some experience. Recently a Craft, Design and Technology (CDT) class in Cornwall, working within the National Curriculum, was asked to design a gypsy's bender tent; this provided opportunities to consider as many sociological as technological issues.

Trying to get a comprehensive picture of developments in multicultural education is difficult. This Chapter shows that the picture of the region's schools built up by large numbers of student teachers (see Note 1) is dramatically different from, and more negative than, the one that is given by LEA senior staff. Without a data bank of reliable statistics, one is at the mercy of the vested interest of the respondent who answers the questions. County councillors and local government officers quote from official policies, while student-teachers ask questions of individual pupils and schoolteachers. Although Devon has had a 'multi-cultural education policy' since 1989, many of its teachers still claim no knowledge of it. An update contained within the wider policy of equal opportunities is on the way, and a draft version of this was submitted to the appropriate senior officer some time ago, but it still awaits approval. The LEA produced a comprehensive document (DCC, 1992) on the teaching of religious education which ought to put multi-faith issues into the mainstream of every school's work in this subject area. This policy is designed to foster a deeper appreciation of each of the mainstream religious faiths. It goes well beyond teaching pupils about beliefs and festivals, and offers a sound basis for developing respectful attitudes towards the daily lifestyles of fellow citizens whose private religious beliefs influence their public behaviour. It is likely that Devon's PSE teachers will make extensive use of these guidelines.

AN OVERVIEW OF DEVELOPMENTS IN THE RURAL SHIRES

In her comprehensive overview of developments in predominantly white schools, Tomlinson (1990) found powerful and persisting Anglocentric assumptions underpinning much of the curriculum in such schools, but she was able to report that many schools in the shires were revising their curricula in order to be more responsive to Britain's cultural diversity. One valuable source of up-to-date developments is the journal *Multicultural Teaching*, as it offers practitioners the chance to publicize their initiatives. However, a glance at its contents over the past few years reveals a virtual absence of any reports from mono-ethnic regions, not that that in itself proves anything, as it could indicate *inter alia* inaction or a coyness about publicizing their developments.

Severe financial cutbacks are making investment in multicultural education less and less likely. A retired Dorset LEA inspector (Holman, 1993) has predicted that in future there will be little development in multicultural/anti-racist education in the shires where 'the curriculum will be conformist, safe, banal'. Dorset had tried via the Technical and Vocational Educational Initiative (TVEI) and its global education policies to examine race-related issues, but TVEI funding ends in 1994. The 1993 Education Act envisages LEAs becoming less powerful and perhaps eventually redundant, and this could hasten the shrinking of support services such as museum and library services. These services used to be proactive (not least in multicultural education), but they are now scarcely able to be reactive as their staffing, stocks and funds diminish, and the publicizing of and caring for their artefacts and other teaching aids will become increasingly restricted. Few Teachers' Centres are surviving the cutbacks, and yet their wardens were often key people in across-the-schools in-service work, including multicultural education.

Naidoo (1992) has done much creative work in Dorset and Hampshire. She describes a sustained and coherent programme using adolescent fiction with Year 9 white pupils to explore racial prejudice. She offers useful guidance to social education tutors about how to help pupils transfer their classroom learning about racism into their daily lives. Hobman (1992) comments positively on work in a social science course for Year 9 pupils in a Hertfordshire comprehensive school with few ethnic minority pupils, where the pupils learned how to challenge discriminatory practices and examine inequality 'by recognising reciprocity in rights and responsibilities and respect for human values'.

Many county schools organize study tours to Asian and African countries. These are usually carefully prepared to prevent them from being simply tourist trips, though claims about what pupils learn socially when they participate in exchange programmes can be exaggerated. If trips are to be more than a supplement to the geography or French lesson, the quality of interpersonal interaction with local people during the visit needs to become a key issue, as must the de-briefing after the visit. Shaikh and Hawkins (1992) show how a project on 'strange fruits' helped pupils to consider many wide-ranging and sensitive issues in the realm of interpersonal and inter-community relations. As Advisory Teacher in Multicultural Education in Somerset, Shaikh frequently used the strategy of thematic foci such as 'cricket' or 'recipes', involving various subject areas and giving students the chance to consider the theme from different perspectives. Drama, art, design, music and dance were particularly responsive within this framework. An ESG-funded adviser often proved to be a personal resource, a catalyst and a counsellor who could empower teachers to make use of personal experience, whose educational value might otherwise have been ignored.

ESG-funding has helped to support 'artists in residence' programmes, giving teachers and pupils alike the chance to work on a person-to-person basis with visitors whose cultures provided new knowledge and a vehicle for the effective social development of students. Black visitors to schools, for example, can give white students a new understanding of the African-Caribbean-European slave trade triangle. Such projects often culminate in exhibitions and concerts which are usually well supported by the local adult community. A recent week of gamelan music introduced Exeter teacher trainees to new musical instruments, new rhythms, new harmonies, and gave them the confidence to organize such inputs into their own school teaching, not least as a way of increasing an appreciation of the aesthetic achievements of a culture of which they had had little previous knowledge. However, although the charisma of the visitors and the novelty of residence make the experience memorable, it may be the exotica that is remembered rather than its potential contribution to reducing racism.

Simulations are well-tested learning vehicles. Children in a rural village were recently asked to draw up plans for building a *gurdwara* in their community. They learnt about Sikhism, but also about why a local farmer was not keen to sell one of his fields for this purpose or why planning permission was held up. Giving children a town trail which requires finding out about non-Anglo-Saxon local landmarks can be a way of learning something new about the child's familiar everyday environment. For example, the 'foreign' restaurant just around the corner is Thai, and the Thai family are pleased to answer the pupils' questions, not just about cuisine but also about lifestyles, customs and their being part of the local community. Such strategies have been, and will continue to be, used by schools in the rural shires. This may be seen by some as tokenistic, especially since these projects tend not to influence the curriculum once they have been completed, but they can leave an indelible and positive impression on some of the children. With the extra funding and staffing from ESG now gone, educationists in the rural regions are finding it difficult to sustain the impetus that has been a characteristic of their work in the past five years.

The ESG programme raised awareness, developed knowledge, provided resources, and introduced multicultural concerns to relatively monocultural schools. It discovered committed individuals who, hopefully, will retain their commitment. It draws to a close, leaving an air of despondency, not least because this coincides with the localizing of funds, the shrinking of overall budgets and, some would say, a lack of political will to retain a high profile for multicultural education. Without ESG, multicultural education might never have appeared in some rural regions and the future looks uncertain without it.

EXAMPLES OF GOOD PRACTICE IN THE SOUTHWEST

Work in two Plymouth schools is selected to illustrate what may be regarded in the south-west as examples of good practice.

In one dockland school, there is a whole-school commitment to the 'international curriculum'. Every room and corridor displays multicultural and multinational images. The school's 'European Awareness' booklet is packed with interesting materials which go well beyond geographical data. Pupils of all ages and ability levels make contact via satellite, fax and E-mail with children in various countries in order to exchange information about many topics from the weather to the family. A project on Pakistan included fax correspondence with the cricketer Wasim Akram and direct links with children in Pakistan, the language difference not proving too much of a problem. The information technology work is supported by many opportunities for pupils to participate in school exchanges, designed to help to break down ignorance about other cultures. The school's ethos is one of concern for social justice. This is actively and enthusiastically supported by parents and governors who are as concerned about their children's self-esteem as with SATs and school league tables. This school epitomizes the best in Devon's global education programme. Although the school is in an economically depressed part of the city, it is planning to increase its exchange programme – to include the English Midlands as well as new contacts in every continent. The children speak with enthusiasm about their world-wide friendship circle, and accept as natural the cultural differences they learn about through this direct discovery method.

One Catholic girls' comprehensive school has a whole-school commitment to community development, and organizes impressive week-long events. In March 1993 the focus was 'The family of the world'. A multicultural programme involved the entire school and a large number of visitors from many national and cultural backgrounds. The theme permeated every curriculum subject. The school's *News Desk* newsletter for May 1993 comprises twenty pages of detailed reporting of the huge variety of learning that can result – from Sumo wrestling to Mandarin to meeting Gypsies. World-wide culinary delights, prepared by the pupils, provided first-class luncheons. Music and dance from Africa and Asia added sound and colour to the many static displays of artefacts. Multi-faith acts of worship involved Hindus, Behais, Buddhists, Muslims, Humanists and Christians. Here is a superb example of how to immerse an entire school for a week in a rich variety of multicultural experiences, while providing opportunities to meet people who share their cultural traditions with the students. These included nomadic gypsies and overseas students from Malaysia who are studying in one of the city's higher education establishments. Despite the pressures of the National Curriculum, this week-long programme is a regular feature of a school which, while holding firm to its Catholic faith, is committed to giving its pupils an appreciation of and respect for other traditions. Popular with one sixth form group was a study of the role of women in Islam, looking at the Qu'ran alongside national traditions and considering whether a 'typical' Muslim woman is any more a reality than is a 'typical' Catholic woman. The evaluations written by the students and published in the newsletter point to learning that goes well beyond the superficial, tokenistic or sycophantic.

Some teachers and schools can be more flexible than others in accommodating unexpected opportunities into their work-schemes. The 1993 Wimbledon Tennis Tournament coincided with the publication of Arthur Ashe's biography and one West Country school's Year 10 health education unit on AIDS. Pupil interest – not anticipated by the teacher – focused not on Ashe's being HIV positive but on his letter to his daughter Camera in which he tells her about the racial injustice that his family had experienced. The fervour with which the pupils discussed this revealed extensive knowledge of and concern about racism. What had been a health education lesson became an exploration of racism.

Personal friendships grow out of personal experiences. It is common to find individual white pupils including among their best friends the one black child who lives in the village, and still holding decidedly racist attitudes towards black people in general. This can be and often is used as a basis for engaging the young people in a discussion about interpersonal and inter-community relations.

Although local traditions can be parochial, they can also offer opportunities to look beyond parish boundaries. The long-established International Folk Festival in Sidmouth, a small seaside Devon resort, inspired one of the town's nursery schools to focus on the countries from which the festival participants came (Stocker, 1987). This gave very young children not only the chance to rummage around in their attics for artefacts, but also to make face-to-face contact with the actual festival participants themselves. After speaking to people from Sri Lanka and Morocco, the young children demonstrated positive respectful attitudes towards the cultures of these countries. They had learnt that every ethnic group has traditions of which it is proud.

EXPERIENCES OF TEACHER-TRAINING STUDENTS

Most teacher trainees choose to study in their home regions, but many do not. Students whose homes are in multi-ethnic Bradford bring to students from mono-ethnic Truro personal experiences and perceptions which challenge rural complacency, and ensure lively debate about racism during college seminars. There is a perceptibly greater understanding of race relations among today's undergraduates than there was only a few years ago, and multicultural concerns now pervade teacher education programmes. This suggests that as long as teachers are trained in universities, their professional development will increasingly have regard to cultural diversity. If, however, the government places more of the initial training in schools, it is possible that this growing awareness could be stifled, as anecdotal evidence suggests that teachers in the shires are less interested in race issues than are their own pupils or the trainee teachers.

Unpublished research undertaken by students in many rural schools may be unsystematic and statistically dubious, but it builds up a consistent picture of indifference about racism. One student teacher on a Cornish placement recently asked Year 9 pupils to indicate by raising their hands if they would classify themselves as racists. A loaded question! More than half the class raised their hands. The size of this group and its eagerness to admit its belief shocked the student. His shock intensified when, admitting his surprise to the children, he was told that he could never understand how important it was to keep Cornwall Cornish! Shades of ethnic cleansing?

Another student teacher, working in a large rural secondary school not far from the city of Exeter, was interested in pupil mobility and the readiness of young people to tolerate and appreciate people whose lifestyles and beliefs differ from their own. Table 6.4 sets out the questions a Year 8 class was asked as part of a lesson on 'culture'. It illustrates pupils' limited personal experience of life beyond the county's borders, but it also suggests an appreciation of teachers' attempts to prepare them for adult life in a culturally diverse society.

A class of 27 ten-year-olds in another village primary school was asked about the concept of 'minority-ness'. Pupil responses appear in Tables 6.5a and 6.5b. They suggest that the real life of the village may have more influence on the young people's opinions than has the media, despite Hall's contention. The village has about 1,000 inhabitants, and

Table 6.4 *Pupil experience of and opinion about geographical mobility*

Question	Yes (%)	No (%)	Don't know/blank (%)
Have you ever lived outside Devon?	8	92	–
Have you lived outside Britain?	4	94	–
Will you live outside Devon when you are older?	20	40	40
Is it important to learn about other cultures?	80	12	8
Do you learn about other cultures in school?	88	0	12
Do you learn about various world religions?	80	12	8

some of the pupils live on isolated farms or in tiny hamlets of four or five houses. One regular minority group in the village is the tourist, but this group is not perceived as such by the children.

While many schools have no or few ethnic minority pupils, every school has pupils who belong to a cultural minority since every person belongs to a variety of groups, some of which will have few members. The minority-ness of accent or physical impairment may be more real to the world of some schoolchildren than is the minority-ness of ethnicity. The pupil who has a minority hobby may conceal that fact from schoolmates in order to avoid adverse attention such as teasing or bullying. In mono-ethnic schools, can feelings and insights gained from this experience be transferred to the inter-ethnic dynamic, in order to encourage greater inter-ethnic understanding? Or is this transfer too remote for most children? The lively discussion that took place would suggest that this particular group of ten-year-olds could. Each person needs an identity, and ideally a willingness to recognize that other identities exist and need to be respected. Can this awareness be achieved at a young age, and so be relevant to the education of five- as well as fifteen-year-olds? Culture is not static, nor is it discrete. Many of the 27 ten-year-olds stated that they were aware of changing perceptions within the village community, especially differences between the generations, and not least perceptions about ethnicity and nationality.

In January 1994, over 200 PGCE (Post-Graduate Certificate of Education) secondary teacher trainees on teaching practice in the south-west were asked to find out from pupils in the 40 schools in the four LEAs where they were placed what positive pictures pupils had of black people. The exact number of pupils who responded is not known but it is in the region of 3,000, a large proportion of the region's teenager population. Pupils were asked to name well-known living black

Table 6.5a   *Awareness of 'minorities' in the shires*

Category of minority	Number of pupils listing it (Pupils could write down as many examples as they wanted to) (Total number of pupils = 27 ten-year-olds)	
Gypsy	27	(There is a permanent camp site on the edge of the village)
New Age Travellers	9	(This was in the local news at the time)
Attending church	8	(Church-attending is high but still a minority activity)
Conservation group	6	(Green issues are passionately championed by some of the village community)
Physical disability	3	(There is a small number of children in the village in this broad category)
Being black	1	(There are no black Britons in the village and no black pupils in the school. The pupil who gave this reply lives in a hamlet which includes one Iraqi and one American family)

Table 6.5b   *Minorities as 'problems'*

What problems do minorities encounter?	They get laughed at
	They get ignored
	They get forced to go along with the majority
	They get mugged
What can you do to help them?	Protect them from bullies
	Befriend them
Do you want to help them?	The class split equally into yes, no, not sure
What problems do majorities have with minorities?	
	They get embarrassed
	They are threatened
	They want them to go away
	Their colloquialisms
	They might get mugged

males and females, and their responses are summarized in Table 6.6. They were then asked to name well-known British black citizens. The responses have not been quantified, but they include a judge, members of both Houses of Parliament, a trade union leader, wealthy businessmen, TV actors, soccer stars, athletes, pop musicians. This suggests that these teenagers are reasonably well-informed about successful black people.

Table 6.6   *Knowledge of positive black role models*
(based on responses to 200 PGCE student teachers in 40 'white' schools)

Teenagers were asked to name internationally known black males
  45% gave the name of a sportsman
  15%   politician
  12%   writer
  10%   pop musician
   8%   film star
  10% gave no reply
They were asked to do likewise for black females.
  20% gave the name of a sportswoman
  27%   politician
  25%   pop musician
  20%   film star
  10%   writer
   8% gave no reply

Hopefully, this will make them challenge negative stereotypes of black British citizens.

As a major assignment, 62 PGCE students of mathematics, geography and history working in schools in Dorset, Somerset, Cornwall and Devon were asked in March 1994 to find out about their schools' policies and practices in regard to multicultural education, since all were in LEAs which have such policies. Over 90 per cent reported that there was no explicit commitment and that there was widespread ignorance of the existence of the LEAs' policies. Even in schools which have some very committed staff and which have official policies, student teachers have reported both hostility towards and ignorance about school responses to the nation's multi-ethnicity. By interviewing staff other than those who are known to be positive, students can build up a fuller picture of the reality of the school than is provided by an official line. Even when a school does devote some of its staff development time to multicultural/anti-racist issues, there can remain a significant degree of indifference and cynicism among the staff, and attempts to re-visit multicultural issues on future staff development days have met with resistance (Powell, 1993).

The anecdotal, student-based data fully support the concern expressed over a decade ago by Craft (1981) about teacher education needing a rationale for addressing multi-ethnicity, in order to equip the next generation of teachers with a sound theoretical basis on which to tackle the social realities of the schools in which they will teach. Many teacher training institutions in the shires arrange for some of their students to do their teaching practice in multi-ethnic city schools. At Exeter University there is no shortage of volunteer students to go to Birmingham and London schools, even when it means incurring extra financial expense (Taylor, 1993b). Learning from personal experience about the dynamics of a multi-ethnic community and classroom is more potent than learning from books and university seminars. There is an increasing proportion of new teachers entering the profession with a more informed understanding of multi-ethnic Britain, and these are coming from training institutions in the shires as well as from those in the cities. Teacher expectations and assumptions contribute to a school's ethos, and it is to be hoped that the new teachers will convince older colleagues that cultural diversity and racism are proper concerns for schools.

Ackers (1991) reported how in one further education college in the south-west only 15 per cent of the teaching staff saw multicultural issues as an educational priority, although 43 per cent were prepared to consider reviewing their teaching materials in order to address them. However, he described how an attempt to develop appropriate policies and practices had met with considerable hostility and derision. Teachers need to recognize that within every ethnic group there are many subcultures and that cultural norms are constantly adapting and changing. There remains much to be done in the context of teacher education.

The 1976 Race Relations Act is of relevance to all schools; yet there is a virtual ignorance of it in the shires where policies about racial harassment and discrimination are still all too rare, even in further and higher education institutions which have overseas students who have suffered from varying degrees of racist taunts. The absence of policies is rationalized in terms of there being few proven examples of racial harassment within the institution. Yet anecdotes persist: for example, final year teacher training students report having been interviewed for jobs by school governors who suggest to black applicants that because there are no black pupils in the school perhaps they might wish to apply elsewhere.

CONCLUSION

Schools in the rural shires need to anticipate the social context in which their pupils will live as adults. Multi-ethnic Britain is a reality. Black–white friendships, neighbours, colleagues are increasing possibilities. It is a truism that the world is a global village. Migration is a universal phenomenon which is as old as the human race. Rural parents need to anticipate that their children will eventually move away from home, and support schools in preparing them for life in a multi-ethnic community which will enrich rather than threaten them.

Education may not be a panacea for the nation's race-related social ills, but it should have a vision that goes beyond corruption, violence and injustice, and offers the prospect of social harmony and reciprocated respect between persons and communities. It plays a vital part in shaping the personal and social development of an individual, and in giving access to knowledge on which to make informed judgements. For that reason, it is important that the shire schools compensate for societal apathy and mass media distortion by including a multicultural dimension in their curricula and their ethos, using such opportunities as are available in the National Curriculum, and seeking to educate their pupils' parents and extended families to recognize that racism can be part of their community and that it is not confined to far-away cities. There are some grounds for being optimistic about parent governors supporting curriculum developments that are well argued by the school's headteacher; and the prospects for multicultural education in the rural shires will depend to a considerable extent on professional educators being able to argue convincingly against the contention that inserting any form of multicultural education into 'monocultural' schools is to waste time and resources.

CHAPTER 7

The LEA and TEC Context

Monica Taylor and Carl Bagley

This chapter reports a national survey of post-ERA developments in cultural diversity, focusing on Section 11 funding, Ethnic Minority Grants, governor training, and Standing Advisory Councils for Religious Education.

> The Government's fundamental objective is that Britain should be a fair and just society where everyone, irrespective of ethnic origin, is able to participate freely and fully in the economic, social and public life of the nation while having the freedom to maintain their own religious and cultural identity. (GB: HO, 1990a, pp. 2–3)

> Primary teachers should learn how to teach children to read, not waste their time on the politics of gender, race and class. (Prime Minister's speech to the Conservative Party Conference, 1992)

Juxtaposition of these statements raises questions about the consistency of and commitment to public policy. Whilst it may sometimes be politically expedient to espouse another rhetoric, polarizing the teaching of reading and anti-racism sets up an unnecessary and false dichotomy. Moreover, it suggests - perhaps foreshadowing 'back to basics' – that the guiding principle should be assimilationist, with English as the language medium. Such fears were at the heart of concerns voiced by LEA advisers/inspectors with responsibility for multicultural anti-racist education (MC/ARE) and equal opportunities (EO) in a post-ERA (Education Reform Act) national research project reported here.[1]

By contrast, the philosophy of MC/ARE starts from the premise – for which there is much empirical evidence – that racism exists in the predominantly monocultural structures and institutions of society.[2] It aims at a society which is socially just, racially harmonious and where cultural diversity is valued and flourishes. Yet, as much research has shown, racial and cultural discrimination is a reality of daily life for many minority ethnic pupils from their earliest years and disenables their learning. Conversely, many white majority pupils – especially those in 'the white highlands' – both lack awareness of the unethicality of racism and its depersonalizing effects, and often fail to have their cultural horizons extended and enriched.[3] The social and educational debate should not be diverted by issues about the teaching of reading and English, from the main question which is the kind of pluralistic and culturally diverse society in which we wish to live.

RECOGNIZING CONCERNS, CONSTRAINTS AND CHALLENGES

With ERA and subsequent legislation the management, financing, curriculum and delivery of education have been politically reconstructed. Since MC/ARE – a good education for all – has always been politically sensitive, the implementation of statutory changes has raised new concerns, constraints and challenges in the realization of equal opportunities. MC/ARE has itself been subject to specific national re-evaluation, including revisions to the funding and remit of Section 11 and the exclusion of MC/ARE from national priority resourcing. At the same time, LEAs have been required to undertake ethnic monitoring of staff and students 'to help secure equality of opportunity for ethnic minority pupils' (para. 3) and to facilitate learner-centred approaches related to 'basic facts about his or her cultural identity' (para. 12) (GB: DES, 1989; GB: DES&WO, 1989).

Although ERA explicitly charged schools to provide a balanced and broadly based curriculum which 'promotes the . . . cultural development of pupils at the school and of society' (GB: Statutes, 1988, S.1(2)), views were divided on whether its ideology was conservative with respect to cultural diversity. Whilst some have dubbed the National Curriculum (NC) as the 'Nationalistic Curriculum', attempts have also been made to indicate how policy and guidance from the then DES and National Curriculum Council, especially on cross-curricular dimensions and themes (NCC, 1990a,b), could be interpreted to underwrite MC/ARE and to market it as an entitlement curriculum.[4]

However, despite the White Paper's title, *Choice and Diversity: A New Framework for Schools*, (GB: DES&WO, 1989) the absence of any mention of equal opportunities renewed concerns, borne out by the 1993 Education Act and Circular 1/94, *Religious Education and Collective Worship*, that more recent national policy development will do little to stimulate or support multicultural anti-racist practice. Rather it appears as if the legislated inclusion of 'cultural' alongside 'spiritual', 'moral' and 'social', as key elements for inspection of 'The Quality of the School as a Community', is re-focussing review of policies and practice in relation to the experience of pupils, parents and staff (OFSTED,1993). Yet schools have received little guidance, and the Office For Standards in Education, conscious of sensitivities, has been exercised to specify evaluation criteria and what constitutes 'development', and to indicate how schools can offer 'learning opportunities' in these domains.[5]

Characteristic of the management of major educational change induced by the pace of legislation, seems to be a locking into response mode to the agenda and cultural framework set by policy-makers. This is also reflected in educational research. Thus, despite the equal opportunities rhetoric, and in line with the low profile of MC/ARE over the last five years, little major research has been sponsored in this area.[6] Our project, 'Multicultural Anti-racist Education after ERA', sought, at a time of far-reaching structural change, to be diagnostic and responsive, by establishing LEAs' concerns and identifying promising developmental strategies in relation to institutional, training and delivery issues. The research had three phases: a national questionnaire, in-depth interviews and thematic case studies.

Initial survey responses by 89 English and Welsh LEAs in mid-1991, followed up by detailed interviews with MC/ARE advisers/inspectors in 27 LEAs, and further contact with 12 LEAs into 1992, provided a purview on policy development and progress in practice (Taylor, 1992a,b). Key findings include:

> In the immediate post-ERA years the proportion of LEAs with MC/ARE policies increased slightly to two-thirds. Policy status varied, with a trend to policy revision, multiple and diverse policies, often reoriented under EO. Some LEAs had new policies on racial harassment.

> In almost three-fifths of LEAs, respondents reported at least some 'progress' in practice since ERA. Progress related to local policy development, national statements and resources, such as Education Support Grants, and increased local awareness, commitment and support. Practice having 'slipped backwards' was linked mainly to schools' preoccupation with the NC. Other priorities or local retrenchment and/or attitudinal resistance were reasons for practice having 'stayed much the same'.

Serious concerns were shared about the status quo of MC/ARE and constraints upon it. The national educational and political climate was seen as ideologically unpropitious, and reflected in the absence of supporting resources and structures. Governors and elected members were said to lack awareness of the importance of MC/ARE. Low priority in LEA and school policy development, implementation and review was due to constraints on finance, staffing and INSET (in-service teacher education).

Promising lines of development, often *ad hoc* and not institutionalized, included attitudinal, structural and resource-led changes, consultation and community initiatives. In some LEAs, developments in language teaching, curriculum, training and inspection were seen as catalysts for change.

In response to LEAs' interests, the research focused on four themes: revised arrangements for the organization of Section 11 and language teaching; the introduction of the Ethnic Minority Grant (EMG) administered by Training and Enterprise Councils (TECs); equal opportunities in governor training; and cultural diversity in the work of local Standing Advisory Councils for Religious Education (SACREs). These themes are litmus indicators of contemporary developments in education and MC/ARE, demonstrating the central place of language teaching, the increasingly influential role of TECs in local education and training, the shift of managerial responsibility from LEAs to schools and their governors, and renewed emphasis through SACREs on the pre-eminence of Christianity amongst culturally diverse beliefs and values. In this changing institutional and ideological context, the research highlights critical issues and some positive practices of consultation, dialogue and partnership characteristic of a pluralist democracy.

SECTION 11 AND LOCAL EDUCATION AUTHORITIES

At the time of the research, the major funding source for ethnic relations and schooling was through Section 11 of the Local Government Act 1966. This legislation enables grants to be awarded to LEAs to employ staff to work with minority pupils and parents from the New Commonwealth, usually as English as a second language (ESL) teachers, bilingual classroom assistants, and home–school liaison workers. The Home Office currently pays 75 per cent of salary costs,

LEAs the remainder (GB: HO, 1990a).[7]

For LEAs and schools, the Section 11 grant has become the primary means of meeting the additional educational needs of minority ethnic pupils. Indeed, as the only large programme of government expenditure targeted to assist the needs of minority ethnic groups over almost thirty years, the availability and use of Section 11 has played a major part in shaping the geographical location, direction and implementation of race-related policy and practice (Ouseley,1990). Such is the centrality of Section 11, that an investigation of its development and application is a useful barometer of central and local government relationships in race and education (Bagley, 1992).

In October 1990, following an extensive review of Section 11, the Home Office issued revised criteria for its administration and use (GB: HO, 1989; 1990a). These emphasized school-based projects which focused on 'core education' areas of primary and secondary education, notably the provision of ESL. As a result, programmes aimed at raising the achievement of minority ethnic pupils, through multicultural and anti-racist whole-school initiatives, could no longer be Section 11 funded. Advisers/inspectors of multicultural education also expressed concern that this main source of support for the development of anti-discriminatory work with teachers and white pupils would be lost, and with it associated advisory teaching posts. The revised guidelines and criteria for Section 11 did, however, introduce the prospect of some promising lines of development for multicultural and anti-racist education, notably: wider consultation and partnership with minority ethnic groups; more stringent targeting of provision to meet the needs of minority ethnic pupils; and closer project monitoring and evaluation.

Consultation

The opportunity for increased community consultation was welcomed by LEA and Race Equality Council (REC) officers, who nonetheless found the process difficult and often unsatisfactory. Concerns expressed included: poorly attended meetings with minority ethnic groups; insufficient time made available for the consultative process; inadequate information about Section 11 for RECs and minority ethnic groups; and consultation meetings being merely a formality, with RECs and minority ethnic groups expected simply to comment on LEA policy decisions already made. To ensure positive consultation initiatives, a proactive strategy was required by LEAs, as illustrated by one Authority's practice.

In order to obtain the perspectives of local minority ethnic communities on Section 11 provision, the LEA held four consultation afternoons over a two-week period in the Civic Centre, each allocated to a specific group: the Pakistani community, the Afro-Caribbean community, the Bangladeshi community and women only. Displays were mounted to explain the Section 11 bids, and officers and translators recorded comments or proposed amendments. Although consultations were not well attended, the exercise was viewed as a pilot, and it was intended that future consultations would be school- and community-based.

Following the consultations, bids were drafted and prioritized by the LEA, then shared with the REC and minority ethnic communities at a joint consultative committee. In discussing the prioritization of bids, the REC supported the primary concern of the Authority, to maintain and extend existing provision, particularly in education. The REC was invited to participate in the recruitment and selection of an LEA officer, responsible for monitoring Section 11, who would sit both on the Local Authority's committee concerned with Section 11 and that of the REC.

In the short term, establishing effective practices and procedures for consultation requires time and resources. However, by involving minority ethnic communities from the beginning of an initiative, LEAs and schools increase the possibility of getting a project right and being cost-effective by saving on later changes. Just as important is the fact that ongoing consultation facilitates a process of dialogue and accountability in which minority ethnic parents are empowered to participate in the decision-making process which influences the direction and quality of their children's education. Equally necessary is regular feedback from the intended beneficiaries of an initiative as to whether resources are being efficiently used. Moreover, as Home Office encouragement suggests, developing consultation will make LEAs and schools better placed for inspections; and the identification of good practice increases the likelihood of continued Section 11 and other government funding.

Targeting, Monitoring and Evaluation

The new rules meant that, for the first time, the Home Office explicitly defined the types and areas of work for which Section 11 funding would be made available. LEA advisers/ inspectors for multicultural education recognized that it was not easy to defend the previous funding system, which often lacked clearly identifiable results. In this respect there was a consensus on the need to establish targeting, monitoring and evaluation of Section 11 provision.

Guidance from the Home Office on the monitoring of provision is, however, limited, while increasing demands are made on LEA administration. Misuse of Section 11 in schools may still occur if the guidance and funds available to LEAs to undertake effective monitoring are insufficient. In addition, delivery by Section 11 staff may be affected by limitations on LEA resources, restricting available INSET and teaching materials. In a climate of financial stringency, LEAs may be tempted to set unrealistic targets to become more competitive in securing Section 11 funds. Nationally, as use of Section 11 is monitored through OFSTED (1993), it will be necessary to ensure that the experience of inspectors and the frequency of inspections are sufficient to identify any misuse of Section 11.

The initial review undertaken by LEAs in preparing Section 11 applications facilitated identification of potentially discriminatory practices which might have remained hidden, such as the language survey in one LEA which revealed a disproportionately high number of minority ethnic pupils in special schools. Research on developmental planning in 24 multiracial primary schools in three LEAs (McMahon and Wallace, 1993), showed that discrimination could arise through restrictions on application of Section 11 to certain pupils, lack of continuity of provision of Section 11 staff and their career development, and the need for additional resources to enable the active participation of minority ethnic parents in school development.

However, if adequately resourced, with additional guidance and appropriate inspection, revised Section 11 criteria can facilitate a process in which LEAs, schools and minority ethnic groups assist each other in: identification of educational needs; development of projects most appropriate to meet those needs; and the formulation of strategies for monitoring and evaluation – with pre-specified objectives and targets – to ensure that Section 11 funds are being used efficiently, effectively and appropriately.

Section 11 Projects
Arising from the Section 11 changes, three- or five-year school-based projects were scheduled to start in April 1992, although many did

not become operational until October–November 1992. The duties of Section 11 staff working with minority ethnic pupils are wide-ranging and include: collaborative teaching with mainstream colleagues in classrooms; selection and development of appropriate teaching material to provide access to the curriculum; assessment and review of pupils' progress and pastoral needs; provision of English language teaching; and home–school liaison, encouraging parental and community involvement in school.

Since their inception, Section 11 projects have provided a valuable opportunity for schools to enhance the delivery and quality of education for minority ethnic pupils, and, as the following example shows, for all pupils:

> In October 1993 a headteacher reported that, in the previous twelve months, due to the classroom support work of Section 11 staff working with mainstream teachers, the school had witnessed a marked improvement in achievement of the Bangladeshi pupils (who formed 30 per cent of the school roll) in GCSE examinations. This had increased the school's position in the league tables, which, in turn, had raised its standing in the community and boosted staff morale. The results also helped to allay the fears of many white parents, who mistakenly believed that Bangladeshi children's needs for English language teaching might be restricting their own children.
>
> According to the head, racial tensions between white and Asian pupils in the school were also in part alleviated through Section 11 English language teaching. He believed that as Bangladeshi children were able to communicate more effectively in English so cultural barriers were broken down, resulting in greater mutual understanding and respect.
>
> That the school was multiethnic and multicultural was viewed as a positive resource, but its benefit to the educational development of all pupils could only be fully tapped through the deployment of Section 11 staff. The head was concerned that any reduction in or changes to Section 11 funding would result in the loss of these staff and their significant contribution.

As a result of the Government's Public Expenditure Survey in November 1992, proposed cuts were announced in Section 11 funding for 1994–95 and 1995–96, which could lead to a 40 per cent reduction in local government services to minority ethnic communities, mostly in education. A survey by the Local Authorities Race Relations Information Exchange (LARRIE,1993) revealed the initial reactions of Local Authorities, and a further (as yet unpublished) survey has been carried out on the likely impact on staff and services. A cut in the grant rate (from 75 to 57 per cent in 1994–95 and to 50 per cent in 1995–96) would mean the Local Authority contribution would need to rise by 72 and 100 per cent in cash terms respectively, to provide the same level of service. Only 6.7 per cent of Authorities believed an increase beyond the existing 25 per cent contribution would be possible. In June 1993 a national conference on Section 11 was organized by the All-Party Parliamentary Group on Race and Community, the National Union of Teachers and the Runnymede Trust. The conference subsequently issued a statement (1993) condemning the proposed cuts and their announcement just after the three- and five-year projects had begun, predicting an underspend of budgeted Government money; arguing that Local Authorities' difficult management decisions about post deletions would disproportionately affect black and minority ethnic staff employed under Section 11; and challenging the Government's expressed aim (see p. 118) for the full participation of ethnic minority people in the life of the nation. This was followed in October 1993 by a lobby of Parliament, which is ongoing. A special issue of *Multicultural Teaching* (12, 1, Autumn 1993) devoted to Section 11, demonstrates the professionalism and commitment in most current Section 11 work, with evidence of positive practice and its effects for pupils, schools and communities.

ETHNIC MINORITY GRANTS AND TRAINING AND ENTERPRISE COUNCILS

Changes to Section 11 also heralded the introduction of the Ethnic Minority Grant (EMG), administered by Training and Enterprise Councils (TECs) (GB: HO, 1990a). TECs are employer-led organizations which plan and administer training and enterprise programmes, (including youth training, adult training and enterprise allowance schemes), monitor skill shortages, and design and deliver local schemes to promote and support the development of small businesses. In breaking down the 'economic, social and cultural differences' perceived as 'barriers to opportunity', the Government considered that the voluntary sector had 'an important contribution to make in addressing the special needs of ethnic minority communities' (GB: HO, 1990b, p.2). TECs were seen by the Home Office to be ideally situated to act as administrative and financial intermediaries between the voluntary sector and the Home Office in the delivery of EMG.

EMG is governed by the same criteria as Section 11, and can also be used for projects for non-New Commonwealth groups. The grant includes running and salary costs, and in exceptional cases is awarded for more than 75 per cent of costs. The grant is available to the voluntary sector by application for grant via TECs to the Home Office. TECs administer and monitor the finances and the effectiveness of projects. In 1992–93, TECs were allocated £4 million for EMG projects, compared with Local Authorities which received £129 million for Section 11. Funded EMG projects were broadly concerned with vocational training, language training, and business advice and counselling.

EMG and Mainstream Provision
In line with revised Section 11 criteria, EMG cannot sponsor projects promoting the cultures of specific minority ethnic groups or anti-racist work. The limitation of the grant to language and cultural barriers means it cannot be used to address the potentially more serious obstacles of racism and racial discrimination in the labour market.

As a specific grant with clearly defined uses, EMG should not be equated with promoting race equality *per se*, since this risks compartmentalizing and marginalizing the issues, with mainstream training and employment programmes remaining unaffected and potentially discriminatory. TECs need to safeguard against treating the grant as an alternative to developing an effective race equality strategy incorporated in all their activities. The establishment of mainstream race equality procedures and practices is particularly important in a climate in which the existence and level of race-related grant aid is vulnerable to cuts and abolition. Leicestershire TEC (1993), for example, which covers Asian inner city wards with unemployment rates of 25 per cent, has established an Inner City Ethnic Minority Task Force for monthly meetings to discuss practical ways of encouraging and supporting greater take-up of TEC services by minority ethnic groups and meeting their needs. The EMG supports English language training for domestic and business use.

Significantly, early in 1993 the National TEC Council Equal Opportunities and Special Needs Sub-Group commissioned the Institute of Manpower Studies (IMS) to provide an overview of the main issues relating to TECs, equal opportunities and special needs (Meager and Court, 1993; Meager and Honey, 1993). Practical outcomes from this investigation include: the first national TEC conference on equal opportunities and special needs in November 1993; creation of a national development project to take forward the main issues

identified by IMS; and the establishment of a TEC equal opportunities
unit to support development and dissemination of policy and good
practice (National TEC Council Equal Opportunities and Special Needs
Sub-Group, 1993).

The need for TEC mainstream race equality provision, however,
does not detract from the positive aspects of EMG which aim to
assist a wide network of minority ethnic groups through funded
projects in the voluntary sector. In this respect, EMG should be
perceived as a complementary part of any race equality strategy (Bagley,
1993a).

EMG Delivery

In considering the delivery of EMG in its first year (1992–93), it is
noteworthy that it was delivered by recently established organizations
– TECs – collaborating with Local Authorities, minority ethnic groups,
the voluntary sector and the Home Office, all of which possessed very
little or no experience of working together. Moreover, EMG, directed
towards training and employment, evolved from Section 11, which
had developed over twenty-five years primarily in education. Not
surprisingly, the transposition of Section 11 criteria to EMG raised
issues and concerns.

For instance, whilst consultation between TECs, LEAs, minority
ethnic groups and voluntary organizations was seen by the Home
Office as 'essential' to ensure an effective and coordinated approach,
guidelines were vague about the ways in which TECs should consult. In
the majority of the ten TECs (just under 25 per cent of those in receipt of
EMG) involved in our research, the relationship with LEAs with regard
to the delivery of EMG and Section 11 was minimal: it was mostly
restricted to obtaining access to a database of minority ethnic groups.
TEC officers claimed that they had not been informed by the LEA
about Section 11 projects, and LEAs reported a similar lack of liaison
by TECs.

The cursory relationship between TECs and LEAs might, in part,
be explained by the political and policy context in which the process
of Section 11 and EMG bidding occurred. For example, TECs were
under the illusion – which they claimed came from informal Home
Office briefings – that, if necessary, money would be transferred
from Section 11 and LEAs and reallocated to EMG and TECs.
This assumption – given weight by the apparent commitment of
Government to reduce the power and influence of LEAs – whilst

subsequently to prove ill-founded, was prevalent at the time Local Authorities and TECs were constructing their bids. Undoubtedly, such speculation did not engender a climate of mutual cooperation and trust.

Equally, the establishment by TECs of consultation procedures with minority ethnic groups and voluntary organizations was variable. Even so, examples of positive practice could be identified:

One TEC produced an information pack which included: its Corporate Plan; an explanatory letter about TECs and EMG suggesting possible projects a voluntary organisation might consider; and a Commission for Racial Equality resource pack on Section 11 and EMG. Promotional advertisements on the availability of EMG were placed in minority ethnic newspapers, and workshops were held to help voluntary groups draft bids.

In the preliminary identification and assessment of the training needs of minority ethnic groups, three TECs engaged consultants to work with communities and voluntary organizations. Constructive dialogue and collaboration led in one case to a school-based EMG project:

The TEC was already working closely with the LEA to develop education and business partnerships, and the EMG was perceived as another facet of these endeavours. As a result, a secondary school was involved in a project aiming to improve the access of Asian girls to careers, jobs and training in which they were under-represented. A project coordinator based in the school worked with Asian girls, together with teaching and careers staff. Planning and running the project necessitated the TEC, the LEA and the school operating together for the benefit of minority ethnic pupils. Such was the LEA's commitment that it provided additional financial support.

As this example shows, the introduction of EMG alongside Section 11 can provide an opportunity for TECs, LEAs, schools, minority ethnic communities and voluntary organizations to establish networks to cooperate in devising complementary, effective and high-quality school-based strategies for the delivery of education and training. Other TEC-supported initiatives, such as local Education Business Partnerships, Business in the Community, and School Curriculum Industry Partnerships, are an indication that, irrespective of EMG, TECs in the 1990s are likely to have an increasingly influential role in schools and education, further fragmenting and diffusing LEA power. Indeed, from April 1994, some TECs will be in partnership with privatized careers services through the new Pathfinder arrangements, for the delivery of careers education and guidance. Careers services customarily have stated commitments to equal opportunities as cornerstones of professional practice; yet they may neglect to monitor school-leaving destination statistics by ethnicity, even in areas where the unemployment rate of young people of minority ethnic origin is twice that of whites. It remains to be seen whether, as TECs have greater involvement in education, there will be positive implications for race equality, and attempts made to redress imbalances in access to training (see also Chatrik and de Sousa, 1993).

GOVERNOR TRAINING AND EQUAL OPPORTUNITIES

Recent legislation, by increasing the control of school senior managers over the delivery of education, shifts the onus for ensuring good ethnic relations and equality of opportunity from LEA to school, from advisers/inspectors and advisory teachers to headteachers and governors. Governors' extensive responsibilities include: school budgets; health and safety; staff discipline and promotion; staff selection and recruitment; exclusions; school–community links; parent complaints; and delivery of the national curriculum. Each has implications for ethnic relations and equal opportunities, so, to be effective, governors need to understand race equality issues. Basic and specialist training programmes and strategies for minority ethnic governor recruitment are required to facilitate this process.

Survey and Interview Findings

Governor training coordinators in 114 LEAs were requested to supply information on equal opportunity training for governors (including race equality training) and the recruitment of minority ethnic governors in 1990–92 (Bagley, 1993b). Replies from 85 indicated that over this period, three-quarters had offered either specific training courses on race equality or, more likely, equal opportunities courses with a race component. Over one-third of the remainder, which had offered no such courses, cited the course on recruitment and selection as covering equal opportunities. Follow-up interviews with 15 governor training coordinators in London, metropolitan and county LEAs, revealed the generally low demand for race equality and equal opportunities training by governors. Equal opportunities courses may have been offered but they did not necessarily run, and, if they did, attendance was extremely low. Poor take-up had resulted in the cancellation of courses and re-evaluation of provision by many LEAs.

The majority of governor training coordinators, committed to the pro-vision of race equality and equal opportunities training, were dismayed at its lack of priority for governors. Coordinators believed that low demand was due to several factors, including: increasing responsibilities and pressures on governors' time; the low profile and apparent lack of support for race equality and equal opportunities at national and local levels; and governors' reluctance to address a controversial issue, which they did not perceive as relevant.

The Strategy of Permeation

The unpopularity of race equality and equal opportunities courses led many LEAs to include equal opportunities issues within all training. Permeation was perceived as the major strategy for ensuring that race equality and equal opportunities were brought to governors' attention. A wider cross-section of governors were thereby brought into contact with equal opportunities; school-based governing body training was also identified for future development.

Race equality and equal opportunities were most frequently addressed in relation to recruitment and selection, as might be expected, given the legal requirements relating to the appointment and employment of staff. It was nonetheless encouraging that LEAs, even if doing little else in relation to race equality and equal opportunities, at least appear to be training governors in this very important area. Other examples of permeation in general training included: a health and safety course which looked at racial harassment; a course on buildings and premises which considered their use by community groups; and a course on finance which examined the setting of priorities for additional expenditure.

Ideally, permeation should augment specific race equality and equal opportunities training provision. In reality, permeation has increasingly been perceived as an alternative to specific courses. But are general courses enabling governors to develop sufficient awareness of race equality issues to be of use in school management? Will the somewhat intangible nature of permeation be used by less committed LEAs to disguise inaction?

In order to safeguard against dissipation of the issues, one Authority had included on all its course evaluation sheets, to be completed by governors after each training session, the question 'How effectively did the course promote equal opportunities issues?'. Responses entered on a database were monitored by the Authority's equal opportunities unit and reviewed with the training coordinator. This LEA has recently commended governors for their role in assisting schools with systems for data collection for ethnic monitoring and in representing the interest of parents in this sensitive, but successful exercise.

Ethnic Minority Governors

Relevant to understanding the trend towards permeation is the fact that the overwhelming majority of governors are white (Keys and Fernandes, 1990). Black and ethnic minority people who have experienced racial discrimination, harassment and violence and who may be more likely to pressurize national and local government and schools for multicultural and anti-racist initiatives, are significantly under-represented on governing bodies. Thus, important voices and perspectives are absent from school management debates. If schools are to respond positively to the educational needs and ambitions of minority ethnic pupils and parents, governing bodies will need to more closely resemble the multi-ethnic nature of the communities they serve. To achieve this, LEAs will need to take positive action measures such as those illustrated:

> Some LEAs had carried out surveys to determine the degree of under-representation. Others were contemplating introducing ethnic monitoring. Several LEAs had conducted specific drives to recruit minority ethnic governors and had produced promotional leaflets, posters and audio-visual material in community languages. Conferences on school governance and equality were held in several LEAs with Chief Education Officers, Chairs of Education Committees and minority ethnic governors as speakers. Others held workshops with minority ethnic leaders on how to become and work effectively as a minority ethnic governor. One LEA used Urban Programme funding to create a post to work with community groups specifically on governance. Meetings were organised in community centres with interpreters and promotional material in community languages. In another Authority, as part of their home–school liaison work, the

brief of Section 11 staff included encouraging individuals from ethnic minority groups to put themselves forward to become a governor.

But however effective LEA strategies are in gaining nominations from individuals from ethnic minority groups for school governance, there is no guarantee that at school level parents will elect or governing bodies coopt minority ethnic governors. For this reason, specific and permeated race equality and equal opportunities training for all governors – indeed for all those involved in schooling and education – is of paramount importance, if the barriers to just and harmonious ethnic relations are to be broken down.

Funding
With the devolution of funds for training to schools, training pro- grammes sold by LEAs and other agencies may increasingly come to reflect what governors and senior managers perceive as their training needs. Thus, training providers are becoming more responsive to consumer demands. Consequently, training providers, concerned to maintain a market for courses and their employment future, may feel unable to afford to offer unpopular race equality and equal opportunity training, or even to include equality issues in general courses, for fear of alienating potential clients. As a result, such training is further jeopardized and its contribution to race equality in schools in danger of being lost.

In addition, as Urban Programme funding is phased out and the future of Section 11 funding remains uncertain,[8] so initiatives from these grants relating to the recruitment of minority ethnic governors will be dissipated. If past positive work in ethnic relations and education is to be maintained and further developed in the 1990s, then policies and practices will require adequate resourcing. Race equality strategies cannot be left financially reliant upon the tenuous and varying fortunes of grant-aid provision.

SACREs, RE AND CULTURAL DIVERSITY
The establishment of Standing Advisory Councils for Religious Educa- tion (SACREs) was one of the most significant innovations of ERA for cultural diversity, and SACREs have received renewed legislative support with the Education Act 1993. The SACRE offers a consultative structure and a forum for dialogue which is distinctive in the local management of the curriculum. Its importance locally is twofold. First,

it is an advisory body which statutorily comprises representatives of the various 'principal religious traditions of the area' (Group A and B), education professionals and Local Authority members. Thus, the composition of many SACREs already mirrors the diversity of a culturally and ethnically plural Britain. The 1993 Act potentially enhances this by requiring LEAs (which continue to have responsibility for Religious Education (RE)) to review the composition of Group A ('Christian denominations and other religions and denominations of such religions') to 'reflect broadly the proportionate strength of that denomination or religion in the area' (GB Statutes, 1993, para. 255(2)). Despite conceptual and empirical difficulties in establishing the 'strength' of religions and their representation, this offers new opportunities for consultation with minority faith groups and learning from initial experiences in setting up SACREs (Taylor,1991).

Secondly, the SACRE has responsibility to advise on RE in relation to the local Agreed Syllabus (AS) – which it can ask the LEA to review – collective worship (CW), including determinations, and, in particular, teaching methods, choice of materials and teacher training. It should consider what is appropriate for pupils according to their ages, aptitudes, family background and 'particular needs' in the local LEA and school context. In multi-religious, multi-ethnic localities the factors to be taken into account may be in tension; for example, respect for religious freedom may have implications for practice in educational contexts which do not sit well with equal opportunities policies. It is fitting in a liberal democratic society that these issues should provoke strong and concerned debate, as is evident in some SACREs.

Representation, Attendance and Participation

Analysis of SACREs' Annual Reports, meeting minutes, attendance at SACRE meetings, and over a year's case-study of the work of four SACREs across the range of LEA types in some of England's most multi-ethnic localities, including interviews with principal figures and minority faith representatives, has revealed a range of issues concerning awareness of and respect for cultural diversity (Taylor,1994). These are evident not just in the content of SACREs' work, but in the very structure and procedures of the SACRE itself. The involvement of representatives of minority faiths and their ability to influence a SACRE is crucial to its operation as a pluralistic body. Representation, attendance and participation are ongoing concerns.

Where the majority of pupils are from faith backgrounds other than Christianity (in one case-study area, two-thirds of pupils are Muslim), the structural inclusion of, for example, Muslim representatives within Group A may be perceived as continuing to marginalise their interests and limit their decision-making power. The 1993 Act, whilst increasing the chances of proportionate representation of minority faiths, does little to change perceptions of the SACRE as a Christian-dominated body structurally, given that each of the four constituent groups formally has only one vote, even though a greater presence and skills of communication and reception may enhance opportunities to influence discussion. A radical solution, properly responsive to local diversity, would have allowed the inclusion of representatives of denominations of Christianity with the Church of England representatives in Group B, thus leaving Group A to minority faiths, or even to allow the representatives of the principal religious tradition of the area – in this case Islam – to constitute a separate group.

Whilst some SACREs continue to receive applications for membership from religious groups and Humanists – another group suffering discrimination – others experience poor attendance by some minority faith representatives (and others), who may see community interests as more pressing or better served by other organizations, such as RECs. The Chair of a SACRE's awareness and appreciation of religious and cultural diversity is critical to the conduct of meetings, and whether minority faith representatives are empowered to participate, have a voice and exert influence. The operation of many SACREs has already enhanced awareness of cultural diversity, for example, by not holding meetings at religious festivals or on sacred days. But consideration has often still to be given to facilitating attendance at times suitable for those who are not part of the mainstream educational establishment. The INSET of SACRE members about RE and broader educational and cultural matters should be seen as part of a process of enabling the meeting to act as an increasingly accountable and public body with adequate budgetary resourcing.

Collective Worship and RE
In terms of its statutory remit, consideration of the procedure for determinations for exemption from worship 'wholly or mainly of a broadly Christian character' initially preoccupied many SACREs.

LEAs and SACREs across the country took different approaches to this contentious issue, some encouraging schools' applications, after consultation with governors and parents, others deterring or even resisting applications. However, with few well-publicized exceptions, there has not been the number of requests for determinations at first foreseen. The NCC analysis of SACRE reports for 1992 (NCC, 1993b) shows that from 1988 to 1992 a total of 272 determinations were granted. In practice, having a determination, or not, has no clear or consistent meaning. Determinations have, in some cases, allowed the continuation of multi-faith assemblies. In a few places they permit separate acts of worship, supported by faith community members. In some schools a determination has effectively inhibited parental withdrawal from CW.

Neither is there evidence of increased withdrawal from CW or RE, as some predicted. Indeed, there are examples of collaboration and compromise, as in the case of Muslim parents, concerned about arrangements for Muslim prayers, who worked with the headteacher, governors and Church authorities to avoid withdrawal. Where schools have a majority of pupils from faith backgrounds other than Christianity, or none, the requirement of a daily act of worship may still be problematic due to the nature of the concept of 'worship' in a school context, and the recent guidance that CW should include 'some elements which relate specifically to the traditions of Christian belief and which accord a special status to Jesus Christ' (GB: DFE, 1994, para. 63). Many SACREs and LEAs have produced helpful guidelines for schools on CW. A few have issued leaflets in community languages to parents, explaining RE and CW. One or two are undertaking training with members of faith communities to enhance communication skills with pupils, so that they may become a religious education resource. Since CW is now a target for school inspection, it is especially important to keep clear records of CW, whether for whole school, year group or class, to demonstrate content, continuity and progression.

RE has had a long history of being in the vanguard of promoting appreciation of cultural diversity and respect for others' beliefs and values. Ongoing controversy about the status of RE as part of the basic curriculum for all pupils, whilst lacking statutory national guidance, has, since 1988, led to unprecedented activity in many LEAs and SACREs with review or revision of ASs and development of programmes of study and attainment targets, in an attempt to give RE parity of standing with the NC. The amount of time to be devoted to Christianity and the number of other world faiths to be studied; the lack of curriculum time and the poor qualifications of many RE teachers for teaching RE (Gates, 1993); and the ability of LEAs to mount and willingness of schools to support INSET are all key issues.

The Education Act 1993 has given further impetus to these activities and concerns by requiring any LEA that has not adopted a new AS since September 1988 to convene an Agreed Syllabus Conference (ASC) (often in practice similar membership to the SACRE) for that purpose by April 1995 (GB Statutes, 1993, para. 256). ERA requires that an AS should 'reflect the fact that the religious traditions of Great Britain are in the main Christian, whilst taking account of the teaching and practices of the other principal religions represented in Great Britain' (GB Statutes, 1988, S.8). Whilst for the first time legimating the study of world faiths other than Christianity, this has given rise to controversial questions of what, when and how subject-matter in relation to each religion should be taught; and the difficulty of specifying sufficient detail in an AS for it to be clear that teaching is in accordance with ERA (NCC, 1993c).

In an example of good consultative practice, in September 1992 the NCC commenced work on guidance for ASCs on the contents and construction of ASs, by inviting members of six religions – Buddhism, Christianity, Hinduism, Islam, Judaism and Sikhism – to form working groups. Further consultation with professional bodies, the establishment of a monitoring group representing religious traditions and educational interests, and a teachers' group, has resulted in the circulation of six documents, including model ASs, for wider comment (SCAA, 1994). At the same time, a revised Circular for Religious Education and Collective Worship (GB: DFE, 1994) has been issued. Whilst this constitutes guidance, 'not an authoritative legal interpretation', of the Acts, the emphasis that 'as a whole and at each key stage, the relative content devoted to Christianity in the syllabus should predominate' (para. 35), and that RE should 'ensure that pupils gain both a thorough knowledge of Christianity reflecting the Christian heritage of this country, and knowledge of the other principal religions represented in Great Britain' (para. 7), indicates divisiveness by degree, separate study of religions, and dismays those committed to cultural pluralism. However, the AS, as a whole, must include all principal religions in the country; and attention is drawn to the need to take account of the local school population and parents' wishes in determining the precise balance of religions. This also suggests consultative opportunities which should be grasped by LEAs and ASCs in order to preserve local flexibility.

Ensuring Quality and Equality

The Government remains concerned about the fact that in some schools RE and CW 'do not take place with the frequency required or to the standard which pupils deserve' (GB: DFE, 1994, para. 5). The SACRE holds a pivotal place as the local watchdog for quality and equality in RE and CW during retrenchment of local educational resourcing. Teachers and RE advisers/inspectors have a special part to play in professionalizing the SACRE, which is the key to long-term support for RE (Taylor, 1992d). Where it works well, the SACRE has proved itself a useful consultative structure, with collaborative groups engaged in locally appropriate curricular developments, a forum for debate, an ally, and, like the National Association of SACREs (NASACRE), a pressure group for RE and CW. In such cases, the SACRE has raised the status of RE locally and contributed to cultural pluralism.

For the most part, however, to date SACREs have had a somewhat distant and ambivalent relationship with schools. With the changing power balance between LEAs and schools, the SACRE needs to enhance its public image, develop a closer partnership with schools and demonstrate that it has teeth. It needs to monitor provision and practice on behalf of pupils, as some have already done by initiating surveys, linked with securing access to GEST (Grants for Education Support and Training) funds for AS implementation, and ensuring that RE and CW receive a fair share of the school INSET budget. Moreover, the emerging focus on spiritual, moral, social and cultural development, in inspection – to which RE and CW make a significant contribution – gives the SACRE an opportunity to sustain its momentum, broaden its links and deepen its impact. Its special position, drawing on the wealth of cultural experience and standing of its community members, should also place it at the forefront of facilitating much-needed dialogue between schools and parents about the values which schools promote, and ways in which partnerships which enhanced intercultural appreciation can be fostered.

MULTICULTURAL ANTI-RACIST EDUCATION INTO THE TWENTY-FIRST CENTURY

Implementation of recent legislative changes has presented new challenges to providing a good multicultural anti-racist education. Yet, despite its national thrust, the policy agenda set is in part open to local interpretation and institutionalization in LEA, TEC and school structures and programmes. The extent to which multicultural anti-racist practice permeates education and training, and receives active support, may well depend on local political will and ongoing review in response to financial constraints. However, in the climate of market forces, of standards and accountability to clients, if the rhetoric is not to be exposed as merely hollow, equal opportunities policies, with their legislative underpinning, could be made a focus for delivery of quality and equality; thus rendering it all the more important for LEAs, TECs and schools to document, demonstrate and disseminate positive practice, where, to be responsive to local needs, educational institutions consult, converse and work in partnership with parents and communities. In a society which is patently multi-ethnic and culturally diverse, these strengths need to be harnessed for the management of change to be effective.

CHAPTER 8

The Local Management of Schools and Racial Equality

Barry Troyna[1]

The weakening of Local Education Authorities is a major feature of current educational change, and in this chapter, Barry Troyna critically assesses its impact on equal opportunities and multicultural education.

In this chapter I want to argue that the status of racial equality on the agenda of Local Education Authorities (LEAs) and their schools has been crucially influenced by the Conservative Government's education legislation, particularly the 1988 Education Reform Act (ERA). Among other things, this established a new relationship between central and local government which, in turn, has had serious implications for what goes on in schools. This argument will be exemplified by a consideration of how the relocation of policy and decision-making in education has negative consequences for the promotion and diffusion of anti-racist education in English and Welsh schools. Without wishing to portray teachers as disenfranchised by the disappearance of LEA policy frameworks for anti-racism, a central theme in this chapter is that the present-day challenge to anti-racism as an orthodoxy in education derives largely from central government's systematic erosion of LEA responsibilities for providing the policy (and financial) co-ordinates for what takes place in schools.

Of course, the volatile nature of the Conservative Government's relationship with education means that any arguments must be provisional. But despite this caveat there is sufficient evidence, both direct and circumstantial, to indicate that anti-racist initiatives are receding in prominence on the educational landscape. It is worth recalling, for instance, John Major's insistence at the 1992 Annual Conservative Party Conference that: 'Primary teachers should learn how to teach children to read, not waste their time on the politics of gender, race and class'. This testifies to the view that what is currently being witnessed is the consolidation and orchestration of a new ideology, what Kate Myers (1990) call 'equiphobia', 'an irrational hatred and fear of anything to do with equal opportunities' (p. 295).

'THE HUB' AND 'THE RIM'

It is now customary in analyses of the antecedents and framing of the ERA to acknowledge its celebration of two diverse, ostensibly contradictory, ideological trajectories and to account for their articulation within the legislative package. This discontinuity was almost inevitable, given that the origins of educational and other Thatcherite reforms in social welfare during the 1980s were to be found in the eclecticism of that ideological orthodoxy popularly termed the 'New Right' (see Hindess, 1990). As Caroline Cox, a prominent New Right ideologue, has pointed out, 'many tributaries go into that river' (cited in S. Ball, 1990, p. 44), and what flows out has been distilled into two distinctive channels of intellectual thought: neo-conservatism which emphasizes a strong, interventionist central state, and neo-liberalism which champions decentralization.

In his book *Politics and Policymaking in Education* (1990), Stephen Ball has graphically illustrated the power struggle amongst 'New Rightists' in their efforts to ensure that their favoured ideological stance assumed centre-stage in the legislation. There is no need to rehearse those arguments here. Suffice to say, compromise prevailed. The National Curriculum, formal student assessment, initially with targets of attainment at 7, 11, 14 and 16, stringent directives for the content and orientation of teacher education courses, alongside the strengthening of categorical or prescriptive funding for in-service education, draw their inspiration and rationale from neo-conservatism. They represent the intrusion of the central state into educational matters, and the determination to rigidify and legitimate particular conceptions of education. Neo-liberals, on the other hand, inspired the moves towards the local management of schools (LMS); the opportunity for schools to assume grant maintained status (GMS) and to 'opt out' of their LEA to receive funding directly from Whitehall; open enrolment; and the creation of City Technology Colleges. Ostensibly, at least, these represent a 'rolling back' of central and local government's influence on what goes on in schools.

It has been argued elsewhere (Troyna, 1993) that what gives coherence and structure to these seemingly disconnected initiatives is that they coalesce around an especially potent policy objective: the weakening, and ultimately dismantling, of LEA influence. This objective, established under Margaret Thatcher's administrations, has been pursued with almost equal vigour by her successor, John Major. The 1993 Education Act is, for instance, further testimony to this ongoing commitment to marginalize Local Authority influence. Even the most cursory glance at the speeches, commentaries and justifications enunciated by New Rightists before and since the passing of the ERA reveals that it is this conviction in particular which has mobilized the Conservative Party project in education, and elsewhere for that matter (Butcher *et al.*, 1990). The determination to expel LEAs from active participation in policy and decision-making after the ERA was emphasized by Kenneth Baker, the Secretary of State responsible for the legislation, during the initial framing of the Act. For Baker, the ERA was intended to sanction a scenario in which

> Central government, at the hub, had to take greater control of the curriculum. At the same time, at the rim of the wheel, the schools and the parents (not the local authorities) had to have a greater say in administration. (*Guardian*, 6 December 1986)

On this view, ERA was designed to make LEAs agents of central government and 'providers of services in competition with others' (Esp, 1989, p. 176), and it has been pretty effective. In the words of Gordon Hutchinson (1993), Director of Education for the London Borough of Enfield, the ERA and subsequent legislation, including of course the 1993 Education Act, marks 'the death of the LEA in its present form' (p. 9). The ERA, therefore, was neither fragmented nor lacking in coherence. Whilst its intellectual stimuli might have been diverse, they were premised on and geared towards a uniform policy objective. What compels attention now is the question: why should the diminution of LEA influence lead to a decline in the status of anti-racist education in Britain?

The rise of 'equiphobia' in the early 1990s and the correlative demise of anti-racism on the agenda of LEAs and individual schools, heightens the temptation to look back on the burgeoning of anti-racist education (ARE) in local settings during the 1980s through rose-tinted spectacles. Certainly, this educational orthodoxy assumed a significant role in in-service education and training courses for LEA officers in this period. What is more, an increasing number of LEAs and schools use anti-racism and social justice principles, in general, as a framework within which decisions were reached about the curriculum, relationships with parents and students, the recruitment and promotion of staff, and priorities for the allocation of human and material resources.

Nostalgia in this instance is misplaced, however. Indeed, there are now some fairly persuasive critiques of how anti-racism was conceived in some Local Authorities skilled in left-wing gesture politics. There are also critical assessments of its limited impact on challenging racial inequality in education. Out of these, two substantive criticisms may be levelled at the way anti-racism was operationalized in the local state during its heyday. First, as Paul Gilroy (1990) has argued, common interpretations of anti-racism in the 1980s tended to rest on naive, if not entirely spurious grounds. In his view, it legitimated a 'coat of paint' theory of racism in which racism was conceived as 'an unfortunate excrescence on a democratic polity which is essentially sound' (p. 195. See also Troyna and Williams, 1986). A more effective approach to ARE would have encouraged policy-makers 'to cohere "race", class and gender inequalities into a more broadly conceived programme', and compelled them to identify 'more precisely the role of education in the generation and reproduction of racism' (Troyna, 1992, p. 87). The consequence of artificially separating anti-racism from a broader approach to tackling structural inequalities in education was revealed by the enquiry into the tragic events at Burnage High School in Manchester in September 1986. The failure of so-called anti-racist teachers, community workers and LEA officers to assuage tensions in the school after the murder of Ahmed Iqbal Ullah supports Gilroy's critique, (see Macdonald *et al.*, 1989; Troyna and Hatcher, 1992).

The second criticism derives from the body of research which, in the 1980s, revealed that LEAs and individual schools tended to view the publication of their policies as the destination not launching pad for ARE. This was especially, though not exclusively, true for educational institutions in predominantly white areas (Troyna, 1989). Flourishing as they did after the 1981 urban disturbances, LEA anti-racist policies often amounted to little more than a cynical ploy to assuage the anxieties of black parents that their children were getting a raw educational deal.

As a vociferous critic of these policies, it would be hypocritical now to assume the role of an apologist. At the same time, it remains true that the structurally decentralized education system in the years prior to the ERA provided LEAs with the space to consult with local communities, and to develop policies and support services aimed at removing the most blatant forms of racism in education. As Robin

Richardson put it in 1983, LEA policies had the *potential* to realize four important goals:

> First, they may facilitate the provision of new, or a redistribution of existing, resources for the development of multicultural/antiracist initiatives in the local context. Secondly, policies may lead to desired structural, procedural and cognitive changes in the local education department and committee. Thirdly, they may constitute a valuable resource for teachers already engaged in integrating multicultural/antiracist perspectives into their routine practices, and who wish to mobilize the concern and involvement of others in the process. Finally, pressure groups may use the policy statement as a campaigning instrument. (Cited in Troyna and Ball, 1985, p. 166)

Of course, these purposes were rarely achieved, and many LEAs only scratched the surface in promoting and effecting educational changes along anti-racist lines. However, the important point is that while central government continued to ignore calls to put its weight behind a policy, it was in the setting of local government that space was available for the discussion, formulation and implementation of ARE education initiatives. And LEA policies provided the potential for the encouragement of ARE, even amongst those teachers, initially indifferent and sometimes hostile to this educational ideology. Although Carol Adams (1993), Director of Education for Wolverhampton, reckons that the 1988 and 1993 legislation offers LEAs the opportunity to act as 'watchdogs for equality', this seems idealistic. The displacement of LEAs' relative autonomy under the ERA means that anti-racists are compelled to look to the central state and individual school governing bodies for structural support and legitimation of racial equality imperatives.

The former provides no solace. Madeleine Arnot (1989–90), Leone Burton and Gaby Weiner (1990), and Richard Hatcher and I (Troyna and Hatcher, 1991) have all shown that the National Curriculum Council (NCC) and its subject working parties made little attempt to 'speak to' anti-racist education and related themes of equal opportunities and social justice in their documents. Furthermore, Arnot (1989–90) demonstrates quite clearly that the consultation exercise mounted by the NCC reinforced the marginality of black groups and women, undermining still further the avowed commitment to provide education for all. At best, the NCC documents only legitimate the continuation of ARE and social justice principles by those teachers (and governors) already firmly committed to those ideals. The subordination of those principles, however, in a new agenda dominated by the National Curriculum and testing consumes teachers' time, compels LEAs to follow suit in drawing up their own priorities, and provides few opportunities for ARE to impact decisively on the new educational landscape. Nor has subsequent legislation redressed the balance. On the contrary, as a review of the 1992 White Paper, *Choice and Diversity*, now the 1993 Education Act, revealed, despite the emphasis on 'the importance of education and schools to the future of society. . . . Strikingly, there is no mention at all in the 64 pages of equal opportunities' (Darlington, 1992, p. 251).

The effect of the central state's exclusion of social justice principles from its curriculum package has been exacerbated by radical changes in Section 11 funding for anti-racist education. This section of the 1966 Local Government Act empowered the Home Secretary to provide payments to Local Authorities 'who in his opinion are required to make special provision in the exercise of any of their functions in consequence of the presence within their areas of substantial numbers of immigrants from the Commonwealth whose language or customs differ from those of the community' (cited in Dorn and Hibbert, 1987, p. 59). Historically, then, Section 11 funding,the bulk of which has always been claimed by education departments within the Local Authority, has been geared towards the employment of extra teaching and advisory staff in response to the presumed 'special needs' of black students. It was claimed that these students constituted an exceptional burden *per se* on Local Authorities. Despite the highly problematic nature of the rationale underpinning Section 11 funding, and the widespread abuse of financial resources made available to LEAs through this channel, the availability of this grant enabled LEAs to set up support services to promote and diffuse anti-racist education as a principle relevant to all schools, irrespective of their location or the ethnic mix of their student population. Furthermore, it allowed LEAs to provide resources for the teaching of community languages, minority arts and other things.

New Rightists have not been blind to the potential use of Section 11 funding for more broadly conceived attacks on racial inequality in education. In 1990, the Ethnic Harmony Campaign comprising leading New Right spokespersons called for the scrapping of Section 11 grants, because they were being used for allegedly contentious anti-racist and multicultural education practices by Local Authorities with leftist credentials. Although not going quite to the extent of abolishing Section 11 funding, the scope of programmes permissible under this grant has been progressively limited by recent central government directives on how this money may be spent.[2] Thus, neither community languages nor minority arts can be funded through Section 11 grants. What prevails is a conception of black students as 'trainee whites', to use John Eggleston's phrase. The imperative is to change the parental culture and bring it more in line with that of the school: in short, to put flesh on the bones of assimilationist ideas in which 'acquisition involves loss' for ethnic minority groups (Cashmore and Troyna, 1990).

These stringent guidelines constitute a regressive educational offensive in which race-related initiatives are eligible for funding only if they comply with highly limited (and limiting) conceptions of equality of opportunity in education. Not only does this assimilationist ideology challenge the orthodoxy of anti-racist education, it flies in the face of the government-sponsored Swann Report (DES, 1985), which championed the concept of education for all and advocated the spread of anti-racist principles throughout the British educational system.

But if developments at the central state level provide little hope for the maintenance or augmentation of the (albeit limited) gains achieved by anti-racists in the 1980s, what of the utilization of the power residing in individual schools in the post-ERA years? Brian Caldwell (1990) notes in his review of the international trend towards school-based decision-making and management that this move represents 'a shift to the school level of authority and responsibility to make certain decisions which were made at the system or central level' (p. 13). On the face of it, then, this would seem to provide anti-racists with the legitimate space to ensure that principles of social justice inform the routine practices, procedures and organizational arrangements at the 'chalk face'.

ADMINISTRATION OR MANAGEMENT?

Hans Weiler (1990) suggests that decentralization in educational governance is motivated by various factors, which for expediency can be crystallized around three distinctive classifications. The 'redistribution' model is based on the sharing of power; the 'efficiency' model is concerned primarily with the cost-effectiveness of the education system through a more efficient deployment and management of resources. Finally, the 'cultures of learning' model emphasizes the decentralization of educational content (Weiler, 1990, p. 44–50). Considering how prominently slogans such as 'parent power', 'choice' and related 'symbolic political language' (Edelman, 1977) have loomed in Conservative Party justifications for the ERA, the introduction of LMS and the development of a market-orientated educational system, it is tempting to assume that these initiatives stem from the 'redistribution' model, which is framed in terms of 'empowerment,' 'enfranchisement' and similar labels.

But despite the seductive properties of this rhetoric, it is clear from the political and fiscal conditions associated with LMS that the scheme is premised on economic rationalist grounds, and is sanctioned by what Weiler refers to as the 'efficiency' model of decentralization. The demonization of LEAs, and the accelerated drive along the road of prescriptive funding in the years leading up to the ERA, exemplified the Government's determination to weaken LEAs' power to subvert Thatcherite conceptions of education while being in receipt of centrally derived grants. Those 'apostles of mediocrity and bigots of indoctrination' is how Kenneth Baker characterized LEAs at the Conservative Party Annual conference in 1988, echoing Margaret Thatcher's indictment expressed a year earlier in her interview with David English, editor of the *Daily Mail*. There she made clear that she was no longer willing to tolerate the allegedly inefficient and misdirected allocation of funds by LEAs. If elected to a third term of office in the impending General Election, Thatcher committed the Conservative Party to

> going further with education than we have ever thought of doing before. When we've spent all that money per pupil, and with more teachers, there is still so much wrong, so we are going to do something about it . . . There is going to be a revolution in the running of the schools. (*Daily Mail*, 13 May 1987)

LMS, then, was conceived primarily in terms of enhancing the cost-effectiveness of the educational system, and expediting greater compatibility between central government's conceptions of education and those operating routinely in schools. As indicated later in this chapter, by determining the formula for the ways in which schools are funded, central government has increased its allocative and regulatory powers, ensuring a correlative decline in those previously invested in LEAs. By securing these powers it shapes and constrains the decision-making matrix, limiting the course of action available to decision-makers at the school level. In the words of Hilda Kean (1991), the function of school governing bodies is more or less restricted to 'juggling meagre resources between competing demands, or fund-raising through poaching children . . . from other schools' (p. 148).

Following Terri Seddon and her colleagues (1990), it is useful to view and interpret the reconstituted relationship between the central state and local schools through the conceptual lens of 'frame factors', an idea which has been developed by Kallos and Lundgren (1979). According to Seddon and her associates, the concept of a frame 'defines those tangible features within educational systems which constrain and direct the character of pedagogical and administrative activity' (Seddon *et al.*, 1990, p. 31). On this view, school governing bodies operate within 'proximal' frames which are at the level adjacent to personnel in the immediate context of school and classroom. Factors at this level help to 'define the space of options and form the immediate base for instructional planning by teachers' (Kallos and Lundgren, 1979, p. 30). However, decisions taken here are not free-floating; they are circumscribed and directed by decisions at the 'higher order' frame level. These are outside the control of actors operating in the school and classroom context – the 'proximal level'. In sum, the notion of 'frame' functions as an explanatory concept. Frames 'define an operational space for planning and subsequent actions by teachers and students' (Kallos and Lundgren, 1979, p. 32).

Against this background, it is unlikely that LMS and the devolution of responsibilities to school governors will be a means through which anti-racist and other social justice objectives might be more effectively realized. This is for the following reasons: firstly, because the most important decisions (including of course, the size of the budget allocated to schools) are reached at the higher order level. LMS, then, accords more power to 'the hub' than to 'the rim' of educational governance. Secondly, this view of LMS focuses exclusively on the 'proximal level', ignoring the 'bigger picture' which the frame factor analysis implies. Of course, it is true that some school governing bodies have exploited their relative autonomy and reached decisions about staffing, disciplinary matters, resource priorities, and even curricular matters which are compatible with anti-racist goals. In general, however, their hands are tied by the *Zeitgeist* orchestrated at the 'higher order' and the decisions taken at this level. In this scenario, LMS represents a strategic weapon in the central state's ideological arsenal. What is more, school governing bodies have far less room to manoeuvre than LEAs. Whereas LEAs could, and did, challenge the anti-egalitarian thrust of Thatcherite educational initiatives by supplementing centrally received grants with the rates – at least until the Local Government Finance Act – school governors, especially those in working-class areas, have fewer sources of income available to them.

Accordingly, the claim that LMS presages a 'change at school level . . . from administration (of centrally determined programmes) to management (of local resources)' is both simplistic and deceptive (Coopers and Lybrand, 1988, p. 8). The next section of this chapter elaborates this argument by illustrating more precisely how and why the decisions taken by governing bodies are unlikely to strengthen racial equality in education.

'THE PURSUIT OF EGALITARIANISM IS OVER'

As has already been indicated, LMS has implications not only for the responsibilities assumed by school governing bodies, but also for the status of LEAs as creative partners in educational decision and policy-making. In sanctioning the redistribution of resources from LEAs to schools, LMS weakens the financial and power base of LEAs. Alongside the reappraisal of rules governing Section 11 funding, the Damoclean threat of charge-capping, the strengthening of categorical funding and the inducements offered to schools to 'opt-out', LEAs are compelled to operate at a reduced budget, and to ensure that their priorities are no longer at variance with political conceptions of a 'good education'. Generally, this demands both their abandonment of independent local priorities and the loosening of a commitment to ensuring adherence to LEA-wide policies and principles.

A recent study looked at the effect of ERA and related initiatives in Manchester, a Labour-controlled LEA which, throughout the 1980s, nurtured an increasingly high profile on anti-racist matters (Ball, Gulam and Troyna, 1990). The findings confirmed the research team's worst fears. Firstly, with its declining budget and the need to respond to the 'new realism' of the Labour Party in the 1990s, the LEA has been forced to adopt a more cautious approach to anti-racist education, confining its activities to working in partnership with those schools and colleges which *seek* its support. In consequence, and in stark contrast to the more initiating role assumed by the LEA in the 1980s, schools which have insisted that there is 'no problem here' now have the freedom to eschew any involvement with anti-racist matters. This means that race-related concerns are likely to be on the agenda only in those schools which perceive its relevance simply in terms of the number of black students on roll. Secondly, in the face of a contracting budget, Manchester LEA has been forced to place emphasis on preserving face-to-face staff rather than sustaining, let along increasing members of specialist, detached units.

It was argued in the study that the experiences of the Manchester Education Authority were illustrative rather than unique. The authors showed, for instance, how the dissolution of the Inner London Education Authority – then the largest Authority and one of the most prominent anti-racist LEAs in Britain – and its replacement by 13 London Boroughs with responsibility for local services in inner London, was the harbinger of a more patchy and circumscribed commitment to racial equality issues in this area. Recent developments in the London Borough of Brent, which witnessed the closure of the Development Programme for Racial Equality in 1991 (Richardson, 1992), in Haringey, where the country's first multicultural education centre for schools closed in 1993, and in Avon (Guy and Menter, 1992) confirm this trend.

At the current stage of evolution of LMS, a number of schools are still in the relatively early days of devolved management and decision-making. Similarly, research into the ways in which schools are spending their budgets is at a preliminary stage. Against this background, then, it is impossible to establish definitively the relationship between decentralized management and the status of anti-racist education matters. However, we are in a position to infer from the principles governing the allocation of school budgets, the relatively low significance accorded to racial equality.

By 1993, at least 85 per cent of the Potential Schools Budget had to be removed from the LEAs and placed directly in the hands of school governing bodies. For the new Inner London LEAs this came into force two years later. The allocation of budgets is based on a universalizing principle of funding which requires that at least 75 per cent of the money allocated to schools (the Aggregated School Budget) is determined by the age and number of students. This is expected to increase to 80 per cent from 1995. LEAs submit their formula-funding arrangements to the Secretary of State whose agreement is essential and decision non-negotiable. The rationale for the formula derives from a commitment to 'horizontal equity' (Dixon, 1991), characteristic of liberal versions of equality of opportunity. Here, rules which are procedurally just and equitable are established, and inequality of outcome is predominant and inevitable (Turner, 1986). Equality means sameness in this political perspective.

The operation of this single formula necessarily constrains the potential for LEA officers to exercise fully their professional judgement about the needs of individual schools, and to intervene accordingly in an effort to pre-empt inequalities of outcome deriving from class, ethnic and ability factors. The pre-eminence of so-called 'objective' criteria as the determinant of budget allocation strengthens the role of the central state in mapping out the terrain on which decisions made at the school level are achieved. At the same time, it effectively prevents LEAs from pursuing policies of preferential funding in accordance with more radical conceptions of equality of opportunity.

It is an arithmetical truth that fundamental changes in funding policy will benefit some schools to the detriment of others. The emerging pattern seems to confirm Haviland's (1988) worst fears that LMS will strengthen the 'divide between those (schools) in affluent and those in poor areas' and result in 'the creation of a large number of "sink" schools' (1988, p. 164). Will Guy and Ian Menter's (1992) case-study of how Avon LEA initially calculated the budget for its local schools clearly demonstrates the likelihood that, in the absence of an understanding of social justice principles, LMS can precipitate a redistribution of resources from inner urban schools to those in suburban and rural areas of the county. The strength of the campaign mounted by inner urban and Labour Party governors in Avon mitigated the most disastrous effects of the original submission. Nonetheless, it remains the case that the abandonment of preferential funding in favour of equal treatment must be 'disproportionately damaging to inner urban schools' (Guy and Menter, 1992, p. 165).

As noted, at the time of writing up to 25 per cent of the Aggregated School Budget (reducing to 20 per cent from 1995) may be allocated to schools on a basis other than age-weighted pupil numbers.[3] The eligibility variables here are non-pupil-led factors: variations in premises costs, small schools and special educational needs, including the incidence of 'social deprivation' among students in different schools. The current picture reveals that most LEAs have attempted to make provision for special educational needs and/or 'social deprivation' under this element of the formula (Lee, 1990). However, it is important not to overestimate the significance of this provision. First, in one of the largest LEAs in Britain the social deprivation factors account for only 1.5 per cent of the total Aggregated Schools Budget. Second, the criteria used for interpreting 'social deprivation' are highly questionable. According to a survey carried out by the National Union of Teachers, 52 of the 104 LEAs in England and Wales, excluding the newly formed London Boroughs, measured 'social deprivation' exclusively in terms of free school meals. Indeed, this proportion increases from 50 to almost 60 per cent when the 16 LEAs which at the time of the survey either did not have, or had not made available, their criteria for 'social deprivation' are omitted. Now, whilst 'social deprivation' is a diffuse, politically contested and intrinsically problematic concept, it can be shown that inferring its existence exclusively from the criterion of free school meals is likely to further discriminate against schools with significant numbers of students from Afro-Caribbean and South Asian backgrounds.

Thatcherite reforms in the 1980s accelerated the trend away from a universal school meals service to one 'in which costs are increasingly borne by parents, with means-tested exemptions for the poorest families' (Glendinning, 1983, p. 50). Co-terminous with this has been the introduction of increasingly restrictive welfare rights legislation, especially the 1986 Social Security Act, confining even further the number entitled to free school meals. In 1986, for instance, it was estimated that one and a half million children were eligible for a free school meal (Berger, 1990, p. 76). By May 1990 this had dropped to a little over one million (*Hansard*, 22 July 1991). What is more, there is a marked and persistent discrepancy between entitlement and take-up for which a number of explanations may be adduced: parental uncertainty about their eligibility, related, of course, to the paucity of information both in terms of its public availability and language; fears about being stigmatized (Berger, 1990; Kumar, 1993); and the inappropriateness, for cultural reasons, of the food offered. According to the Junior Minister of Education, over 24 per cent of children entitled to free school meals in May 1990 did not receive them (*Hansard*, 22 July 1991).

This discrepancy assumes a more insidious character once it is recognized that the use of free school meals as an index of social deprivation derives in a significant number of cases from *take-up*, not eligibility. Although there are no clear-cut empirical data documenting the differential take-up of free school meals by black and white students, there are clear indications that eligible black students are less likely to have free school meals than their white counterparts. This is partly for cultural reasons. Students of South Asian origin or affiliated to Rastafari will not necessarily have their dietary requirements satisfied by local school meals services. Secondly, only a limited number of LEAs and schools provide details about entitlement to free school meals; even fewer translate those notices into the appropriate local community languages.

In sum, the application of crude measures of social deprivation, on the one hand, and variability in the criteria used in deciding about how to resource social/educational disadvantage, on the other, militates against the provision of reasonable and equitably distributed resources to schools.

'ON THE BACK BURNER'?

Is there a glimmer of hope peeking through the almost uniformly bleak picture which has been sketched out? Well, it could be contested that, whilst it is appropriate to acknowledge that the ERA consolidates a hierarchical power relationship between those operating at the 'hub' (central government) and the 'rim' (individual schools and LEAs), the analysis tends to underplay the significance of school governors in the implementation of the Act. As Rosemary Deem argues: 'So far as [sic] issues to do with gender and race are concerned, governors are likely to exert a major influence over whether or not concerns about gender and racial equality continue to be prioritised and pursued in schools' (1989, pp. 247–8). Recently, the DES (now Department for Education) has distributed to all governors a note outlining their responsibilities with regard to the Sex Discrimination Act (1975) and Race Relations Act (1976) in relation to pupils and staff matters. However, the available evidence suggests that governors will be unlikely, or unwilling, to challenge effectively the anti-egalitarian trajectory of the ERA, despite the fact that they have more influence over the education of pupils than at any time since the 1944 Education Act.

Although it is by no means true that it relies on the presence of black or female governors to ensure that anti-racist and other social justice principles figure on the agenda of governing bodies, existing studies of the composition and dynamics of school governance confirm Deem's argument that it tends to operate 'very much within a white, patriarchal and middle-class framework' (1989, p. 258). To begin with, there is a significant under-representation of black (and women) governors (CDC, 1990; Deem, 1989; Jeffries and Streatfield, 1989; Webb, 1991). Secondly, few LEAs appear to take an active role in ameliorating this position by enhancing the number of black governors (CDC, 1990, p. 4–6). Finally, although, as Deem points out, the 1986 Education Act requires LEAs to make training available to governors, the research available suggests that courses related to equal opportunities issues are few and far between (CDC, 1990). Moreover, Anne Webb's research in Coventry indicated that 'training in equal opportunities and multicultural education was not perceived as a priority by local governors' (1991, p. 15). The combination of these factors has been that governors committed to anti-racist education find that their policy proposals tend to fall on deaf ears. Recent research carried out for the Commission for Racial Equality (CRE) in 'Woodshire' LEA and four of its local secondary schools also confirms these patterns.[4] Of particular significance in this research was the finding that the overwhelming majority of LEA officers, multicultural education support staff, and local Racial Equality Council workers interviewed in the study believed that racial equality and other social justice issues were now firmly on the 'back burner' in the LEA and its schools.

This is not altogether surprising. Despite the rhetoric, LMS is a divisive tool which, implicitly at least, aims to ensure that the relationship between schools assumes a more competitive edge: in short, its intention is to divide and fool. The increasing emphasis on age-weighted pupil numbers in the formula, in association with the introduction of open enrolment, encourages (some might say compels) schools to channel their limited resources into improving their academic performance profiles. This is seen as a means to an end: to attract students from neighbouring schools, thus ensuring survival if not an increase in their budget. The statutory requirement for schools to publish their GCSE and 'A' level results reinforces this 'survival of the fittest' ideology, and confirms the view that LMS constitutes a voucher system, at least in embryonic form.

As a result of these pressures, concern with social justice principles or, more precisely, the allocation of resources to promote these concerns as an organizational, procedural and pedagogic norm, have been de-prioritized in a significant number of schools and the LEAs. Of course, it is naive to believe that a school's academic profile is the sole criterion which determines where parents send their children (Ball, 1993; Couldron and Bolton, 1991). Nonetheless, the impact of the 'anti-antiracist' campaign orchestrated by the New Right in the 1980s, the consequent rise of 'equiphobia', and the enduring and seductive powers of the 'tightening bond' thesis that holds that 'good' qualifications lead to a 'good' job (Troyna, 1984) all testify to the view that for those parents in a position to operate choice there is intense pressure to send their children to academically successful schools. This does not augur well for the survival and future security of inner urban schools which are likely to be even less well-resourced with the move towards what is termed euphemistically as 'direct assessment measures' (Wainwright, 1993, p. 6); or for the enfranchisement of black working-class parents and their children, or the integration of anti-racist principles into the educational agenda for the 1990s and beyond.

CHAPTER 9

School Governors, 'Race' and Racism

Kevin Brehony

The role of school governors has acquired greater salience under the current educational reforms, and this chapter sets out to explore some of the more significant implications for ethnic relations.

Governors of schools are confronted by and interact with the structural inequalities associated with 'race', ethnicity and racism in at least two different ways. Firstly, in their own practices, governors can significantly affect the representation of black, Asian and other minority social groups in the field of school governance. Secondly, they are responsible for decisions that might either enhance or diminish the opportunities for black, Asian and other minority pupils, teachers and other staff. In order to explore these and some of the other issues arising from the impact of the structures of 'race', ethnicity and racism, this chapter draws upon data collected during the course of an ESRC-supported project on 'The Reform of School Governing Bodies – a sociological investigation'.[1] The project researchers, in addition to myself, were my co-director Professor Rosemary Deem of Lancaster University and our research assistants Ms Sue Hemmings and Ms Suzanne Heath. What we were signalling by the use of the term 'sociological' in the title of the project was the importance, in our view, of the concepts of class, gender, ethnicity and 'race' in understanding the social relations reproduced and potentially transformed through the day-to-day work of school governors. For the purposes of this discussion, I have linked the terms 'race', 'ethnicity' and 'racism' to refer to structure, and black and Asian to refer to agents. At the same time, I recognize that as Cole (1993) has pointed out, the terms 'black and Asian' are far from unproblematic, but in this context there is no better alternative.

In the use of the term 'structure', I follow Bhaskar (1989) who speaks, from a critical realist position, of the social world as being composed of underlying structures which generate patterns of events and discourses. Furthermore, he argues, only social science can reveal the nature of the structures as they possess an ontological depth from which it follows that structures are not simply reducible to what may be observed on the surface. Moreover, according to Bhaskar, all social structures are relational. That is to say, they presuppose social relations which pre-exist the individuals that enter into them. Among such social relations we may include those between black and Asian people on the one hand, and white people on the other. In this country these social relations are generally characterized by racism and by relations of domination and subordination, and thus they correspond to what Sayer (1992) calls internal or necessary relations. However, these relations take many different forms and provide, along with other structures like class and gender, the materials by means of which people reproduce and change society. They achieve this through intentional action, in school governing bodies just as in any other institution or area of social life (Craib, 1992). In this view, the underlying structures do not determine the actions of agents. The relation as described by Porter (1993) is 'generative', the structures provide the conditions for actions but are themselves, sometimes unintentionally, produced by the actions of agents.

Before discussing the actions and intentions of governors I shall provide a brief description of the research project. After that, I shall consider some of the issues around the notion of representation, in the political sense, and that of ethnic minorities on school governing bodies in particular. I shall then look at a number of aspects of the work of the governing bodies studied which relate to the perpetuation of the structures of 'race', ethnicity and racism. Specifically, I shall consider how governors dealt with problems arising from the funding of schools since the Education Reform Act of 1988: the phenomenon of 'white flight', changes in the way Section 11 funds are distributed and the policy of ethnic monitoring.

THE RESEARCH PROJECT

The Reform of School Governing Bodies Project began as a pilot study in October 1988, when the new governing bodies were formed after the 1986 Education Act. From the autumn of 1988 we attended all the formal meetings and some sub-committee or working group meetings of fifteen governing bodies in two LEAs, which we call Northshire and Southshire. After April 1990 we reduced the number of governing bodies being studied to ten, both to allow us to focus in more depth and to reflect the proliferation of sub-committees and working groups in many of them. The two LEAs related to governing bodies in very different ways. Northshire took a fairly paternalistic attitude to its governing bodies but also offered them a lot of support, Southshire had a 'hands off' approach but also provided correspondingly less support and guidance to governors. Both LEAs had fairly high-profile but contrasting policies on 'race'.

The differences between the two LEAs and the consequences for their governing bodies are further explored in Brehony and Deem (1990). Some governing bodies consisted almost entirely of governors new to the task in 1988, others had mostly experienced governors. The schools to which the governing bodies were attached covered both primary and secondary, represented a range of sizes, and included affluent suburban as well as poor 'inner city' working-class areas. The schools were on a continuum, at the ends of which were all-white schools and schools with a substantial proportion of black and Asian students. In one of the schools, a project connected to the LEA's race policy was being conducted.

The research project was a multi-site, case-study. We cannot claim that our governing bodies and our 170 governors are in any sense statistically representative of all governing bodies and governors, although our data is not out of line with either other case-study evidence (Golby and Brigley, 1989) or national survey evidence (Streatfield and Jefferies, 1989). Case-study research is generalizable principally to theoretical propositions and the sites studied, rather than to whole populations (Bryman, 1988). The methods we used included the observation of meetings, sub-committees and working groups; attendance at governor training sessions; and two questionnaires sent in the summer of 1989 to all 254 members of the fifteen pilot case-study bodies, and in 1992 to all members of the ten governing bodies which constituted the main project. On both occasions the response rate achieved was in the region of 50 per cent. We carried out semi-structured interviews with 43 governors: headteachers, chairs of governing bodies, chairs of finance and other sub-committees, parent, LEA, co-opted and teacher governors. We collected a range of documentation including agendas, meeting and briefing papers. This form of research has many strengths, not the least of which is that it takes seriously the meanings attributed to actions by the actors in the situation. We were interested in how the governors made sense or attempted to make sense of 'doing' school governance. But like Porter (1993), we feel that 'understanding actor's viewpoints may be a necessary condition for social knowledge, but it is not a sufficient one', for the explanation of actions requires the elucidation of the structures that underlie them.

REPRESENTATION

School governing bodies may be thought of as institutions, similar to others in a liberal democratic society, that function to provide a space for decision-making and also to regulate conflict. In order to even begin to do this they must extend to potentially conflicting interests the right of representation. Typically, in liberal democratic societies, interests are held to gain representation through the person of elected representatives. Those who share an interest or a spectrum of interests with others seek to promote them by getting their representative elected to deliberative bodies. However, not all representation occurs through election. Interests in corporatist arrangements such as 'quangos' are represented by people selected by power-holders who, by so doing, exercise a degree of control not only over the range of interests represented but also the representatives.

The composition of school governing bodies is organized in such a way as to secure the representation of the headteacher, other teachers, parents, the Local Education Authority (where relevant the Minor Authority such as a Parish Council), and representatives of the community. Only the representatives of parents and teachers are elected. Even then, there are grounds to doubt the view that parent and teacher governors do represent, in any meaningful way, the interests of parents and teachers. For such a heterogeneous category as parents it is debatable whether they have any interests in common beyond a general desire to secure for their children a good education, and even that cannot be assumed in every case. However, even where communities of parents are relatively homogeneous in terms of social class and ethnicity, a further question arises of how parent governors could possibly represent the views and interests of all the parents of pupils at a school, especially if the school is a large one.

LEA and co-opted governors gain their places on governing bodies through a process that in many ways parallels corporatist arrangements. LEA-appointed governors go through a selection process of a kind which varies widely in its scope and rigour, and is usually conducted by the political party (or parties) having a majority on the council. The final category are co-opted governors selected by the other governors who must, according to the 1986 Education (No. 2) Act, have regard to the extent to which they and those they are considering for co-option are members of the local business community.

Co-option of specific interests to bodies with power within the education system has a long history. Typically, as in Prime Minister Balfour's speech on the 1902 Education Act (Brehony, 1985), it has been legitimated by an appeal to the argument that there is a need for 'experts' to be given a voice. Specifically, the requirement to co-opt representatives of the local business community to governing bodies may be presented as signifying the existence or desirability of a partnership between schools and business; or it may, as right-wing ideologists have portrayed it, represent an attempt to shift power in the education system from producer interests (teachers and Local Education Authorities) to consumer interests (parents and business persons).

It may be seen from the preceding account that interests based on social class, gender or ethnicity are not recognized as requiring representation. This is not, however, the view of many governors. A teacher governor we interviewed, for example, was one among many who thought that ethnic minorities *should* be represented. He said,

> I'd like far more ethnic minority governors than we've got, and that's not something that's prescribed in the Act. When I came there were none. We now have three, we need twice as many as that for it to represent the balance of the youngsters in the school. We should have four Asian governors and two Afro-Caribbean governors.

The lack of any mechanism for representing social categories is hardly surprising, given that the ideological framework in which the legislation restructuring governing bodies was located was one which gave prominence to the market, and saw society only as consisting of atomized individuals who acted either as producers or consumers.

THE SOCIAL COMPOSITION OF GOVERNING BODIES

Class, gender and ethnicity do more, however, than form the basis upon which interests that require representation may arise. As major structures that generate social inequalities, they operate in such a way as to favour, as elsewhere in the political system, the representation on governing bodies of certain social groups and the exclusion of others. It is important to note this dual operation of structures. They are not simply negative in their consequences as they both enable and constrain, and the structure of ethnic relations, 'race' and racism is no exception. Both the NFER (National Foundation for Education Research) study by Keys and Fernandes (1990) and our own reveal that the majority of governors are male, white and from professional and managerial or executive backgrounds. Thus, the structures of race, gender and social class work to generate a pattern of outcomes that includes this white, male professional group but excludes others.

Turning specifically to the question of the ethnic composition of governing bodies, the NFER survey (Streatfield and Jefferies, 1989) conducted immediately after the recomposition of the governing bodies in 1988 and based on a stratified random sample of 500 schools in ten different LEAs, found that 41 per cent of governors in those schools were women but less than 3 per cent were black or Asian. Of the approximately 250 governors in our pilot study, just 33 per cent were women but 8 per cent black or Asian. This means that in our case-study, black and Asian governors were over-represented; in the 1991 Census just over 5 per cent of the population was described as being members of 'ethnic minorities'. As might have been expected, in view of the fact that the black and Asian population is not evenly distributed at a national level, it was not distributed evenly within the areas of our case-study schools. Owing to the resignation of a number of governors and their replacement during the course of each year of the study, the number of black and Asian governors fluctuated a little, but in 1991–92, for example, out of the ten governing bodies studied only four had black or Asian governors. Three of these governing bodies were of schools in overwhelmingly working-class areas, though one other school in a working-class area had no black or Asian governors. On one governing body in that year 68 per cent of the governors were Asian, and thus the governors from that governing body constituted 65 per cent of all the black and Asian governors in the case study for 1991–92. The concentration of black and Asian school governors in certain areas and the preponderance of Asian males among them that we observed, replicates the pattern found by Geddes (1993) in local government.

Decisions made by governing bodies often originate outside the full governing body meeting, so that representation at that meeting is not always sufficient to ensure that an interest is fully represented in the decision-making process. The picture regarding representation and the composition of governing bodies is further complicated by the sub-committee structure that most of them adopted. Most governing bodies established working parties at an early stage, and some of these became sub committees after the 1989 revised Regulations permitted their establishment. After LMS (local management of schools), where the sub-committee structure functioned fully, the finance committee frequently made day-to-day decisions which were then endorsed by the full governing body. This was, in most governing bodies, the most powerful of the sub-committees, and also the one least likely to contain black and Asian governors where they were in a minority. Representation is therefore not merely a question of gaining access to sites where decisions may be taken. It is also bound up with questions to do with power once representation has been gained.

The numbers dealt with were very small and so statistical generalization is ruled out. But it is worth recording perhaps, for the benefit of future researchers, that roughly equal numbers of black and Asian governors were either co-opted or parent governors, and around three-quarters of all black and Asian governors fell into these categories. If this pattern is typical of school governing bodies elsewhere where a black and Asian population is present, it seems reasonable to assume that one outcome of the Tory reforms relating to school governing bodies is an increase in the absolute number of black and Asian school governors because parent and co-opted governors are the categories that have expanded most as a consequence of them. Nevertheless, although (as in local government) the number of black and Asian governors is likely to have grown in recent years, the black and Asian population as a whole may still be seriously under-represented.

Representation: sources of conflict
Under the heading of the representation of ethnic minority communities there are at least two separate issues: the national representation of governors from all the ethnic minorities, and the representation of governors in terms of the ethnic composition of their particular student and parent body. Regarding the first issue, until the proportion of black and Asian governors reaches 5 per cent (or whatever proportion of the total population the black and Asian population happens to be), then the black and Asian population may be said to be under-represented. The second issue is potentially more conflictual, as it concerns the appropriateness and the justice of members of one ethnic community governing a school where the pupils belong to another. Conflict over

representation in this sense broke out in 1992 at Slough and Eton, a Church of England secondary school. There the Asian governors sent a petition to the Berkshire LEA which, ironically, was one of the few LEAs to adopt an anti-racist policy in the early 1980s, complaining that the majority of governors were white whereas 98 per cent of the pupils in the school were Asian (*The Times*, 24 July 1992).

Writing at the beginning of the 1980s, Ben-Tovim *et al.* (1982) argued for 'the extension of forms of democratization within formal institutions of the state to accommodate the active involvement of the Afro-Caribbean and Asian communities in decisions over funding, distribution of resources etc.' It could be argued that the post-1986 governing bodies do, indeed, represent an extension of the democratization called for in the area of schooling, because they allow lay minorities to become involved in school government and to challenge the professional ideologies held by teachers. This appears to have been partly what happened at Stratford East (Deem and Brehony, 1993), at Slough and Eton, and at Stepney Green. In the last-named school where some 94 per cent of the pupils were Asian, the Asian governors in 1990 tried to sack the head, an event that drew from the *Evening Standard* the egregiously insulting title to its story, 'Moslems in bid to sack school head' (Rogers, 1990). In all three of these schools, and in one in the case study, Asian governors came into conflict with the head and, in some instances, members of the teaching staff also. These were cases in which the majority of governors were Asian. On school governing bodies where black and Asian governors were in a minority the situation was different, and conflicts between them and the head did not arise.

Governors' views about representation
In our interviews with governors we asked if they felt that any social groups were excluded from representation on governing bodies. Significantly, many in their answers did not refer to ethnic minorities. Several governors however, mainly heads, took the opportunity presented by the question to do so. One head of a school with a significant proportion of black and Asian pupils, when asked if the legislation on governing bodies had made the school more accountable to the community through the composition of the governing body replied:

I couldn't put my hand on my heart and say 'yes it has' yet. I mean we've struggled to get parents from, what one would say, ethnic minority groups onto the Governing Body and we did succeed. Unfortunately, that has fallen away because of the lack of commitment of those two individuals, but I will be more pleased when I see the Governing Body reflecting the composition of the school which it's far from doing at the moment.

Many of the governors interviewed thought that governing bodies in general were not very representative of their school's local community. For example, this governor of a school in an area with a large black and Asian population commented:

when we look at the governing body in terms of origins and racial differences, ethnic minorities representation, it doesn't represent the local community at all. I'm not suggesting it necessarily has to reflect exactly the balance in the community. The representation does seem very different to the balance within the community, with only two governors who are of Asian origin. I've a feeling that one of them I haven't met. Yes I haven't met one, he obviously wasn't there at that meeting. And I'm not confident that I've met the other one either. And it was something that struck me on the day of the interviews and actually was commented on by the candidates. That it does seem rather odd that a lot of the emphasis in the interviews was to do with the balance in the community and some of the problems that that's brought to the school, but that wasn't reflected in the personnel involved both in the governors and the staff.

Another governor in a predominantly white area felt that his governing body was representative, but that:

further afield in other places, not necessarily in [Northshire] but beyond, there are some groups who, although they make up the community are not represented. You know we're talking about those from a different ethnic group, or those who are perhaps socially under-privileged find it very difficult to put themselves forward and are not keen to be put forward by somebody else, to become part of a Governing Body. I mean the statistics research will probably show that there are very few black Governors and there are very few Governors who are probably out of work and all this business. So in a general point I would think that Governing Bodies are not truly representative of the people that are served by their schools.

Many governors advanced other explanations of why this might be. A head we interviewed, rather than blaming the commitment of individuals, indicated that the problem lay more with the governing bodies and the way they were constituted and structured. He said that, 'very often people from ethnic minorities do not think it is a fit place for them. So that's a sort of subversive exclusion'. A teacher governor in a secondary school addressing the question of how to increase the representation of ethnic minorities and women combined both an individual and a structural explanation by saying that:

> I'm against positive discrimination because I seriously feel that if you put people in to pay lip-service to the notion of equality, either of race or gender, and those people are not confident in being there, then in fact they won't represent anyone because they'll say nothing. On the other hand, the converse side to that argument is, if you don't give them the experience, they won't get the experience.

Getting sufficient governors, particularly co-opted and parent governors, was a major problem for some schools in working-class areas. The chair of governors at one of these schools conflated parents with people from ethnic minorities in his answer to a question specifically about the representation of ethnic minorities:

> I mean there's only two parents nominated to take two parents' places and that's it. There's no more you can do. I mean we did more than was necessary to get Parent Governors. I mean we didn't just send a note out. We sent information that it was coming up, we sent notes home, information letters. I think parents must have been told about five times before the actual nomination forms were sent home, they were told that they could nominate themselves. We still only had the two, what more can you do?

While recruiting and retaining governors in the working-class areas in the case-study was more of a problem than in the more affluent areas, we have frequently drawn attention to the fact that once on a governing body certain categories of governors were often silent during the meetings. In other words, only some voices were being heard and hence only some interests represented. The literature of social psychology (Brown, 1988) attests to the fact that this is nearly always the case in group interactions. However, silence did not appear to be a characteristic randomly distributed. Typically, it was working-class parent governors who were silent, and also women and black and

Asian governors when they were in a minority on a governing body. It would seem from this that black and Asian governors do not lack the confidence to speak about matters that concern governors, but they are constrained from speaking when they are the only non-white governors or one of only two non-white governors present.

RACISM

One possible explanation for silence is the anticipation of a racist reaction from the other governors. The revelation that we had observed behaviour classifiable as racist on some of the governing bodies (Deem, 1989; Deem, Brehony and Hemmings, 1992) has proven to be one of the least acceptable of our findings. Walter Ulrich, the leading figure in the National Association of Governors and Managers and who, while he was at the Department of Education and Science, was reportedly the main architect of the current regulations controlling governing bodies, is only one of several who have challenged them. Ulrich was reported to have said that, 'you need a lot of evidence' for the claim that governors are racist and sexist (Holdsworth, 1983). Ada Fordham, chair of Action for Governors' Information and Training, the other national organization claiming to represent governors, also focused on the small scale of the study, and argued that our evidence should not be taken to imply that these practices are widespread. In fact we have never made this claim, and we have reported only that some instances of racism were observed.

The use of the term 'racism', as Cashmore and Troyna (1990) caution, can degenerate into sloganizing if used to describe every instance of injustice or inequity involving ethnic minorities. In the absence of any evidence of why reports of racist behaviour in governing bodies prove so unpalatable as to provoke vigorous denials of its existence, we may only speculate about the roots of this reaction. Partly the problem lies with the inflation of the terms 'racist' and 'racism' to the point where they become virtually devoid of meaning. Furthermore, racist behaviour in popular imagery is strongly associated with young white males with skinhead haircuts and swastikas tattooed on their arms. As governing bodies generally contain few if any of that social group then, so the argument runs, they cannot contain racists. But the most likely explanation for incredulity in the face of evidence of racism lies elsewhere. Arguably it is to be found in the liberal utopian vision of governing bodies, which were intentionally constructed to represent potentially hostile interests, as being free from conflict and other consequences of social divisions; a vision encapsulated in the much promoted image of governors and teachers in partnership. Racist behaviour for holders of this view constitutes an intolerable threat to a partnership of equals engaged in rational discourse. Overtly racist behaviour was, however, comparatively rare. Racism in a more implicit manifestation was much more evident when, in conjunction with 'race' and ethnicity, it structured a number of racialized policy issues that affected the governors.

POLICIES

In their book on racism and education reform, Troyna and Carrington (1990) make the point that much of the purpose of recent reform in education has been the diminution, if not the destruction, of local education authority (LEA) power and influence. While recognizing the limitations of LEA policies on 'race' they note that following the Education Reform Act the terrain has changed. Now, they write, 'In the absence of the regulatory functions of the LEA, each governing body will need to be convinced of the value and efficacy of anti-racist education' (Troyna and Carrington, 1990). Our evidence suggests that while this is undoubtedly so, each governing body needs to be convinced that *any* positive policy on 'race' has value and efficacy. I shall now turn to three racialized policy issues that the governing bodies were confronted with. The way they responded illustrates the extent to which the attack on the LEAs has significantly worsened the chances that anti-racist policies may be adopted by schools.

Ethnic monitoring

During the period of the project, one of our two LEAs asked governors to help with the conduct of ethnic monitoring. The item appeared on their agendas as a matter for consideration 'at the request of the Local Authority'. However, the LEA was merely responding to the Department of Education and Science (DES) Circular 16/89 which made it mandatory for all LEA maintained schools to collect ethnically based data on pupils from September 1990. As Gordon (1992) has explained, the impulse for what was, in effect, the re-introduction of ethnic monitoring in schools stemmed from dissatisfaction among ethnic minority group communities. This dissatisfaction found expression in the reports prepared by the committees chaired by Rampton and Swann (DES, 1981; 1985). Moreover, the move to ethnic monitoring also arose from the recognition among policy-makers, particularly after the urban disorders of the early 1980s, that racial discrimination and inequality could lead to serious disruption of the social order. In our study, the LEA concerned presented the case for the collection of ethnically based statistics in a document made available to governors. The supporting arguments were cast in terms of the increased effectiveness of educational provision, a greater awareness of the communities it served, the educational implications of ethnicity and the possible targeting of resources to improve the education of ethnic minority children.

What did governors make of the LEA's approach to ethnic monitoring? At one governors' meeting in January 1991 in a largely white, suburban school, the head introduced the issue and told governors that the LEA wanted schools to send the names of first-year pupils to the LEA. The adviser for multicultural education would then, on the basis of the names provided, carry out a survey of selected parents. Several of the governors expressed disquiet at this, and one argued that names alone were not sufficient to determine a pupil's ethnicity. Two governors felt that this was a sensitive issue which might put the position of the school at risk; it was then very popular with parents. Another governor said that he had 'experience of the Census here where you ask four-year-olds to translate for the family', and asked if 'this is a touch of the race relations industry?'. A governor who was also a Conservative councillor remarked that she had a friend with a Huguenot name whose family had been here for three hundred years, and asked how this would be dealt with. Throughout the debate, which lasted for almost twenty minutes, none of the governors said anything in support of the exercise. The lack of promised details and guidance notes from the adviser clearly did not help, but the only argument that could be construed as carrying any weight in favour of the collection of ethnically based statistics was that the governors had a statutory duty to ensure the information was collected. This view carried the day and the governing body reluctantly agreed to co-operate.

At a meeting in 1992 of an almost all-white primary school, the ethnic monitoring item was placed on the agenda for 'information only'. Nevertheless, some discussion took place after the item was introduced by the head who explained that in the school there were 'very few children who come into this category'. A governor who was also a Conservative local councillor asked about the purpose of the exercise. In the course of responding, the head said that in another town with a different social composition, 'monitoring is very different from ours'. A co-opted governor from business caused much laughter by replying that, 'they count the British there don't they?', which was followed by another LEA governor making a fatuous remark about Scottish devolution. The minutes of this meeting recorded that 'only 6 children were of ethnic origin' in the school but none were of the required age for monitoring. This conflation of ethnic and black sums up well the operation of the structures of 'race', ethnicity and racism within that governing body.

On the other governing body where the issue arose, the majority of governors were Asian. Again, the head introduced the item and the chair asked about the purposes of the monitoring. The head replied that, hopefully, it was 'to give out resources'. This led to the chair questioning the head about the number of ethnic minority children in the school, to which the reply given was 90 per cent Asian, 0.5 per cent West Indian. The chair responded by asking how many teachers were from ethnic minorities, and when he was told that there were only two implied that he felt there should be more by observing that, 'this does not reflect the situation'.

All three of these governing bodies responded negatively to the ethnic monitoring initiative. Partly this was because the LEA's approach was a little unsubtle, but there is also little doubt that few governors were convinced of the value of a positive policy on 'race'. This was as true of the governing body dominated by Asians as it was of the others. This was not because the Asian governors were unaware of the salience of 'race' in the school they governed or in the education system generally. It was more that they had different strategies to deal with it.

SECTION 11

The reaction of many of the governors in the case-study to the change in the arrangements regulating the administration of the Section 11 grant supports the findings of Guy and Menter (1992) who, writing of the introduction of formula-funding by the Avon LEA, described inner-city school governors as being 'overwhelmed and demoralised' by an 'avalanche of complex documents' and lacking some of the skills and resources required to cope with their predicament. In October 1990, the Home Office issued Circular 78/1990 which contained the new regulations governing the award of the grant. This money was to be made available to meet the 'special needs' of ethnic minority pupils of New Commonwealth origin where linguistic or cultural barriers prevent such pupils gaining full access to mainstream educational provision. As Section 11 is outside the terms of reference of Local Management of Schools budget delegation, it was the LEAs which had to apply for the grant by putting forward projects aimed at raising the achievement of ethnic minority pupils in various curriculum areas.

Three schools in the case-study stood to be directly affected by the change in the purposes permitted under previous regulations, and in two instances staff were to be lost. None of the three schools could be described as anything other than under-resourced, and teachers struggled hard to combat the widespread material disadvantages that affected their pupils and parents. In one of the schools, a large primary situated in a bleak estate with a high proportion of black and Asian pupils, Securicor were hired in an effort to combat persistent vandalism. The overall atmosphere of the school and the area was one of inner-city deprivation. The head reported at one meeting of the governors that the reading books used in the school went back to the 1950s and 1960s, and that geography books referring to the Belgian Congo had only recently been thrown away. In classes above Year 3, there was no construction material with which to teach National Curriculum technology. The arrangements for the school carnival in 1991 excluded parents on the grounds that in the past fighting had broken out among them. In the school, over a third of the pupils had been classified as having special needs, and a teacher governor told the governing body that she had taught in many schools but had never encountered such a high proportion of children classified as having special needs at Warnock stage 3.

From the discussions of the governors it became clear that the LEA had in the past recognized the problems faced by the school when it was allocating funds. The change in the Section 11 criteria coming together with financial delegation and a reduction in the overall budget allocation, meant that the school was, in the terminology of LMS, about to become a 'loser'. Specifically, the jobs of welfare assistants employed under Section 11 with contracts at the school were put into jeopardy as a result of the changes. The LEA, in order to secure its bid, offered the welfare assistants training in Punjabi if the bid was unsuccessful. The governors were told by an LEA official they would all be in a 'really difficult ball game'. Even if the LEA bid was accepted, the school stood to lose 2.2 Section 11 staff who, if they had attended the second language course, would be redeployed.

The governors also understood that the school was in deficit, but it was difficult to establish the real position as the new accounting systems employed by the LEA to administer LMS were not working very well. This led to the school's budget being charged for all the travelling expenses of Section 11 staff in the town, and while the school had only one paraffin heater £4,000 was set against the budget for oil for heating.

A special meeting of the governors was called to discuss the Section 11 situation. The governors were highly supportive of the staff of the school and sympathized with their predicament. One said, 'even if they put me in court' I would not vote to cut staff. Another governor, highlighting the contradiction between devolution of powers to schools while funding allocations were ever more concentrated at the centre, said 'we are just doing the dirty work which we were set up for. The person we should really be attacking is the Secretary of State'.

In one of the other schools, the changes in Section 11 led to the reduction of funding from three teachers to two. Here also the governors were supportive, but could not understand why the money for Section 11 still came from the government and why they had to 'fight for it again and again'. An Asian governor who was a teacher at another school, said that, 'the main problem is that it's a fact that our children need Section 11 help. Where the money comes from is not the main thing. No one has the right to take it away, that's the main thing'. This view was representative of that of all the black and Asian governors in the case-study schools affected by the changes.

White flight

The changes in the funding of Section 11 hit hardest the schools that could least afford to lose resources. LMS and the introduction of a quasi-market (Le Grand and Bartlett, 1993) in education has also put a lot of pressure on teachers and governors in such relatively unpopular schools. These pressures are at their most acute if the school is in the secondary sector. Unpopularity among parents and pupils may arise for a number of reasons, but schools with a sizeable proportion of working-class and black and Asian pupils are often perceived to be at a disadvantage in the competition for age-weighted pupil units (AWPUs). The head of such a school explained:

The thing that's changed the accountability is open enrolment; and that's something which is a very serious issue for a school like this, which is, put as negatively as possible, a small secondary [school] with a significant ethnic minority, and based in the heartland of white racism, not quite *à la* Cheltenham but the same problem, mixed in a Jaguar belt of the south-east, surrounded by schools in all-white areas in places like [Hightown] and [Lowtown]. And it's increased the accountability because you've got to get kids in through the gate because the kids are the vouchers, and if you don't get the kids in through your gate, you are on a sticky wicket and as you know we're going to work next year's budget today, and if I get 15 less Year Eight youngsters than I'm hoping I shall get, it'll cost me a member of staff. That's a fairly sharp kind of accountability.

At the head's instigation, the governors of this school held a special meeting to discuss the possibility of a move to another site in a location with a higher social class clientèle as a solution to the problem of pupil numbers. Like most of the situations described in connection with Section 11 funding this was not simply a 'race' issue, it also had much to do with social class and the class-associated selection functions of schooling. Nevertheless, 'race' was implicated as the head's remarks demonstrate; but perhaps because of the presence of two Asian governors, who said almost nothing in the meeting, it never surfaced in the discussion whereas 'socio-economic group' did.

ETHNIC MINORITY GOVERNORS' SUPPORT FOR REFORMS

What was striking about the black and Asian governors observed was the extent to which many welcomed much of the Tory reform programme, which provided further evidence for the phenomenon noted by Blair, and Whitty *et al.* (Blair, 1993; Whitty, *et al.*, 1993). An Afro-Caribbean parent governor of a primary school, for example, expressed strong support for the National Curriculum assessment procedures (SATs) on the grounds that parents like to know what their children are achieving. The mainly Asian governors of another primary school wanted the pilot SATs results to be published, even though this was not a requirement, so that, as one put it, an incentive to raise standards would be provided and parents would be informed as to how the school was performing. This orientation towards some of the Tory themes was also evident in the hostility of many of the Asian governors to mother-tongue teaching and other aspects of the multicultural approach to schooling. An Asian chair of governors articulated this position by arguing that children had to compete, and that as the competition was conducted in English this is what they needed. He also claimed that otherwise, 'they will still be as we, doing the manual jobs irrespective of their intellectual ability'.

Control of schools by governors was something many of them took very literally, and yet, as the changes to the Section 11 funding and their consequences show, governors' actual control is highly circumscribed. That this was recognized is evident from this reply given in an interview by an Asian governor following a question about accountability:

> whether it is in mainstream staff, whether it is Section 11 staff, whether it is support staff, whichever it is, the focus for the centre of the making of decisions does not lie with the governors, the focus for making decisions lies somewhere else. As long as that line is somewhere else, the institution cannot be accountable to the community. Very much so the community wants it done but the community is not the decision-making instrument, the decision-making instrument is somewhere else. Now if it is the wish of the local authority – as of central government – they should make it sure, it ought to be made sure that if these schools are going to be accountable to the community the decision-making process shall lie in the community.

CONCLUSION

The changes in the way schools are governed, together with those brought about by other policies intended to restructure the state education system have, on this evidence, offered to the black and Asian communities the appearance of new opportunities to influence decision making processes that relate to schools. As we have seen, several governors from minority communities support some of these changes. Nevertheless, as the last quotation indicates, the promise of power for consumers has remained just a promise for black and Asian governors. Paradoxically, a policy that was designed to take power away from the producers and place it in the hands of the consumers may well yet produce almost the opposite of what was intended. Heads of schools, in alliance with (mainly white) male chairs are still very much in control of those areas of school life that they do have discretion over. This does not mean that they are, as a consequence, necessarily hostile to black and Asian communities but it does mean that they are rarely accountable to them.

Several suggestions for tackling the problem of under-representation have been proposed, including some by a group headed by the National Consumer Council(1990). While many of its proposals were sound, it seems likely that they would do little if implemented to transform the structures of 'race', ethnicity and racism which account for much of the evidence presented here. Neither would its proposals do anything about the amount of the resources, over which the governors of inner-city schools have little control. Racist policies that lead to severe reductions in resources through the restructuring of Section 11 and through the creation of a context where 'choice' (for which read 'white flight') is encouraged, cannot be countered simply through increased representation on school governing bodies in an increasingly fragmented school system. The powerlessness felt by the governors at one of the schools hit by the cut in Section 11 funding was tangible; as was the frustration at being cast in the role of executors of policies they fundamentally disagreed with.

Turning to the prospects for anti-racist education in an era of LEA decline, the signs observed in the case-study are not at all propitious. Those white governors who were not openly hostile to members of ethnic minorities, and very few were, showed very little understanding of the educational issues which coalesce around ethnicity. There were few signs either that the heads, who have had to bear much of the load of introducing governors to the world of schooling in general, were going to introduce governors to these particular issues. In an increasingly marketized educational world where lay governors are being given increasingly extensive powers, policies intended to promote social equality and justice have, it would seem, little chance of success.

CHAPTER 10

School, Community and Ethnic Minority Parents

Carol Vincent

The role of parents, long recognized to be a vital element in effective schooling, is examined in this chapter with particular reference to culturally diverse schools in a changing climate.

INTRODUCTION

Since the late 1960s, relations between schools and the surrounding community have been the focus of considerable rhetoric, if perhaps rather less action. This chapter examines several issues relevant to this topic. The first section outlines the societal context in which relationships between ethnic minority parents and teachers are conducted. Secondly, the chapter moves to consider the predominant usage of the term 'community' which, it is argued, presents a misleading image of a fixed and static entity. The third section analyses recent government policy which seeks to redefine and redirect the relationship between schools and parents through the publication of another limited concept: the parent-as-consumer. Drawing on recent case study data, the fourth section explores examples of actual relationships between ethnic minority parents and teachers. The chapter concludes with suggestions for the future development of home–school links, which include within this general policy aim a specific appeal made by schools to minority parents.

ETHNIC MINORITY PARENTS AND SCHOOLS

In any consideration of the interaction between ethnic minority parents and schools, it is important to emphasize that relationships are conducted 'within a society still marked by racial and cultural antagonisms' (Tomlinson, 1993, p.144). Evidence of such tensions relating to education can be found in a number of sources. Ethnographic research studies have consistently identified stereotypical and negative opinions which some teachers hold concerning their black pupils, (Tomlinson,

1984; Wright, 1987; Mac an Ghaill, 1988; Gee, 1989; Gillborn, 1990; 1994; Mirza, 1992). This situation is corroborated by data on exclusions. It has been argued recently that the number of black students being permanently excluded is four times greater than their proportion within the school population (Gillborn, 1994).

It seems unavoidable that some of these same attitudes will spill over to the children's families (Mac an Ghaill, 1988; Mirza, 1992). Indeed, when Barbara Tizard and her colleagues (1988) asked white teachers about their experience of black parents, 70 per cent mentioned a negative attribute in reply. Neo-conservative perceptions of 'dysfunctional' families are often thinly veiled references to African-Caribbean families (David, 1993). As Mirza points out, this discourse emphasizes 'family composition' (e.g. one-parent families) rather than 'family disposition' (e.g. attitudes and values) (Mirza, 1992, p.176). Indeed, supplementary schools and classes, first established by African-Caribbean groups who were concerned that their children were being failed by state education, are largely ignored by both mainstream practitioners and the literature on home–school relations. In addition, some studies have highlighted a general lack of knowledge amongst teachers (a predominantly white middle-class workforce) of cultures, religions, and lifestyles that differ from their own (Tizard *et al.*, 1988; Tomlinson and Hutchison, 1991).

Finally, there have also been cases, relatively few in number but highly publicized and ultimately successful, involving white parents who seek to segregate their children from black pupils, and who have received tacit approval from the courts and/or Local Education Authorities (LEAs) for their actions. The Commission for Racial Equality took one such case against Cleveland LEA as far as the Court of Appeal before it was finally dismissed. Despite the apparent clash with the spirit if not the requirements of the 1976 Race Relations Act, the judiciary concluded that 'parental preference . . . should be supreme' (Vincent, 1992, p.439).

It is incidents and attitudes such as these that establish the climate in which parent–teacher interactions are conducted. Unsurprisingly, black groups and individuals often respond with disillusionment and suspicion of the white-dominated education system (see ACER, 1986). Indeed, the tone employed by 1960s compensatory education initiatives apparently lingers on. One relatively recent project featured home–school liaison teachers who visited Asian parents at home in order to 'explain school policy and practice' (Macleod, 1985, p.2). Here the parents were construed as the passive recipients of approved school knowledge.

The project booklet even contains advice for the workers on dealing with those parents who 'fail to conform' (see also Mac an Ghaill, 1988; Mirza, 1992).

REDUCTIONISM AND SIMPLIFICATION: 'THE PARENT' AND 'THE COMMUNITY'

Consideration of ethnicity does not feature highly in the majority of the literature on home–school relations. The common presentation of 'the parent' is as a homogeneous figure, a portrayal which ignores an individual's positioning within the dynamics not only of ethnicity, but also of social class and gender (on the latter, see David, 1993). Questions of power relationships are marginalized in this process. As schools are informed by the dominant social values of the white middle class (Musgrave, 1979), this prevailing ethos disadvantages those groups whose beliefs and practices differ. Furthermore, it is these groups who are particularly vulnerable to attempts by educators to change 'parenting', and particularly, mothering, practices to make them fit accepted norms. Omitting consideration of these issues from the debate on home–school practice risks rendering the discussion superficial and perfunctory.

The inclusion of the dimensions of gender and class in addition to ethnicity is important, as it serves to counteract the process of essentialism that is reflected in the common usage of the phrase, 'the black community'. The assumption here is that black people will display uniform attitudes and beliefs which arise from their shared experience of being black. Thus, potential diversity in perspective, arising from class, gender, ethnic, religious or generational differences, is denied. Brar, making a similar point, comments that,

> in many inner-city areas, the 'black' community is often seen as a single, homogeneous community, usually for ease of identification, narrowly confined to a particular geographical location, somehow spatially separate from the school community and often assessed against an idealised notion of a unitary white community. (Brar, 1991, p.33)

Brar's point is further elaborated by Cameron McCarthy (1990) in his development of the concept of *nonsynchrony*. He argues that inequality in education demands,

> a response . . . that recognizes that minorities are not simply oppressed as racial subjects, but are positioned as classed and

gendered subjects as well. These dynamics of race, class and gender are interwoven, in an uneven manner, into the social fabric of the institutions and structures of . . . society. . . . This uneven interaction of race, with other variables, namely class and gender – a process that I have called nonsynchrony – is a practical matter that defines the daily encounter of minority and majority actors in institutional and social settings. (McCarthy, 1990, p.117)

It is arguable that over-simplification and reductionism, similar to that identified by McCarthy, can also be seen in the common usage of the term 'community'. Its application often assumes traditional organic groupings, consisting of a population that shares common values and interests as well as a place of residence. A prime example of an organic community is that portrayed by Young and Willmott (1957) in London's East End. It is a moot point as to whether such communities were pervaded by the degree of closeness and harmony that the public imagination often associates with them, or whether their portrayals were heavily influenced by the discourse of 'romantic localism' (Rizvi, 1993, p.155). In any case, the concept of organic communities seems increasingly inadequate as a means of describing the spatial organization of urban areas. It is too one-dimensional an idea, unsuited to the situation of one locality containing several different social groupings which may have little contact with each other (Thomas, 1986). Instead, Willis (1990) suggests that we are seeing the development of 'proto-communities', consisting of people who share the same interests and aspirations, and who are brought together by these subjective circumstances, rather than objective criteria such as living in the same area, working in the same factory, or presumably having children who attend the same school. However, schools, particularly those designated as 'community' institutions, have a tendency to assume the existence of area-based relationships, which they then endeavour to exploit, in an effort to break down barriers between 'the community' and the school (Vincent, 1993b).

GOVERNMENT CONCEPTIONS OF THE PARENTAL ROLE

The previous section has argued against the use of a simplistic, one-dimensional model to explain individuals' relationships with their surroundings or with each other. Despite this, however, government policies and pronouncements suggest the adoption of a new homogeneous construction of 'the parent': 'the parent-as-consumer'. The rhetoric argues for the diminution of the entrenched power of educational administrators and teachers, leaving individual parents with the task that is rightfully theirs: to make choices about the education their child receives. This ideal is embedded in the Parents' Charter (DFE, 1991), and the 1988 and 1993 Education Acts. It is also supplemented by a neo-conservative emphasis on the duties of the 'responsible' parent (DFE, 1992).[1] The possibility of some parents being denied access to a complete range of choices because of their geographical location, social class and/or ethnicity is ignored.

However, the parent-as-consumer has a limited role once an initial choice of school is made. Parents, with the exception of the tiny minority of parent governors, are then expected to revert to a more passive model, which concentrates on supporting and helping the professionals. The Parents' Charter suggests that appropriate parental duties consist of ensuring the punctuality of their children, attending school events, and reading with their children. Thus, parents are expected to be concerned only with their individual child's progress rather than, say, the conditions his/her class works in. Their voice impinges upon daily school life only on specific occasions, and in situations where they can learn from the professionals. The Charter therefore does nothing to support those parents who for various reasons find it difficult to approach the school. Nor does it create a more equal relationship between teachers and parents. The two 'camps' are still kept apart. Indeed, such a division is crucial, if parents are to act in accordance with their government-ordained role as regulators of the education process, expected to create pressure for the use of traditional educational methods and curriculum content.

RESEARCH ON HOME–SCHOOL RELATIONS

This chapter now turns to empirical data to illustrate some of the earlier points. Research carried out by Tizard, Mortimore and Burchell (1988) highlights some salient issues affecting the involvement of ethnic minority parents. They note that few teachers visit minority parents at home or spend time in local social or religious centres (see also Mac an Ghaill, 1988). They describe the monocultural nature of many schools in terms of curriculum, staffing and ethos, where racial prejudice may go unnoticed. It is, they conclude, hardly surprising if some minority parents view their child's school with a mixture of wariness, bemusement and anger. Although multicultural approaches to education became more common during the 1980s, many schools include such strategies as one-off events rather than as part of an on-going programme (Brar, 1991). Tizard and her colleagues suggest that teachers need to make links with individual parents, perhaps through home visits, and that schools need to make links with community groups. They argue that minority parents, sometimes educated in different and often more formal school systems, may have serious reservations about child-centred education, especially learning through play. They comment that schools need to listen to these viewpoints, discuss them and go some way towards meeting them. They might also have noted that although many schools have at least a nominal equal opportunities policy to tackle issues such as verbal abuse, parents are rarely involved in its planning. Additionally, alterations to the political climate since Tizard's study have rendered equal opportunities issues marginal for many practitioners (Epstein, 1993).

Tomlinson and Hutchison's (1991) study, based on interviews with Bangladeshi parents in London, draws similar conclusions. They found that parents felt insufficiently informed about the progress of their children and about curriculum issues in general. Teachers had varying, and in many cases inadequate, knowledge of Bengali culture, religion or language. Some teachers equated lack of fluency in English with lack of literacy. Whilst some parent-respondents felt that local schools had improved over time in many aspects, including teacher expectations and acceptance of cultural differences, others were "'reluctantly satisfied'" in that they felt that as migrants they were not in a position to complain or criticise, and that the school "had all the power'" (Tomlinson and Hutchison, 1991, p.44).

My own recent research focused on parental participation in one inner-city Borough, and the project was based on case-studies of teacher–parent relationships in primary schools and other educational institutions. The data used here derives from semi-structured interviews conducted in two primary schools, Hill Street and Low Road. Both were large schools (300-plus pupils), with predominantly working-class and racially-mixed intakes. Ninety-five parents and all the permanent, full time teachers (31) were interviewed. The respondents included parents from all the main ethnic groups represented in the schools' populations.[2]

Hill Street School provided various opportunities for parents to visit the school, including regular parent–teacher meetings, socials, parent governor surgeries, and a small Parent–Teacher Association. Parental responses varied.[3] During the fieldwork period, the second school, Low

Road, had no parents' association or regular parent–teacher meetings or socials. Neither school had a home–school policy. Between them, the two schools commanded seven places for parent governors; but there was only one black parent governor at Low Road, and two black co-opted governors at Hill Street. There were four black teachers at Hill Street and five at Low Road (two of whom were on temporary placements).

Overall, the interviews revealed a marked degree of alienation and disaffection amongst ethnic minority parents. Some of their concerns were also voiced by white parents at the two schools. These included a perception of their own lack of knowledge concerning teaching methods and curriculum content, and a pervasive feeling of discontent with the resulting dependency on professional judgement. As the following quotations suggest, many parents felt themselves subordinate, in the face of both the teachers' professional knowledge and social class status.

> You have more control [at home]. You can actually choose what your child does, you can choose the books. I choose black books for my kids, but I also have lots of different books. I choose when they eat and when they don't, when they go out to play and when they don't. Here [at school] it's all been taken from you, you don't have the right to say 'my child doesn't go to school today'. If you do, you are in trouble. (African-Caribbean mother, Hill Street)

> They take more notice of the teacher, and you take second place . . . you're not as important as the teacher, and they've got to do things the teacher's way. (African-Caribbean mother, Hill Street)

Another woman described how she resisted the show of automatic deference which she felt was expected of her as a parent when in conversation with a teacher.

> I tend to treat the teacher not as the teacher but as someone to talk to. I've always been on first name terms with the teacher. I don't like saying 'miss', because I find it makes you inferior, as if they are better than you. (white mother, Hill Street)

As noted above, these experiences and perceptions were common to parents of all ethnic groups. However, it was often the case that black parents felt the problems were compounded by differences in language or culture, or a suspicion of racial prejudice. This chapter now turns to consider several issues affecting relations between ethnic minority parents and teachers at Hill Street and Low Road.

Teacher–parent relationships: Bangladeshi parents at Low Road
Nearly 30 per cent of Low Road's population came from Bangladeshi families. All the parents interviewed for this study expressed frustration that they did not know what sort of work their children did at school, or how they were getting on. During the research period the school had only one Bengali/Sylhetti-speaking teacher. As she was a class teacher she was often unavailable to parents, despite her efforts to maintain links with them. Therefore, many parents relied on their children to translate, an ineffective form of communication where younger children are involved, especially when the subject for discussion is the child itself. As there were no regular parent–teacher meetings, informal communication was the most common type of teacher–parent interaction at Low Road. This effectively excluded those Bangladeshi parents who spoke little English. Thus, parent-respondents commented that they would appreciate a particular invitation and occasion to visit. Their information about school life was reduced by the irregularity of translated letters home.

The Bangladeshi parents who participated in the study noted that Low Road had no books in Bengali (it actually had a few and was ordering more), no Bengali classes, and only one Bengali-speaker on the staff. The school appeared to take little account of Islam; it had not, for example, celebrated Id-ul-Fitr during the previous year. Shortly after the main fieldwork period, another Bengali/Sylhetti-speaker was appointed to the staff. He felt strongly that Bangladeshi culture and Islam should be more prominent in school life, and he had organized a celebration of Id. He found that the other teachers did not oppose such developments, but had not previously initiated any. Such inaction, he commented, was in itself an action. For the Bangladeshi parent-respondents, the school's ethos was formed by those who had their origin in a different social class and ethnic group, spoke a different language, and were influenced by a different religion.

Community–school relations: South Asian Muslim parents at Hill Street
Other ethnic minority parents also offered accounts of their relationship with the school, which suggested that they felt their concerns and opinions were marginalized. Taken together, the range of incidents and

events which they highlight is indicative of the level of institutional neglect of issues related to ethnicity. This section provides a further illustration through its focus on relations between Hill Street School and two community associations run by members of the Asian Muslim community.

Through the promptings of a Muslim governor and with the support of a nearby mosque, Hill Street School instituted bi-weekly separate assemblies for Muslim children, a move welcomed by those of their parents who took part in the study. These were later reduced to one a week because as a teacher put it, the necessary organisational arrangements were 'intrusive'. The school also hosted Gujerati and Urdu lessons during the day for Asian children. Teachers were obtained through one of the local Islamic centres. However, no steps were taken to include them in the main staff body. They took lessons in a shabby, uninviting room (which was nominally the Parents' Room) and then left, having little contact with other teachers or children (see also Macdonald *et al.*, 1989 ch.22, for similar examples). One Hill Street teacher did work very hard to establish links with local community groups, particularly the two nearby Islamic associations. However, the school as a whole had no coherent idea of the sort of liaison it wished to establish. The issue, in fact, was not discussed, as visiting the centres was seen as an end in itself. Thus, the community groups were used as resource centres, places that could provide translations, information and teachers for language lessons. Pressure of work on all those involved meant that such contact remained limited and infrequent. Thus, opportunities to establish a more interactive, pervasive link between Hill Street School and the community centres were lost.

Furthermore, the attitudes of some of the teachers concerning Asian parents veered towards paternalism. For example, the neighbouring Coronation School hosted Saturday English lessons and other activities for Asian women and children. One teacher thought that involving Hill Street parents would be advantageous to home–school relationships, because 'If they [Asian parents] see something being done to help them, then hopefully they will see the school as a useful place.' However, the Asian communities, particularly the local Muslim community, were very well-established, and had their own thriving community groups. Thus, they were unlikely to see themselves as needing 'help'. Simply offering lessons, without establishing the existence of any demand for them is unlikely to result in an enthusiastic response. This, in turn, may be seen as providing further evidence that the parents are apathetic and uninterested in education.

Discipline and behaviour: African-Caribbean parents at Hill Street and Bangladeshi parents at Low Road

Given the high rate of exclusions affecting African-Caribbean children, especially boys, discipline and behaviour in schools is often a controversial topic. As noted above, several research studies have concluded that teachers may be influenced in their judgements of black children's ability by their behaviour rather than their school work (Wright, 1987; Mac an Ghaill, 1988). Gillborn (1990) identifies 'the myth of an Afro-Caribbean challenge to authority' (p.19). He concludes that many conflicts arise out of the teachers' expectations of disruptive or challenging behaviour from African-Caribbean boys, and also their ethnocentric interpretations of the forms of dress, speech or even ways of walking adopted by the pupils (p.200).[4]

The following account details a relatively minor incident and its consequences in terms of parental attitudes towards Hill Street School. I suggest that in the hothouse atmosphere of a pressurized school day, events such as this one may not be investigated fully, or even taken very seriously by the school authorities. However, this can lead to parents feeling that their concerns or complaints are largely ignored, which, in turn contributes to a perception of dislocation between school and home.

A black woman, Ms Abrahams, describing the conflict between her son and his teacher, said she felt that the teacher concentrated on criticizing her son's behaviour, and not paying enough attention to his academic performance. She believed the teacher reacted to the child in a negative manner, and had once attempted to humiliate him by 'calling him like a dog'.[5] After this incident Ms Abrahams insisted that the boy be moved to another class. Although she focused her comments on her differences with this particular teacher, the event had clearly affected Ms Abrahams' view of the school as a whole. This mistrust was also conveyed by another woman who mentioned the same incident. In the following passage, the second woman, Ms Watson, uses 'we' to denote a small group of black women who were friends. It also emphasizes their separateness from the school establishment.

> The teacher – when we first heard of it, we thought it was just a one-off thing and it was the child – but we found she was picking on the black children in her group. There was an incident where she . . . said [to the child] that this is the way she'd treat her dog. And

other little things we felt were wrong, were racist basically. . . . It was specifically aimed at the black kids, if we thought it was the white kids as well we wouldn't have made too much fuss. . . . We tried to put that over to the head but she said the teacher said she didn't do it that way [ie talk to the child in a way that was offensive] . . . she [the head] doesn't pay much attention to what you are saying . . . I don't feel comfortable around that teacher now. I don't have much contact with her now . . . [But] I think apart from that particular teacher and the head . . . all the others have done their best to be aware of all the different cultures and teach in the class to suit everyone and get all the kids involved. That teacher is just one, they're not all like that. (Ms Watson, Hill Street)

The child's version of the incident and the teacher's obviously differ markedly. However, the important point in this context is that, irrespective of what exactly happened, the parents' perceptions of the school were adversely affected. Although both Ms Abrahams and Ms Watson stressed that they had not adopted a uniformly negative view, they remained unhappy with the school's response, and maintained a distance between themselves and the staff. I would argue that such incidents are not atypical, and that these relatively minor events, which have no major reverberations (such as formal complaints to the governing body or LEA) may nonetheless be common and effective contributors to cool home–school relations.

Indiscipline and, in particular, playground behaviour were issues of concern for the Bangladeshi parents at Low Road. Indeed, they were subjects frequently mentioned by other Low Road parents. My interpreter endeavoured to find out whether the Bangladeshi respondents felt their children suffered from racial abuse and harassment. The responses were mixed, some said yes, the fighting and name-calling were directed at Bangladeshi children more than at other groups of children. Others said no, there was a generally high level of indiscipline involving children indiscriminately; of course, children may not always tell their parents about racist incidents (Troyna and Hatcher, 1992). The Bangladeshi parents, however, shared a general perception that teachers rarely followed up incidents or complaints from children, a criticism made by many parent-respondents from all ethnic groups. In fact, the school did have a procedure for dealing with fighting and name-calling; all incidents were meant to be recorded and sent to the head. Parents appeared largely unaware of this system, which emphasizes the need for clear procedures, known to all staff, parents and children, for dealing with transgressions.

Hill Street and Low Road both had anti-racist policies, although at neither institution did the documents have a very high profile. The two schools were reactive rather than proactive in their attitudes towards any racial incidents (Gillborn, 1993). At Low Road especially, occasional displays of overt racism from some white parents or children were clearly visible. However, the school made few overt attempts to encourage a climate which might militate against such behaviour.

In conclusion, many black and ethnic minority parents in this study responded with a sense of disaffection to their children's apparently insular ethnocentric schools. However, this focus on ethnicity should not be taken as suggesting that the different ethnic groups held homogeneous opinions of the schools. Although most parent-respondents also shared the same gender and class groups, other factors were pertinent in determining their attitudes towards the school. These included familiarity with the English primary education system, perceptions of their children's progress, religious affiliations and so on. Similarly, many white working-class parents who took part in the study also argued that the schools neglected their needs and concerns. Therefore, it is important to stress that the differing reactions and relations of actors in any educational setting cannot be explained in terms of ethnicity alone (McCarthy, 1990).

Parental responses

Data from this research project suggests the existence of three main types of response from the parents interviewed.[6] The first group are *school-supportive* parents. This group had become incorporated to some extent into the school structure. They could be relied upon to attend school events when summoned, and they took the initiative in forging a relationship with their child's teachers. They felt strongly that parents should not leave education to the school, did 'school' work at home with their children, and attempted to monitor their progress. Twelve out of the 45 Hill Street parents clearly fitted into this category, whereas only 4 out of 50 did so at Low Road. The latter group is small because there were no regular parent-teacher meetings or socials at Low Road, and thus fewer opportunities for a clearly identifiable group of supportive parents to emerge. At both schools, this group was mostly, but not exclusively, composed of white parents.

The second group is the *detached* parents. A small number of parents at both schools believed it was not part of their role to have much interaction with the school. Eight parents (out of 45) at Hill Street and 9 (out of 50) at Low Road fell clearly into this category. They felt that the acquisition of 'school knowledge' was the teachers' province. They had little and irregular contact with the school. They were not uninterested in their children's progress, but did not see themselves as educators. The schools' somewhat weak attempts to encourage them otherwise had passed them by. They had not, however, abdicated responsibility as parents, seeing it as their part to aid their children's development in other ways, such as regulating their behaviour, introducing them to cultural and religious mores, or preparing them for the adult world. This group of parents was composed of working-class adults from across all ethnic groups.

A far larger group of parents expressed a desire to get more involved with the school, but were hindered from doing so for a variety of reasons. These *independent* parents maintained minimal contact with the schools. In some cases this was prompted by a conscious decision, arising from their disaffection with the school, an attitude characterized as 'active non-participation' by Pugh and De'Ath (1989). Alternatively, 'passive non-participation' describes a parent who may wish to have more contact with the school, but is prevented from doing so by practical circumstances. For example, she may not be fluent in English, but interpreters are not always present at school events, and there is irregular translation of notes home. She may work long hours. She may have small children and no child-care. Or she may simply be under a degree of financial and emotional stress that precludes involvement. School-inspired events may not meet parents' concerns or interests; thus a rational decision over the allocation of their time may exclude school meetings (Showstack-Sasson, 1983). Twenty-five parents at Hill Street and 37 at Low Road fell into this category. These parents were often labelled 'apathetic' by staff and other *supportive* parents, because they were not seen at school very often. They rejected the traditional roles of Parent Association member and voluntary helper (where available), perceiving that these made little difference to their children's education. In their relationships with teachers, parents found that they often had to take the initiative, and this they were not always prepared to do. Instead, they made alternative arrangements, working with the children at home without reference to the class teacher, and/or taking them to supplementary classes. However, this group all claimed that they would like closer involvement with the school, and made sporadic efforts to achieve it.

It was also this group of parents who emphasized the inequality which they felt was a defining feature of their relationships with the teaching staff. They spoke of feeling excluded, and saw, except in cases of crisis, no appropriate role for themselves at school. Some parents identified exclusive professional control as being responsible for denying them any significant influence (see quotations on p.180 above). Others were less critical, having so internalized their exclusion that they exhibited considerable uncertainty about approaching teachers.

> Whenever, I've gone to a teacher, she's always said how nice it was to have parents showing an interest. So perhaps some parents don't show any interest, and that's the problem. I don't know, maybe it ain't been put to them to show an interest. Alright, they really should go and fend for themselves. The children have only got one education and you have to make sure it's a good one. But maybe some people don't think of that, maybe they think well, the teacher might be busy or they might not like to go in the class and look at the work, they might feel a nuisance. (white mother, Low Road)

Arguably, this parental perception of exclusion stems not from a deliberate staff strategy, but rather from the teachers' semi-conscious agenda which gave parents a low priority. There is, therefore, a large constituency of *independent* parents who feel distanced from their child's school in some way. Data from this particular study shows that this group includes parents from all ethnic groups. However, in view of the disaffection of many ethnic minority parents, it is unsurprising that they are over-represented within this category.

THE FUTURE DEVELOPMENT OF HOME–SCHOOL RELATIONS

What then should be the aim of initiatives hoping to improve home-school relations? I would argue that it should not be to 'convert' *independent* and *detached* parents so that they adopt the *school supportive* model. Indeed, many parents had already rejected the latter role, seeing it as an inadequate response to their concerns. Instead, a *participant* model would allow parents access to decision-making power, not just in terms of the inclusion of a few lay individuals as with governing bodies, but by offering parents the opportunity to operate collectively. Such a role would require a range of strategies, in an attempt to establish parental participation at different levels. The *school supportive* parents saw their role as an individual one, focusing mainly on their own child's progress, and on whole-school issues only in terms of organizing fund-raising and socials. The individual parent–teacher relationship is indeed a key one, and could be bolstered by the school introducing simple measures such as regular, private teacher–parent meetings; the provision of clear, accessible information on the organization of the school (including equal opportunity policies) and the delivery of the curriculum; curriculum workshops, home reading and maths schemes; 'open' sessions when parents can visit the classroom during the school day, and so on. However, a role for parents as participants would extend beyond this to include whole-school, and local educational issues. Macbeth (1989) has suggested class or year group meetings when parents are invited to school to talk about the curriculum and organization for that year, meet each other, and perhaps adopt a system of class representatives whereby one parent, known to all, can act as a link between the teacher and other parents with children in the same class.

Sally Tomlinson (1991) has proposed statutorily based Home–School Associations (HSAs), arguing that, firstly, legislation is necessary to raise the status of potential parental contributions; and that, secondly, parents' groups stand a better chance of survival if supported within a structure that gives them legitimacy. Thus, she suggests HSAs would be open to parents, teachers, governors and older pupils, and would discuss educational issues rather than the more peripheral and mundane matters that often dominate the agenda at parent meetings (Hess, 1991). HSAs would be funded by a government grant, and be consulted about educational decisions at local and, through representatives, at national level. Parents would then have the opportunity to participate individually and collectively at different levels – that of the individual child, the class, and the school (Macbeth, 1989).

Such changes would involve great alterations in current relationships between teachers and parents. Several schools in a recent Royal Society of Arts project (Ball, 1994) have attempted innovations along these lines (although developing whole-school parents' groups seems to be a less popular choice by the schools involved). Progress is acknowledged to be slow, as individual schools endeavour to implement reforms that run counter to the dominant tenor of home–school relations (Jones *et al.*, 1992). Although legislation, such as that required to establish a nation-wide network of HSAs, is unlikely to be wholly transformative, it could serve to 'kick-start' the system into reform. Support offered to parents from a source independent of any one institution is also important. A network of parents' centres could offer parents advice and information, develop links between schools and community groups, particularly those concerned with education such as supplementary schools and playgroups, as well as providing parents' groups with facilities and resources. Such centres do exist, but they are few and often plagued by precarious funding (Philips, 1989; Vincent, 1993a).

These suggestions for future developments are designed with all parents in mind, rather than specifically being directed towards ethnic minority parents. However, a number of Bangladeshi parent-respondents at Low Road did suggest separate parents' groups as a solution to their isolation from the school. This is a controversial notion, which fuels fears that such action could have divisive effects. The MacDonald Report, which investigated the events at Burnage High School preceding the tragic murder of Ahmed Iqbal Ullah in 1986, highlighted this danger by quoting the following letter from a London headteacher.

> I would strongly advise that you [the Burnage headteacher] do not set up a separate ethnic system for minority [parent] groups. Two or three schools in the London area have tried it and it has been a fiasco. It is divisive, creates suspicion and can lead to unnecessary squabbles with indigenous white parents who often feel they are being pushed aside. . . . Where there are open discussions with all groups the veil of suspicion is removed. (Quoted in Macdonald *et al*, 1989, p.178)

Such a move is likely to cause particular resentment when there are few opportunities for indigenous parents to be in contact with the school. This was the case at Burnage, and would also apply to the two schools in my research, especially Low Road.

An alternative strategy to increase the level of ethnic minority involvement at Hill Street and Low Road would aim to increase the *general* level of parental involvement. However, given respondents' strong sense of alienation, it is vital that a specific appeal is made within this to minority communities. Preparation for a parents' evening, for example, would include such measures as translating letters into home languages, arranging for interpreters, and inviting people personally. More general contact with community groups, especially those with an educational brief, can expand the insular focus of schools like Hill Street and Low Road.

Ethnic minority and working-class parents have historically been perceived as a 'problem' by the school. Ensuring that these voices are validated by the educational establishment is a long and difficult, but crucial, process. The dominant home–school rhetoric speaks of involving parents as partners. However, despite this discourse which stresses equality, sharing, and mutual obligations and responsibilities, many parents will continue to refuse to invest their time and resources if the actual relationship offered by their children's schools is a profoundly unequal one.

Notes

Chapter 3: Ethnic Relations in the Primary Classroom

The author acknowledges the permission of David Fulton (Publishers) for the reproduction of extracts from her book *Race Relations in the Primary School*, published in 1992.

1 'Black', as used throughout the article, refers to those of South Asian or Afro-Caribbean parentage.
2 This study was conducted as part of a CRE-funded research project.
3 All names used throughout the article are pseudonyms.
4 It was common practice in the schools for the nursery units to be staffed by one or two teachers and several nursery nurses. In the schools, the nursery nurses (often referred to as Care Assistants) worked as support staff in the classroom.
5 'Gonah' is a term used by Moslems to mean sin (in the eyes of Allah).
6 'Statementing' is a formal assessment of a child's cognitive and behaviourial development, normally undertaken by the school and the Psychological Service.
7 Classroom logs were used by teachers in all four schools as a systematic way of recording facts and incidents relating to pupils. They were available for consultation by other staff.

Chapter 4: Ethnic Relations in Secondary Schools

1 This chapter is based on a large-scale study of ethnic relations directed by the writer and published in 1994 as G.K. Verma, P. Zec and G.D. Skinner, *The Ethnic Crucible*, by The Falmer Press, whose permission we acknowledge for the reproduction of several extracts.

Chapter 5: The Schooling of Young Black Women

1 See Cross, Wrench and Barnett, 1990; Drew, Gray and Sime, 1992; Mirza, 1992; Skellington, 1992; *Employment Gazette*, 1993; T. Jones, 1993.
2 Research on black girls in schools during the 1980s can be loosely categorized on the one hand into feminist studies (Fuller, 1982; Phizacklea, 1982; Dex, 1983; Griffin, 1985; Riley, 1985; Weis, 1985; Sharpe, 1987 (1976); Wright, 1986; Wulff, 1988; Coultas, 1989; Reid, 1989), and on the other into the 'male' tradition of liberal race-relations and education research (Driver, 1980; Rutter *et al.*, 1982; Verma and Ashworth, 1985; Eggleston *et al.*, 1986; Mac an Ghaill, 1988; Gillborn, 1990).

3 For a more detailed description of methodology and findings see H. Mirza, *Young Female and Black*, Routledge, 1992.

4 See Fryer, 1984; Gilroy, 1987; Solomos 1993.

5 In addition, 30 young women from a school in Trinidad (aged 16–18 years) and 16 young women from youth clubs and community centres in South London (aged 18+) participated in semi-structured interviews concerning their career choices and attitudes to marriage and relationships.

6 See, for example, McRobbie and Garber, 1976; Willis, 1977; Brake, 1985; Lees, 1986; Brown, 1987, Wallace, 1987; McRobbie, 1990.

7 Teachers provide easy targets, offering tangible and powerful evidence against themselves. It is not surprising, therefore, that they are assumed by many social commentators to be the central link in the transmission of social and racial inequality (Wright, 1987; Gillborn, 1990; Mac an Ghaill, 1988). However, as Foster (1991) points out, this is a tentative link founded upon the inherent methodological shortcomings of ethnography which are highly interpretative and speculative. Foster's perspective has aroused a great deal of controversy, the response to which can be found in Wright, 1990; Troyna, 1991; Hammersley, 1992; Gillborn and Drew, 1992; 1993; Hammersley and Gomm, 1993.

8 Dex, 1982; Rutter *et al.*, 1982; Eggleston *et al.*, 1986; Cross, Wrench and Barnett, 1990; Drew, Gray and Sime, 1992; *Employment Gazette*, 1993.

9 The media has taken a particular interest in the subject of the 'black superwoman' ('Flying Colours', *Guardian*, 12 June 1991; 'Black Men: Losers in a One-Sided Sexcess Story', *Voice*, 18 June 1991; 'Sisters are Doing it for Themselves', *The Times*, 31 Mrch 1992; 'Race Relationships', *Sunday Times*, 24 May 1992). Offering a sensational interpretation of the 1991 labour force statistics, these newspapers mischievously suggest that black women are more successful than their male counterparts. But as I have argued (*Guardian*, 12 May 1992), black women are not more successful than black men. This is a divisive interpretation of a simple fact: black men are locked into a racially limited area of the labour market where there is less opportunity for educational mobility than in those open to black women.

10 Wilson's (1987) study of the black condition in America is just such an example of this cultural redirection. He argues that public policy initiatives aimed at stemming the tide of the growing black 'underclass' should be directed towards displacing the female-headed household by restoring the economically successful, self-assured, black, male breadwinner.

11 See Moynihan, 1967; Murray, 1984; Wilson, 1987.

12 Eggleston *et al.* (1986:95) show African Caribbean boys least likely of all ethnic and white groups to want their wives to stay at home upon having a child. Similarly, research in the USA has shown that black husbands have a 'permissive' attitude to their wives working (Landry and Jendrek, 1978).

13 The majority of Britain's ethnic minorities live in the large urban conurbations, 42 per cent of all ethnic minorities live in the London and Greater London area alone. 63 per cent of African Caribbeans live in the

London area, with 30 per cent in the West Midlands region and Metropolitan County (T. Jones, 1993).

Chapter 6: Ethnic Relations in All-White Schools

1 This chapter refers to the education system in England and Wales. Scotland and Northern Ireland have somewhat different systems.

2 After this chapter was commissioned every opportunity was taken to collect data from a large number of schools in the south-western counties by using student teachers. This gives an up-to-date picture of how pupils and ordinary teachers see some of the issues. I am indebted to the many undergraduate and postgraduate teacher-trainee students who have done so much to put a multicultural awareness into so many subjects in so many secondary schools in the south-west of England, and I am pleased to highlight their contribution in this chapter.

Chapter 7: The LEA and TEC Context

1 This chapter is based on a two-year research project, 'Multicultural Education After ERA: Concerns and Challenges for the 1990s', sponsored by the Council for Local Education Authorities at the National Foundation for Educational Research, April 1991 – March 1993, and updated by other research. For further methodological details see the authors' respective published papers.

2 See, for example, Braham, Rattansi and Skellington, 1992; Jones, 1993.

3 See, for example, on racial harassment in and around schools, the Swann Report (GBP: HofC, 1985), the Commission for Racial Equality's Report, *Learning in Terror* (1988); and for experience in 'white' schools (Taylor, 1992a; Troyna and Hatcher, 1992).

4 See, for example, on the 'nationalistic' curriculum, Tomlinson (1993). Others have, however, attempted to demonstrate a multicultural dimension to the national, basic and whole curriculum and in cross-curricular themes, at primary and secondary levels (see King and Reiss, 1993; and the four-volume series edited by Pumfrey and Verma, 1993). A notable curriculum development project, led by the Runnymede Trust, with wide consultation, *Equality Assurance in Schools*, issued a handbook of guidance on issues of cultural diversity and race equality in the curriculum, school organization and management (Runnymede Trust, 1993). See also the policy and teacher support materials on cultural diversity in Wales, which promotes the curriculum Cymreig (CCW, 1991, 1993).

5 More explicit guidance has been issued to schools on spiritual and moral development (NCC, 1993a) than on cultural development. OFSTED (1994) has also just taken the unusual step of issuing a discussion paper on spiritual, moral social and cultural development and inviting comment. It remains to be seen what weighting will eventually be given to cultural preservation, cultural maintenance and appreciation of cultural diversity.

6 The Economic and Social Research Council also sponsored several projects in

The Educational Needs of a Multicultural Society Initiative, from 1988. The *Intercultural Education Project*, funded by the European Commission and managed by DFE, to improve the education of children from ethnic minority families, is focussing on early years, bilingual teaching and learning, and the involvement of parents. A UK database of contacts and information on Section 11 and other work with ethnic minority families to support their children's learning is being established.

7 Since our Section 11 research, a Private Member's Bill extending the scope of Section 11 to include non-New Commonwealth groups was enacted in 1993. Reductions in the level of Section 11 funding have also been signalled by the Home Office after 1994 (see below for further discussion).

8 Since this chapter was written, the Government has decided that all Section 11 funding will come within a new Single Regeneration Budget. From 1994, local authorities will be expected to bid for Section 11 funding alongside other priorities.

Chapter 8: The Local Management of Schools and Racial Equality

1 Earlier versions of this chapter were presented at the Ontario Institute for Studies in Education; James Cook University; Queensland University of Technology; University of Keele and the 8th ERA Research Network Seminar at the University of Warwick. Thanks to Andy Hargreaves, Michael Singh, Erica McWilliam and Fazal Rizvi, Dennis Gleeson and David Halpin, respectively, for providing an opportunity to give the arguments a trial run.

I would also like to thank Denise Anderson (National Union of Teachers), Fran Bennett (Child Poverty Action Group), Will Guy, Richard Hatcher, Vinod Kumar (National Children's Bureau), Ian Menter, Rosalind Levacic, Sarah Palmer (LARRIE) and Nargis Rashid for their time and efforts in helping me collect material for this chapter.

2 For further details about the proposed and actual changes to Section 11 funding in recent years see the special issue of *Multicultural Teaching*, vol. 12, no. 1, 1993, and the *Times Educational Supplement* (25 March 1994, p. 10).

3 Donald MacLeod, Education Correspondent for the *Guardian* wrote in July 1993 of the Government's intention to increase the significance of pupil numbers (with a correlative decline in social and economic factors) in determining grants to LEAs and schools. Accordingly, 'the greater use of pupil numbers to determine school budgets has shifted money away from schools in deprived areas towards more prosperous catchment areas, as councils lose their scope for discretionary help' (MacLeod, 1993, p. 4).

4 'Woodshire' is, of course, a pseudonym.

Chapter 9: School Governors, 'Race' and Racism

1 The research project described here was funded by an Economic and Social Research Council Grant (R000 23 1799). I am indebted to my co-director of the project, Professor Rosemary Deem of Lancaster University, and to

Suzanne J. Heath and Sue Hemmings both of whom worked on the project as research assistants. I am also grateful to the governing bodies involved in the study for all the help and assistance they gave us.

Chapter 10: School, Community and Ethnic Minority Parents

1 At the 1993 Conservative Party Conference, the Secretary of State for Education, John Patten, declared: 'Home is where . . . values are learnt. Being a parent is a privilege, one that must never be squandered. Parents must not walk away from their children and their responsibilities. . . . Parents must provide the caring and disciplined home environment', quoted in the *TES*, 8 October 1993. Similarly, the RSA *Start Right* report (Ball, 1994) suggests linking the receipt of child benefit with attendance at parent training sessions (*TES*, 18 March, 1994).

2 At Hill Street, 10 parent-respondents were African-Caribbean in origin, 8 South Asian, 8 Turkish or Cypriot, and 19 English, Welsh, Scots or Irish (ESWI). At Low Road, 11 parent-respondents were African-Caribbean in origin, 15 were Bangladeshi, 1 was Arabic, and 23 ESWI; 20 were male and 75 female.

3 For example, parent governor surgeries were poorly attended. Reasons for this included a general uncertainty about the status of parent governors, as well as the reluctance of some parents to seek out an individual they did not know.

4 In the detention book at Hill Street, most entries were for fighting and swearing. However, one child was given a detention for 'walking insolently', and another for 'attitude problems' (see Gillborn, 1990, ch.2).

5 After an incident between two children, the teacher apparently called the boy over to her, suggesting by her words and tone of voice that he was a dog. The teacher told Ms Abrahams that she was joking with the child.

6 In view of the above comment that the differing reactions and relations of actors in any educational setting cannot be explained in terms of ethnicity alone, the following typology includes parents of *all* ethnic origins.

References

Chapter 1: Education for All in the 1990s

Commission for Racial Equality (1989) *Racial Segregation in Education: report of an investigation into Cleveland LEA*, London: Commission for Racial Equality.

Cox, B. (1991) *Cox on Cox: an English curriculum for the 1990s*, London: Hodder and Stoughton.

Dearing, R. (1994) *The National Curriculum and its Assessment*, London: School Curriculum and Assessment Authority.

(DES) Department of Education and Science (1977) *Education in Schools: a consultative document*, London: HMSO.

DES (1981a) *West Indian Children in our Schools*, Report of the Committee of Inquiry into the Education of Ethnic Minority Children, London: HMSO (Rampton Report) cmd. 8273.

DES (1981b) *The School Curriculum*, London: HMSO.

DES (1985) *Education for All*, London: HMSO (Swann Report) cmnd. 9453.

DES (1988) Letter to National Curriculum Council from Kenneth Baker, Secretary of State for Education, York: NCC.

Education Reform Act (ERA) (1988) London, HMSO.

Ghuman, P.A.S., and Gallop, R. (1981) 'Educational attitudes of Bengali families in Cardiff', *Journal of Multicultural and Multilingual Development*, vol. 2, no. 2, pp. 127–44.

Ghuman, P.A.S., and Wong, R. (1989) 'Chinese parents and English education', *Educational Research*, vol. 31, no. 2, pp. 134–40.

Graham, D. (1993) *A Lesson for Us All: the making of the National Curriculum*, London: Routledge.

Joseph, K. (1985) 'Education for an ethnically mixed society', speech on leaving office, May 1985, reproduced in *Multicultural Teaching*, vol. 4, no. 3, pp. 6–8.

Labour Party (1989) *Multicultural Education: Labour's policy for schools*, London: Labour Party.

MacDonald, I. (1988) *Murder in the Playground*, Manchester: Longsight.

Modood, T. (1993) 'The number of ethnic minority students in British higher education: some grounds for optimism', *Oxford Review of Education*, vol. 19, no. 2, pp. 67–82.

'Plowden Report' (1967) *Children and their Primary Schools*, London: HMSO.

Smith, H. (1994) 'Key lessons every child must learn', London: *Evening Standard*, 9 April 1994.

Taylor, P. (1992) 'Ethnic group data and applications to higher education', *Higher Education Quarterly*, vol. 46, no. 4, pp. 359–74.

Taylor P. (1993) 'Minority groups and gender in access to higher education', *New Community*, vol. 19, no. 3, pp. 425–40.

TES (Times Educational Supplement), (1990) 'Editorial', 8 June, p. A23.

Tomlinson, S. (1993) 'The Multicultural Task Group: the Group that never was' in A.S. King and M.J. Reiss (eds) *The Multicultural Dimension of the National Curriculum*, Sussex: Falmer.

Chapter 2: The National Curriculum and Ethnic Relations

Adams, A. (1993) 'English' in A. King and M. Reiss (eds) *The Multicultural Dimension of the National Curriculum*, London: Falmer.

Ashraf, S.A. (1988) 'A view of education: an Islamic perspective' in B. O'Keeffe (ed.) *Schools for Tomorrow: Building Walls or Building Bridges*, London: Falmer.

Bishop, A. (1993) 'Culturalising mathematics teaching' in A. King and M. Reiss (eds) *The Multicultural Dimension of the National Curriculum*, London: Falmer.

Booth, M. (1993) 'History' in A. King and M. Reiss (eds) *The multicultural Dimension of the National Curriculum*, London: Falmer.

Booth, M. and C. Husbands (1993) 'The History National Curriculum in England and Wales; assessment at Key Stage 3', *The Curriculum Journal*, vol. 4, No. 1, Spring.

Cox, B. (1991) *Cox on Cox; an English curriculum for the 1990s*, London: Hodder & Stoughton.

Dearing, R. (1994) *The National Curriculum and its Assessment*, London: Schools Curriculum and Assessment Authority.

DES (Department of Education and Science) (1989) *National Curriculum: from policy into practice*, London: DES.

DES (1992) *Standard Assessment Task 1992. The Spelling Test: going swimming*, London: HMSO.

DFE (1992) *Choice and Diversity: a new framework for schools*, London: HMSO.

DFE (1994) *Religious Education and Collective Worship Circ. 1/94*, London: DFE.

Ditchfield, C. (ed.) (1987) *Better Science Working for a Multicultural Society*, London: Heinemann.

Donald, J. and Rattansi, A. (1992) *'Race', Culture and Difference*, London: Sage.

Eco, U. (1992) 'Overinterpreting texts' in S. Collini (ed.) *Interpretation and Over-interpretation*, Cambridge: Cambridge University Press.

Eggleston, S.J. (1990) 'Can anti-racist education survive the 1988 Education Act?' *Multicultural Teaching*, vol. 8, no. 3.

Figueroa, P. (1993) 'History: policy issues', in P.D. Pumpfrey and G.K. Verma (eds) *Cultural Diversity and the Curriculum, Vol. 1*, London: Falmer.

Fines, J. (1993) 'History and the challenge of multicultural education' in A. Fyfe and P. Figueroa (eds) *Education for Cultural Diversity*, London: Routledge.

Foster, P. (1993) 'Report on education and training', *New Community*, vol. 20, no. 1. (Commission for Racial Equality).

Fyfe, A. (1993) 'Multicultural or anti-racist education: the irrelevant debate', in A. Fyfe and P. Figueroa (eds) *Education for Cultural Diversity*, London: Routledge.

Gill, D. (1993) 'Geography' in P.D. Pumpfrey and G.K. Verma (eds) *Cultural Diversity and the Curriculum, Vol. 1*, London: Falmer.

Gill, D., Mayor, B. and Blair, M. (eds) (1992) *Racism and Education: structures and strategies*, London: Sage.

Gillborn, D. and Drew, D. (1992) '"Race", class and school effects', *New Community*, vol. 18, no. 4 (Commission for Racial Equality).

Halstead, J.M. (1988) *Education, Justice and Cultural Diversity: an examination of the Honeyford Affair*, London: Falmer.

Halstead, J. M. (1992) 'Ethical dimensions of controversial events in multicultural education' in M. Leicester and M. Taylor (eds) *Ethics, Ethnicity and Education*, London: Kogan Page.

Hammersley, M. and Gomm, R. (1993) 'A response to Gillborn and Drew on "race", class and school effects', *New Community*, vol. 19, No. 2 (Commission for Racial Equality).

Hardy, J. and Vieler-Porter, C. (1990) 'Race, schooling and the 1988 Education Reform Act' in M. Flude and M. Hammer (eds) *The Education Reform Act 1988: its origins and implications*, London: Falmer.

Hargreaves, D.H. (1991) 'Coherence and manageability: reflections of the National Curriculum and cross-curricular provision', *Curriculum Journal*, vol. 2, No. 1, Spring.

Hirst, P.H. (1985) 'Education and diversity of belief' in M.C. Felderhof (ed) *Religious Education in a Pluralistic Society*, London: Hodder & Stoughton.

HMI (1992) *Report on Education in England 1990/91*, London: HMSO.

HMI (1993) *Report on Education in England 1991/92*, London: HMSO.

Hull, J. (1989) *The Act Unpacked*, Derby: Christian Education Movement.

Islamic Academy, The (1991) *Faith as the Basis of Education in a Multi-Faith, Multi-Cultural Country: Discussion Document II*, Cambridge: The Islamic Academy.

Kernaghan, P. (1993) *The Crusades*, Cambridge: Cambridge University Press.

King, A. and Reiss, M. (eds) (1993) *The Multicultural Dimension of the National Curriculum*, London: Falmer.

Mabud, S.A. (1992) 'A Muslim response to the Education Reform, Act 1988', *British Journal of Religious Education*, vol. 14, No. 2, Spring.

Marland, M. (1993) 'Cultures, Literatures and English' in A. Fyfe and P. Figueroa (eds) *Education for Cultural Diversity*, London: Routledge.

Mathematical Association, The (1992) *1992 GCSE Mathematics Papers: do the questions show gender and cultural bias?* Leicester: The Mathematical Association.

Mitchell, P. (1993) 'Religious Education and the Multicultural Perspective' in A. King and M. Reiss (eds) (1993) *The Multicultural Dimension of the National Curriculum*, London: Falmer.

Moon, B. and Mortimore, P. (1989) *The National Curriculum: straightjacket or safety net?* Ginger Paper 5, London: Education Reform Group.

NCC (1990) *Curriculum Guidance 8: Education for Citizenship*, York: National Curriculum Council.

NCC (1991) *NCC News* No. 5 February 1991.

NCC (1992) *Starting out with the National Curriculum*, York: National Curriculum Council.

OFSTED (1993) *Standards and Quality in Education 1992–93*, London: HMSO.

Parrinder, P. (1993) 'War of Words', *The Times Higher Education Supplement*, 1 April.

Piper, B. (1992) 'Black parents, the National Curriculum and the new management of schools: what can antiracist teachers do?' *Multicultural Teaching*, vol. 10, no. 3, pp. 7–10.

Pring, R. (1992) 'Education for a pluralist society' in M. Leicester and M. Taylor (eds) *Ethics, Ethnicity and Education*, London: Kogan Page.

Pumfrey, P.D. and Verma, G.K. (eds) (1993) *Cultural Diversity and the Curriculum*, vols 1 to 4, London, Falmer.

Rattansi, A. (1992) 'Changing the subject? Racism, culture and education' in J. Donald and A. Rattansi, 'Race', Culture and Difference, London: Sage.

Reiss, M. (1993a) 'Science' in A. King and M. Reiss (eds) *The Multicultural Dimension of the National Curriculum*, London: Falmer.

Reiss, M. (1993b) *Science Education for a Pluralist Society*, Buckingham: Open University Press.

Richardson, R. (1993) 'Bias and insults in examination questions: a case study', *Multicultural Teaching*, vol. 12, no. 1, Autumn, pp. 44–5.

Rorty, R. (1992) 'The pragmatist's progress' in S. Collini (ed.) *Interpretation and Overinterpretation*, Cambridge: Cambridge University Press.

Runnymede Trust (1993) *Equality Assurance in Schools*, London: Trentham Books with The Runnymede Trust.

Savva, H. (1990) 'The multilingual classroom' in J. Harris and J. Wilkinson (eds) *A Guide to English Language in the National Curriculum*, Cheltenham: Stanley Thornes.

SEAC (1992) *Specification for the Development of Tests in History for Pupils at the End of the Third Key Stage of the National Curriculum*, London: SEAC.

Semple, M. (1993) 'Physical education and dance' in A. King and M. Reiss (eds) *The Multicultural Dimension of the National Curriculum*, London: Falmer.

Smith, D. and Tomlinson, S. (1989) *The School Effect: A study of multi-racial comprehensives*, London: Policy Studies Institute.

Tomlinson, S. (1993) 'The Multicultural Task group: the Group that never was', in A. King and M. Reiss (eds) *The Multicultural Dimension of the National Curriculum*, London: Falmer.

Troyna, B. (1993) *Racism and Education*, Buckingham: Open University Press.

Verma, G.K. (1993) 'Cultural diversity in secondary Schools' in P.D. Pumfrey and G.K. Verma (eds) *Cultural Diversity and the Curriculum, vol 1*, London: Falmer.

Walford, R. (1993) 'Geography' in A. King and M. Reiss *The Multicultural Dimension of the National Curriculum*, London: Falmer.

Watts, S. (1993) 'Science in the National Curriculum: developing an anti-racist and multicultural perspective' in A. Fyfe and P. Figueroa, *Education for Cultural Diversity*, London: Routledge.

Webster, A. and Adelman, C. (1993) 'Education for citizenship' in G. Verma and P. Pumfrey (eds) *Cultural Diversity and the Curriculum, Vol. 2*, London: Falmer.

White, J. (1988) 'An unconstitutional National Curriculum' in D. Lawton and C. Chitty (eds) *The National Curriculum*, London: Institute of Education, London University.

Chapter 3: Ethnic Relations in the Primary Classroom

Alexander, R.J. (1984) *Primary Teaching*, London: Holt, Rinehart & Winston.

Banks, J. and Lynch, J. (eds) (1986) *Multicultural Education in Western Societies*, London: Holt.

Becker, H.S. (1952) 'Social class variations in the teacher–pupil relationship', *Journal of Educational Sociology*, 25, pp. 451–65.

Brah, A. and Minhas, R. (1988) 'Structural racism or cultural difference: schooling for Asian girls' in M. Woodhouse and A. McGrath (eds) *Family, School and Society* (pp. 215–22), London: Hodder & Stoughton.

Burrell, G. and Morgan, G. (1979) *Sociological Paradigms and Organizational Analysis*, London: Heinemann Educational.

Carrington, B. (1983) 'Sport as a side-track: an analysis of West Indian involvement in extra-curricular sport' in L. Barton and S. Walker (eds) *Race, Class and Education*, London: Croom, Helm.

Carrington, B. and Short, G. (1989) *'Race' and the Primary School*, Slough: NFER-Nelson.

Driver, G. (1977) 'Cultural competence, social power and school achievement; West Indian secondary school pupils in the West Midlands', *New Community*, 5 (4) pp. 553–9.

Driver, G. (1979) 'Classroom stress and school achievement: West Indian adolescents and their teachers', in V.S. Khan (ed.) *Minority Families in Britain: support and stress*, London: Macmillan.

Driver, G. (1980) *Beyond Underachievement: case studies of English, West*

Indian and Asian school leavers at sixteen plus, London: Commission for Racial Equality.

Foster, P. (1990) 'Cases not proven: an evaluation of two studies of teacher racism', *British Educational Research Journal*, 16 (4), pp. 335–50.

Fuller, M. (1980) 'Black girls in a London comprehensive school' in R. Deem (ed.) *Schooling for Women's Work*, London: Routledge.

Furlong, J. (1984) 'Black resistance in liberal comprehensives' in S. Delamont (ed.) *Readings in Interaction in The Classroom*, London: Methuen.

Gillborn, D.A. (1988) 'Ethnicity and educational opportunity: case studies of West Indian male–white teacher relationships', *British Journal of Sociology of Education*, 9 (4), pp., 371–85.

Gillborn, D.A. (1990) *'Race' Ethnicity and Education*, London: Unwin Hyman.

Gillborn, D.A. and Drew, D. (1992) '"Race", class and school effects', *New Community*, 18 (4), pp. 551–65.

Gray, J., McPherson, A.F. and Raffe, D. (1983) *Reconstructions of Secondary Education: theory, myth and practice since the war*, London: Routledge.

Green, P.A. (1985) 'Multi-ethnic teaching and pupils' self-concepts', Annex to ch. 2 of *Education for All*, the final report of the Committee of Inquiry into the Education of Children from Ethnic Minority Groups, London: HMSO.

Grugeon, E. and Woods, P. (1990) *Educating All: multicultural perspectives in the primary school*, London: Routledge.

Hargreaves, D.H., Hester, S.K. and Mellor, F.J. (1975) *Deviance in Classrooms*, London: Routledge.

Leaman, O. and Carrington, B. (1985) 'Athleticism and the reproduction of gender and ethnic statuses', *Leisure Studies*, p. 214.

Leiter, K.C.W. (1974) 'Ad hocing in the schools' in A.V. Cicourel (ed.) *Language Use and School Performance*, New York: Academic.

Mac an Ghaill, M. (1988) *Young, Gifted and Black: student–teacher relations in the schooling of black youth*, Milton Keynes: Open University Press.

Mac an Ghaill, M. (1992) 'Coming of age in 1980s England: reconceptualising black students' schooling experience', in D. Gill, B. Mayor and M. Blair (eds) *Racism and Education: structure and strategies*, London: Sage.

Massey, I. (1991) *More than Skin Deep: developing anti-racist multicultural education in school*, Sevenoaks: Hodder & Stoughton.

Mortimore, P., Sammons, P., Stoll, L., Lewis, D. and Ecob, R. (1988) *School Matters: the junior years*, Wells, Somerset: Open Books.

Nuttall, D. and Goldstein, H. (1990) *Differences in Examination Performance*, RS 1277/90, London: ILEA Research and Statistics Branch.

Parekh, B. (1985) 'Background to the West Indian tragedy', *Times Educational Supplement*, 22 March.

Rist, R.C. (1970) 'Student social class and teacher expectations: the self-fulfilling prophecy in ghetto eduction', *Harvard Education Review*, 40, pp. 411–51.

Rutter, M., Maugham, B., Mortimore, P. and Ouston, J. (1979) *Fifteen Thousand Hours*, London: Open Books.

Schutz, A. (1970) *On Phenomenology and Social Relations: selected writings*, ed. H.R. Wagner, Chicago: Chicago University Press.

Sharp, R. and Green, A. (1975) *Education and Social Control: a study in progressive primary education*, London: Routledge.

Smith, D. and Tomlinson, S. (1989) *The School Effect*, London: PSI/Heinemann.

Tomlinson, D. (1984) *Home and School in Multicultural Britain*, London: Batsford.

Troyna, B. (ed.) (1987) *Racial Inequality in Education*, London: Tavistock.

Troyna, B. and Hatcher, R. (1992) *Racism in Children's Lives*, London: Routledge.

Wright, C. (1987) 'Black students – white teachers' in B. Troyna (ed.) *Racial Inequality in Education*, London: Tavistock.

Wright, C. (1992) *Race Relations in the Primary School*, London: David Fulton.

Wright, C. (1993) 'Early education: multiracial primary school classrooms' in R. Gomm and P. Woods (eds) *Educational Research in Action*, Milton Keynes: Open University Press.

Chapter 4: Ethnic Relations in Secondary Schools

DES (Department of Education and Science) (1985) *Education for All*, report of the Committee of Inquiry into the Education of Children from Ethnic Minority Groups (Swann Report), London: HMSO.

Parekh, B. (1990) 'Britain and the Social Logic of Pluralism' in Commission for Racial Equality, *Britain: A Plural Society*, London: CRE.

Pumfrey, P. and Verma, G.K. (1992) (eds) *Cultural Diversity and the National Curriculum: Volume 1 – The Foundation Subjects and RE in Secondary Schools*, London: Falmer.

Pumfrey, P. and Verma, G.K. (1993) (eds) *Cultural Diversity and the National Curriculum: Volume 3 – The Foundation Subjects and RE in Primary Schools*, London: Falmer.

Rex, J. and Tomlinson, S. (1979) *Colonial Immigrants in a British City*, London: Routledge.

Tomlinson, S. (1990) 'Race relations and the urban context' in P.D. Pumfrey and G.K. Verma (eds), *Race Relations and Urban Education: Contexts and Promising Practices*, London: Falmer.

Verma, G.K. (1990) 'Inter-ethnic relationships in schools', report based on a study of schools in Greater Manchester, University of Manchester.

Verma, G.K. (1992) 'Cultural diversity in secondary schools: its nature, extent and curricular implications' in P. Pumfrey and G.K. Verma (eds), *Cultural Diversity and the National Curriculum: Volume 1 – The Foundation Subjects and RE in Secondary Schools*, London: Falmer.

Verma, G.K. and Pumfrey, P. (1992) (eds) *Cultural Diversity and the National*

Curriculum: Volume 2 - Cross-Curricular Themes in Secondary Schools, London: Falmer.

Verma, G.K. and Pumfrey, P. (1994) (eds) *Cultural Diversity and the National Curriculum: Volume 4 – Cross-Curricular Themes in Primary Schools*, London, Falmer.

Verma, G.K., Zec, P. and Skinner, G.D. (1994) *The Ethnic Crucible*, London: Falmer.

Chapter 5: The Schooling of Young Black Women

Ainley, P. (1988) *From School to YTS: education and training in England and Wales 1944–1987*, Milton Keynes: Open University Press.

Alba, R.D. (1985) (ed.) *Ethnicity and Race in the U.S.A: toward the twenty-first century*, London: Routledge.

Allen, S. (1987) 'Gender, race, and class in the 1980s', in C. Husband (ed.) *Race in Britain, Continuity and Change: the second edition*, London: Hutchinson.

Amos, V., and Parmar, P. (1981) 'Resistances and responses: experiences of black girls in Britain', in A. McRobbie and T. McCabe (eds) *Feminism for Girls: an adventure story*, London: Routledge.

Barrett, M., and McIntosh, M. (1982) *The Anti-Social Family*, London: Verso.

Barrow, C. (1986) 'Finding support: strategies for survival', *Social and Economic Studies*, special number; J. Massiah (ed.) *Women in the Caribbean* (Part 1): Institute of Social and Economic Research, University of the West Indies, vol. 35, no. 2.

Besson, J. (1993) 'Reputation and respectability reconsidered: a new perspective on Afro-Caribbean peasant women', in J.H. Momsen (ed.) *Women and Change in the Caribbean*, London: James Currey.

Bettelheim, B., and Janowitz, M. (1977) 'The Consequences of Social Mobility' in J. Stone (ed.) *Race, Ethnicity and Social Change*, North Scituate, Mass.: Duxbury.

Brah, A. (1992) 'Difference, diversity and differentiation' in J. Donald and A. Rattansi (eds) 'Race', Culture and Difference, London: Sage.

Brake, M. (1985) *Comparative Youth Culture: The Sociology of Youth Subcultures in America, Britain and Canada*, London: Routledge.

Brown, P. (1987) *Schooling Ordinary Kids: Inequality, Unemployment, and the New Vocationalism*, London: Tavistock.

Bryan, B., Dadzie, S., and Scafe, S. (1985) *The Heart of the Race: Black Women's Lives in Britain*, London: Virago.

Carby, H.V. (1982a) 'Schooling in Babylon' in CCCS, *The Empire Strikes Back: Race and Racism in 70s Britain*, London: Hutchinson.

Carby, H.V. (1982b) 'White woman listen! Black feminism and the boundaries of sisterhood' in CCCS, *The Empire Strikes Back: Race and Racism in 70s Britain*, London: Hutchinson.

Chevannes, M. (1979) 'The Black Arrow Supplementary School Project', *The Social Science Teacher*, vol. 8, no. 4.

Clark, R.M. (1983) *Family Life and School Achievement: why poor black children succeed or fail*, Chicago: University of Chicago Press.

Collins, H.P. (1990) *Black Feminist Thought*, London: Unwin Hyman.

Coultas, V. (1989) 'Black girls and self-esteem', *Gender and Education* special issue: Race, Gender and Education, vol. 1, no. 3.

Cross, M., Wrench, J., and Barnett, S. (1990) *Ethnic Minorities and the Career Service: an investigation into processes of assessment and placement*, research paper series no., 78. Employment Department, Sheffield: HMSO.

Davis, A. (1982) *Women, Race and Class*, London: The Women's Press.

Dex, S. (1982) 'West Indians, further education and labour markets', *New Community*, vol. 10, no. 2 (winter) pp. 191–205.

Dex, S. (1983) 'The second generation: West Indian female school leavers' in A. Phizacklea (ed.) *One Way Ticket*, London: Routledge.

Drew, D., and Gray, J. (1991) 'The black and white gap in examination results; a statistical critique of a decade of research', *New Community*, vol. 17, no. 2.

Drew, D., Gray, J., and Sime, N. (1992) *Against the Odds: the education and labour experiences of black young people*, research paper series no. 68, Employment Department, Sheffield: HMSO.

Driver, G. (1980) *Beyond Underachievement: case studies of English, West Indian and Asian school leavers at sixteen plus*, London: Commission for Racial Equality.

Durant-Gonzalez, V. (1982) 'The realm of female familial responsibility' in J. Massiah (ed.) *Women in the Caribbean Research Papers, Vol. 2: Women and the family*, Cave Hill, Barbados: ISER, UWI.

Eggleston, S.J., Dunn, D., Anjali, M., and Wright, C. (1986) *Education for Some: the educational and vocational experiences of 15–18-year-old members of minority ethnic groups*, Stoke-on-Trent: Trentham.

Employment Gazette (1993) 'Ethnic origin and the labour market', London: HMSO, January.

Foner, N. (1979) *Jamaica Farewell: Jamaican migrants in London*, London: Routledge & Kegan Paul.

Foster, P. (1991) 'Case still not proven: a reply to Cecile Wright', *British Educational Research Journal*, vol. 17, no. 2.

Fryer, P. (1984) *Staying Power: the history of black people in Britain*, London: Pluto.

Fuller, M. (1978) 'Dimensions of gender in a school', unpublished PhD thesis, University of Bristol.

Fuller, M. (1980) 'Black girls in a London comprehensive school' in R. Deem (ed.) *Schooling for Womens' Work*, London: Routledge.

Fuller, M. (1982) 'Young, female and black' in E. Cashmore and B. Troyna (eds) *Black Youth in Crisis*, London: George Allen & Unwin.

Gibson, A and Barrow, J. (1986) *The Unequal Struggle; the findings of a West Indian research investigation into the underachievement of West Indian children in British schools*, London: Centre for Caribbean Studies.

Gillborn, D. (1990) *'Race', Ethnicity and Education: teaching and learning in multi-ethnic schools*, London: Unwin Hyman.

Gillborn, D., and Drew, D. (1992) '"Race", class and school effects', *New Community*, vol. 18, no. 4.

Gillborn, D., and Drew, D. (1993) 'The politics of research: some observations on methodological purity', *New Community*, vol. 19, no. 2.

Gilroy, P. (1987) *There Ain't No Black in the Union Jack*, London: Hutchinson.

Gilroy, P. (1990) 'The end of anti-racism', *New Community*, vol. 17, no. 1, October.

Glazer, N., and Moynihan. D.P. (1963) *Beyond the Melting Pot: the Negroes, Puerto Ricans, Jews, Italians and Irish of New York City*, Cambridge, Mass: MIT Press.

Gonzalez, N.S. (1985) 'Household and the family in the Caribbean: some definitions and concepts' in F.C. Steady (ed.) *The Black Woman Cross-Culturally*, Cambridge, Mass: Schenkman.

Griffin, C. (1985) *Typical Girls? Young women from school to the job market*, London: Routledge.

Guy, W., and Menter, I. (1992) 'Local management of resources: who benefits?' in D. Gill, B. Mayor and M. Blair (eds) *Racism and Education*, London: Sage/Open University.

Hall, S. and Jefferson, T. (eds) (1976) *Resistance through Rituals; youth sub-cultures in post war Britain*, London: Hutchinson.

Hammersley, M. (1992) 'A response to Barry Troyna's "Children, 'Race' and racism: the limits of research and policy"', *British Journal of Educational Studies*, vol. 40, no. 2.

Hammersley, M., and Gomm, R. (1993) 'A response to Gillborn and Drew on "Race, class and School effects"', *New Community*, vol. 19, no. 2.

Jones, J. (1985) *Labour of Love, Labour of Sorrow: black women, work and the family, from slavery to the present day*, New York: Vintage.

Jones, T. (1993) *Britain's Ethnic Minorities*, London: PSI.

Justus, J.B. (1985) 'Women's role in West Indian society' in F.C. Steady (ed.) *The Black Woman Cross-Culturally*, Cambridge, Mass.: Schenkman.

Knowles, C. and Mercer, S. (1992) 'Feminism and antiracism: an exploration of the political possibilities' in J. Donald and A. Rattansi (eds) *'Race', Culture and Difference*, London: Sage.

Landry, B., and Jendrek, M. (1978) 'The employment of wives from black middle class families', *Journal of Marriage and the Family*, November.

Lawton, D. (1992) *Education and Politics in the 1990s*, London: Falmer.

Lee, J. (1982) 'Society and culture' in F. Litton (ed.) *Unequal Achievement: the Irish experience 1957–1982*, Dublin: Institute of Public Administration.

Lees, S. (1986) *Losing Out: Sexuality and Adolescent Girls*, London: Hutchinson.

Leicester, M. and Taylor, M. (eds) (1992) *Ethics, Ethnicity and Education*, London: Kogan Page.

Mac an Ghaill, M. (1988) *Young, Gifted and Black: student teacher relations in the schooling of black youth*, Milton Keynes: Open University Press.

Mac an Ghaill, M. (1989) 'Coming of age in 1980s England: reconceptualising black students' schooling experiences, *British Journal of Sociology of Education*, vol. 10, no. 3.

Mac an Ghaill, M. (1993) 'Beyond the white norm: the use of qualitative methods in the study of black youths' schooling in England' in P. Woods and M. Hammersley (eds) *Gender and Ethnicity in Schools: ethnographic accounts*, London: Routledge/Open University.

McAdoo, P.H. (ed.) (1988) *Black Families*, 2nd edn, London: Sage.

McDowell, D.E. (1990) 'Reading family matters' in C.A. Wall (ed.) *Changing Our Own Words*, London: Routledge.

McRobbie, A. (1990) *Feminism and Youth Culture*, London: Macmillan.

McRobbie, A., and Garber, J. (1976) 'Girls and subcultures: an exploration' in S. Hall and T. Jefferson (eds) *Resistance Through Rituals: youth subcultures in post-war Britain*, London: Hutchinson.

Mama, A. (1992) 'Black women and the British state: race, class and gender analysis for the 1990s' in P. Braham *et al.* (ed.) *Racism and Antiracism: inequalities, opportunities and policies*, London: Sage.

Massiah, J. (1986) 'Work in the lives of Caribbean women' *Social and Economic Studies*, special number: J. Massiah (ed.) *Women in the Caribbean* (Part 1): Institute of Social and Economic Research, University of the West Indies, vol. 35, no. 2.

Mirza, H.S. (1992) *Young, Female and Black*, London: Routledge.

Mirza, H.S. (1993) 'The social construction of black womanhood in British educational research: towards a new understanding' in M. Arnot and K. Weiler (eds) *Feminism and Social Justice in Education*, London, Falmer.

Mohammed P. (1988) 'The Caribbean family revisited' in P. Mohammed and C. Shepherd (eds) *Gender in Caribbean Development*, Women and Development Studies Project, St Augustine, Trinidad: University of the West Indies.

Moses, Y.T. (1985) 'Female status, the family, and male dominance in a West Indian community' in F. Steday (ed.) *The Black Woman Cross Culturally*, Cambridge, Mass.: Schenkman.

Moynihan, D. (1967) 'The negro family: a case for national action' in L. Rainwater and W.L. Yancey, *The Moynihan Report and the Politics of Controversy*, Cambridge, Mass.: MIT Press.

Murray, C. (1984) *Losing Ground: American Social Policy 1950–80*, New York: Basic.

OFSTED (Office for Standards in Education) (1993) *Access and Achievement in Urban Education*, London: HMSO.

Palmer, F. (ed.) (1987) *Anti-racism: an assault on education and value*, London: Sherwood.

Pearson, D. (1981) *Race, Class and Political Activism: a study of West Indians in Britain*, Farnborough: Gower.

Phizacklea, A. (1982) 'Migrant women and wage labour: the case of West Indian women in Britain' in J. West (ed.) *Work, Women and the Labour Market*, London: Routledge.

Phizacklea, A. (1983) 'In the front line' in A. Phizacklea (ed.) *One Way Ticket*, London: Routledge.

Phoenix, A. (1987) 'Theories of gender and black families', in G. Weiner and M. Arnot (eds) *Gender Under Scrutiny*, London: Hutchinson/Open University Press.

Powell, D. (1986) 'Caribbean women and their response to familial experiences' *Social and Economic Studies*, special number: J. Massiah (ed.) *Women in the Caribbean* (Part 1): Institute of Social and Economic Research, University of the West Indies, vol. 35, no. 2.

Ratcliffe, P. (1988) 'Race, class and residence: Afro-Caribbean households in Britain' in C. Brock (ed.) *The Caribbean in Europe: aspects of the West Indian experience in Britain, France and the Netherlands*, London: Frank Cass.

Rattansi, A. (1992) 'Changing the subject? Racism, culture and education' in J. Donald and A. Rattansi (eds) *'Race', Culture and Difference*, London, Sage/Open University.

Reid, E. (1989) 'Black girls talking' *Gender and Education*, special issue: *Race, Gender and Education*, vol. 1, no. 3.

Riley, K. (1985) 'Black girls speak for themselves' in G. Weiner (ed.) *Just a Bunch of Girls*, Milton Keynes: Open University.

Rutter, M., Gray, G., Maughan, B., and Smith, A. (1982) 'School experiences and the first year of employment', unpublished report to the DES.

Sharpe, S. (1987) [1976] *Just Like a Girl: how girls learn to be women*, Harmondsworth: Penguin.

Skellington, R. (1992) *'Race' in Britain Today*, London: Sage/Open University.

Solomos, J. (1993) *Race and Racism in Britain*, 2nd edn, London: Routledge.

Stack, C. (1982) [1974] *All Our Kin: strategies for survival in a black community*, New York: Harper & Row.

Stone, K. (1983) 'Motherhood and waged work: West Indian, Asian and white mothers compared' in A. Phizacklea (ed.) *One Way Ticket*, London: Routledge.

Stone, M. (1985) [1981] *The Education of the Black Child: the myth of multicultural education*, London: Fontana.

Sutton, C., and Makiesky-Barrow, S. (1977) 'Social inequality and sexual status in Barbados' in A. Schlegel (ed.) *Sexual Stratification: a cross-cultural view*, New York: Columbia University Press.

Thorogood, N. (1987) 'Race, class and gender: the politics of housework' in J. Brannen and G. Wilson (eds) *Give and Take in Families*, London: Allen & Unwin.

Tomlinson, S. (1982) 'Response of the English education system to the children of immigrant parentage' in M. Leggon (ed.) *Research in Ethnic*

Relations, vol. 3.

Tomlinson, S. (1985) 'The "Black Education" Movement' in M. Arnot (ed.) *Race and Gender*, Oxford: Pergamon Press/Open University.

Tomlinson, S. (1993) 'The Multicultural Task Group: the Group that never was' in A. King and M. Reiss (eds) *The Multicultural Dimension of the National Curriculum*, London: Falmer.

Troyna, B. (1991) 'Children, "race" and racism: the limitations of research and policy', *British Journal of Educational Studies*, vol. 39, no. 4.

Verma, G.K. and Ashworth, B. (1985) *Ethnicity and Educational Achievement*, London: Macmillan.

Wallace, C. (1987) *For Richer for Poorer: growing up in and out of work*, London: Tavistock.

Weis, L. (1985) *Between Two Worlds: black students in an urban community college*, London: Routledge.

Willis, P. (1977) *Learning to Labour: how working class kids get working class jobs*, Farnborough: Saxon House.

Wilson, W.J. (1987) *The Truly Disadvantaged: the inner city, the underclass, and public policy*, Chicago: University of Chicago Press.

Wiltshire-Brodber, R. (1988) 'Gender, race and class in the Caribbean' in P. Mohammed and C. Shepherd (eds) *Gender in Caribbean Development*, Women and Development Studies Project, St Augustine, Trinidad: University of the West Indies.

Wright C. (1986) 'School processes: an ethnographic study' in S.J. Eggleston *et al.*, *Education for Some: the educational and vocational experiences of 15–18-year-old members of ethnic minority groups*, Stoke-on-Trent: Trentham.

Wright, C. (1987) 'The relations between teachers and Afro-Caribbean pupils: Observing multicultural classrooms' in G. Weiner and M. Arnot (eds) *Gender Under Scrutiny*, London: Hutchinson/Open University.

Wright, C. (1990) 'Comments in reply to the article by P. Foster: case not proven', *British Educational Research Journal*, vol. 16, no. 4.

Wulff, H. (1988) *Twenty Girls: growing up, ethnicity and excitement in a south London Microculture*, Stockholm Studies in Anthropology, 21, Stockholm: University of Stockholm.

Chapter 6: Ethnic Relations in All-White Schools

Ackers, L. (1991) 'If you ain't got a puncture, there's no need to mend it', conference report from Southwest Anti-Racist Group, Plymouth.

Anderson, B. (1989) 'Anti-racism and education: strategies for the 1990s', *Multicultural Teaching*, 7 (3), pp. 3–5.

Britain: an official handbook, (1989), London: HMSO.

Census 1991: county reports, London: HMSO.

Craft, M. (1981) *Teaching in a Multicultural Society*, Lewes: Falmer.

DCC (Devon County Council) (1992) *Promoting Quality: RE in the basic curriculum*, Exeter: DCC.

DES (Department of Education and Science) (1987) *Educational Support Grants*, Circular 1/87, London: HMSO.

DES (1989a), *Ethnically-based Statistics on School Pupils*, Circular 16/89, London: HMSO.

DES (1989b), *From Policy To Practice*, London: HMSO.

Diamond, I. and Clarke, S. (1989) *The Changing Population of Britain*, Centre for Economic Policy Research, London: Blackwell.

Hall, S. (1981) 'The whites of their eyes. Racist ideologies and the media' in G. Bridges and R. Hunt (eds) (1981) *Silver Linings*, Lawrence & Wishart.

HMI (Her Majesty's Inspectorate) (1992) *Annual Report 1990–1991*, London: HMSO.

Hobman, J. (1992) 'Teaching about prejudice and discrimination', *Multicultural Teaching*, 10 (3) pp. 19–22.

Holman, F. (1993) '2b or not 2b. Anti-racist education and the demise of the LEAs', *Multicultural Teaching*, 11 (2) pp. 20–5.

Jay, E. (1992) *Keep Them in Birmingham*, London: Commission for Racial Equality.

Klein, G. (1993) *Towards Race Equality*, Stoke-on-Trent: Trentham.

Lawlor, M. (1994) 'This crazy National Curriculum,' *The Observer*, 21 February 1994.

McCarthy, C. (1990) *Race and Curriculum*, London: Falmer.

McFarlan, S. (1993) Complete collection of LEA Policies on Multicultural and Anti-racist Education, located in the library of the University of Plymouth.

McKeith, L. (1988) 'The Olaudah Equiano Bicentenary Project' in *Better to Light A Candle*, Perspectives, 39, University of Exeter.

Naidoo, B. (1992) *Through Whose Eyes?*, Stoke-on-Trent: Trentham

NCC (National Curriculum Council) (1989) *From Policy to Practice*, York: NCC.

NCC (1990a) *The Whole Curriculum, No. 3*, York: NCC.

NCC (1990b) *Curriculum Guidance on Education for Citizenship*, York: NCC.

Notre Dame School, Plymouth (1993) *News Desk*, no. 6.

Parents' Charter, April, 1991.

Popple, K., Harris, D., and Popple, S. (1990) An examination of racism in a 'mono-cultural city', paper given to the British Sociological Association Annual conference, April.

Population Trends (1991), London: HMSO.

Powell, J. (1993) 'Attitudes to multicultural education in a white highlands school', unpublished essay, available from the School of Education, University of Exeter.

Runnymede Trust (1993) *Equality Assurance in Schools*, Stoke-on-Trent: Trentham

Shaikh, M and Hawkins, L., (1992), 'Strange fruit', *Multicultural Teaching*, 10 (1) pp 33–7

Smith, J., (1987), 'Working with the community', in *Ethnicity and Prejudice in 'White Highland' Schools*, Perspectives, 35, University of Exeter.

Social Trends (1993), London: HMSO.

Stocker, G. (1987) 'Working with very young children' in *Ethnicity and Prejudice in 'White Highland' Schools, Perspectives*, 35, University of Exeter.

Taylor, W.H. (1993a) 'Educating British children for European citizenship', *European Journal of Education*, 28 (4), pp. 437–44.

Taylor, W.H. (1993b) 'The multi-ethnic inner city: its teaching practice potential for undergraduate (secondary) students of education in non-city training institutions', *Cambridge Journal of Education*, 23 (3), pp. 305–18.

Tomlinson, S. (1990) *Multicultural Education in White Schools*, London: Batsford.

Chapter 7: The LEA and TEC Context

All-Party Parliamentary Group on Race and Community, National Union of Teachers and Runnymede Trust (1993) *Section 11: the Future of Funding for Race Equality*, London: Runnymede Trust.

Bagley, C.A. (1992) *Back to the Future. Section 11 of the Local Government Act 1966: Local Education Authorities and multicultural/anti-racist education*, Slough: NFER.

Bagley, C.A. (1993a) *An Enterprising Initiative? Training and enterprise councils and the ethnic minority grant*, Slough: NFER.

Bagley, C.A. (1993b) *Governor Training and Equal Opportunities*, Slough: NFER.

Braham, P., Rattansi, A. and Skellington, R. (eds) (1992) *Racism and Anti-racism: inequalities, opportunities and policies*, London: Sage with The Open University.

Chatrik, B. and de Sousa, E. (1993) *Where Are They Now? Black young people and the youth training guarantee*, Nottingham: Black Employment and Training Forum with the Runnymede Trust.

Commission for Racial Equality (1988) *Learning in Terror: a survey of racial harassment in schools and colleges*, London: CRE.

Curriculum Council for Wales (1991) *Community Understanding: a framework for cross-curricular themes in Wales*, Advisory Paper 11, Cardiff: CCW.

Curriculum Council for Wales (1993) *Educating for Cultural Diversity in Wales*, Cardiff: CCW.

Gates, B. (1993) *Time for Religious Education and Teachers to Match. A digest of under-provision*, Lancaster: Religious Education Council.

GB: DES (Great Britain: Department of Education and Science) (1989) *Ethnically-based Statistics on School Pupils*, Circular 16/89, London: DES.

GB: DES & WO (Great Britain: Department of Education and Science and Welsh Office) (1989) *Ethnically-based Statistics on School Teachers*, Circular 8/89 (DES) and 12/89 (Welsh Office), London/Cardiff: DES & WO.

GB: DFE (Great Britain: Department for Education) (1994) *Religious Education and Collective Worship*, Circular 1/94, London: DFE.

GB: DFE & WO (Welsh Office) (1992) *Choice and Diversity. A New Framework for Schools*, London: DFE.

GB: HO (Great Britain: Home Office) (1989) *A Scrutiny of Grants under Section 11 of the Local Government Act: final report, December 1988*, London: Home Office.

GB: HO (1990a) *Section 11 Ethnic Minority Grants: grant administration, policy and guidelines*, London: Home Office.

GB: HO (1990b) *Section 11 of the Local Government Act 1966*, Circular 78/90, London: Home Office.

GB (Great Britain) Statutes (1988) *Education Reform Act 1988*, Chapter 40, London: HMSO.

GB: Statutes (1993) *Education Act 1993*, Chapter 35, London: HMSO.

GBP: HofC (Great Britain Parliament: House of Commons) (1985) *Education for All*, report of the Committee of Inquiry into the Education of Children from Ethnic Minority Groups (Swann Report), Cmnd 9453, London: HMSO.

Jones, T. (1993) *Britain's Ethnic Minorities*, London: Policy Studies Institute.

Keys, W. and Fernandes, C. (1990) *A Survey of School Governing Bodies*, vol. 1, Slough: NFER.

King, A. and Reiss, M. J. (eds) (1993) *The Multicultural Dimension of the National Curriculum*, London: Falmer.

LARRIE (Local Authorities Race Relations Information Exchange) (1993) *Section 11 Survey Report: part one*, London: LARRIE.

Leicestershire TEC (1993) *Annual Report 1992–3*, Leicester: Leicestershire TEC.

McMahon, A. and Wallace, M. (1993) 'Development planning: surprise outcomes for multiracial primary schools', *Management in Education*, / (1), 14–15.

Meager, N. and Court, G. (1993) *TECs and Equal Opportunities: a review paper for the G10 Special Needs and Equal Opportunities Sub-Group*, Brighton: Institute of Manpower Studies.

Meager, N. and Honey, S. (1993) *People with Special Training Needs and TECs: a review paper for the G10 Special Needs Sub-Group*, Brighton: Institute of Manpower Studies.

National TEC Council Equal Opportunities and Special Needs Sub-Group (1993) *Feedback on the Consultation Process*, Brighton: Institute of Manpower Studies.

NCC (National Curriculum Council) (1990a) *The Whole Curriculum*, Curriculum Guidance 3, York: NCC.

NCC (1990b) *Education for Citizenship*, Curriculum Guidance 8, York: NCC.

NCC (1993a) *Spiritual and Moral Development: a discussion paper*, York: NCC.

NCC (1993b) *Analysis of SACRE Reports 1993*, York: NCC.

NCC (1993c) *Analysis of Agreed Syllabuses for Religious Education*, York: NCC.

OFSTED (Office for Standards in Education) (1993) *Handbook for the Inspection of Schools*, London: OFSTED.

OFSTED (1994) *Spiritual, Moral, Social and Cultural Development*, Discussion Paper, London: OFSTED.

Ouseley, H. (1990) 'Resisting institutional change' in W. Ball and J. Solomos, J. (eds) *Race and Local Politics*, London: Macmillan.

Pumfrey, P. and Verma, G. (eds) (1993) *The Foundation Subjects and Religious Education in Primary Schools*, London: Falmer.

Runnymede Trust (1993) *Equality Assurance in Schools: quality, identity, society*, Stoke-on-Trent: Trentham.

SCAA (School Curriculum and Assessment Authority) (1994) *Model Syllabuses for Religious Education Consultation Document: Introduction; Model 1; Model 2; Model Attainment Targets; Working Group Reports; and Glossary of Terms*, London: SCAA.

Taylor, M.J. (1991) *SACREs: their formation, composition, operation and role on RE and worship*, Slough: NFER.

Taylor, M.J. (1992a) 'Learning fairness through empathy: pupils' perspectives on putting policy into practice' in M. LEICESTER and M.J. TAYLOR (eds) *Ethics, Education and Ethnicity*, London: Kogan Page.

Taylor, M.J. (1992b) *Multicultural Antiracist Education After ERA: concerns, constraints and challenges*, Slough: NFER.

Taylor, M.J. (1992c) *Equality after ERA?* Slough: NFER.

Taylor, M.J. (1992d) 'Empowering SACREs to support RE', *Resource*, 15 (1), 2–4.

Taylor, M.J. (1994, forthcoming) *SACREs: current controversies and cultural diversity*, Slough: NFER.

Tomlinson, S. (1993) A nationalistic curriculum for white superiority?, *ACE Bulletin*, 51, 10–11.

Troyna, B. and Hatcher, R. (1992) *Racism in Children's Lives: a study of mainly white primary schools*, London: Routledge.

Verma, G. and Pumfrey, P. (eds) (1993) *Cross Curricular Contexts: themes and dimensions in primary schools*, London: Falmer.

Verma, G. and Pumfrey, P. (eds) (1993) *Cross Curricular Contexts: themes and dimensions in secondary schools*, London: Falmer.

Chapter 8: The Local Management of Schools and Racial Equality

Adams, C. (1993) 'Week By Week', *Education*, 4 June, p. 427.

Arnot, M. (1989–90) 'Consultation or legitimation? Race and gender politics and the making of the National Curriculum', *Critical Social Policy*, 27, pp. 20–38.

Bagley, C. (1992) *Back to the Future. Section 11 of the Local Government Act 1966: LEAs and multicultural/anti-racist education*, Slough: NFER.

Ball, S. (1990) *Politics and Policy Making in Education*, London: Routledge.

Ball, S. (1993) 'Education markets, choice and social class: the market as a class strategy in the UK and USA', *British Journal of Sociology of Education*, 14, 1, pp. 3–20.

Ball, W., Gulam, W., and Troyna, B. (1990) 'Pragmatism or retreat? Funding policy, local government and the marginalisation of anti-racist education' in W. Ball and J. Solomos (eds) *Race and Local Politics*, London: Macmillan, pp. 78–94.

Berger, N. (1990) *The School Meals Service*, Plymouth: Northcote House.

Briault, E. (1976) 'A distributed system of educational administration', *International Review of Education*, 22, 4, pp. 429–39.

Burton, L., and Weiner, G. (1990) 'Social justice and the National Curriculum', *Research Papers in Education*, 5, 3, pp. 203–27.

Butcher, H. *et al.* (1990) *Local Government and Thatcherism*, London: Routledge.

Caldwell, B. (199) 'School-based decision-making and management: international developments' in J. Chapman (ed.) *School-Based Decision-Making and Management*, Lewes: Falmer, pp. 3–28.

Cashmore, E., and Troyna, B. (1990) *Introduction to Race Relations*, 2nd edn, Lewes: Falmer.

CDC (Community Development Council) (1990) *Minority Ethnic Communities and School Governing Bodies*, London: CDC/NCC/AGIT.

Coopers and Lybrand (1988) *Local Management of Schools: A Report to the Department of Education and Science*, London: HMSO.

Couldron, J., and Boulton, P. (1991) '"Happiness" as a criterion of parents' choice of school', *Journal of Education Policy*, 6, 2, pp. 169–78.

Dale, R. (1989) *The State and Education Policy*, Milton Keynes: Open University Press.

Darlington, S. (1992) 'What about the losers?' *Education*, 25 September, p. 251.

Deem, R. (1989) 'The new school governing bodies: are gender and race on the agenda?' *Gender and Education*, 1, 3, pp. 247–60.

Deem, R. (1993) 'Educational reform and school governing bodies in England 1986–1992' in M. Preedy (ed.) *Managing the Effective School*, London: Paul Chapman, pp. 204–19.

DES (Department of Education and Science) (1985) *Education for All*, London: HMSO (Swann Report).

Dixon, R. (1991) 'Repercussions of LMS', *Educational Management and Administration*, 19, 1, pp. 52–61.

Dorn, A. and Hibbert, P. (1987) 'A comedy of errors: Section 11 funding and education' in B. Troyna (ed.) *Racial Inequality in Education*, London: Tavistock, pp. 59–76.

Edelman, M. (1977) *Political Language: Words that Succeed and Policies that Fail*, New York: Academic.

Esp, D. (1989) 'The Changed Role of the LEA under Financial Delegation' in R. Levacic (ed.) *Financial Management in Education*, Milton Keynes: Open University Press, pp. 170–8.

Gilroy, P. (1990) 'The end of anti-racism' in W. Ball and J. Solomos (eds) *Race and Local Politics*, London: Macmillan, pp. 191–209.

Glendinning, C. (1983) 'School meals: privatisation, stigma and "local" autonomy' in D. Bull and P. Wilding (eds) *Thatcherism and the Poor*, London: CPAG, pp. 48–52.

Guy, W., and Menter, I. (1992) 'Local management: who benefits?' in D. Gill, B. Mayor and M. Blair (eds) *Racism and Education: structures and strategies*, London: Sage, pp. 151–68.

Haviland, J. (ed.) (1988) *Take Care, Mr. Baker!*, London: Fourth Estate.

Hindess, B. (ed.) (1990) *Reactions to the Right*, London: Routledge.

Hutchinson, G. (1993) 'To boldly go: shaping the future without the LEA', *Local Government Policy Making*, 19, 5, pp. 9–14.

Jeffries, G. and Streatfield, D. (1989) *The Reconstruction of School Governing Bodies*, Slough: NFER.

Kallos, D., and Lundgren, U. (1979) *Curriculum as a Pedagogical Problem*, Stockholm: GWK Gleerup.

Kean, H. (1991) 'Managing Education: the local authority dimension', *Journal of Education Policy*, 6, 2, pp. 145–54.

Kumar, V. (1993) *Poverty and Inequality in the UK: the effects on children*, London: National Children's Bureau.

Lee, T. (1990) *Formula Funding and Social Disadvantage: summary of LEA methods*, Centre for the Analysis of Social Policy, University of Bath.

Macdonald, I., *et al*. (1989) *Murder in the Playground*, London: Longsight.

MacLeod, D. (1993) 'Cities face school spending squeeze', *Guardian*, 26 July, p. 4.

Myers, K. (1990) 'Review of "Equal opportunities in the new era"', *Education*, 5 October, p. 295.

Richardson, R. (1992) 'Race policies and programmes under attack: two case-studies for the 1990s' in D. Gill, B. Mayor and M. Blair (eds) *Racism and Education: structures and strategies*, London: Sage, pp. 134–50.

Seddon, T., Angus, L. and Poole, M. (1990) 'Pressures on the move to school-based decision-making and management' in J. Chapman (ed.) *School-Based Decision-Making and Management*, Lewes: Falmer, pp. 29–54.

Troyna, B. (1984) 'Multicultural education? Emancipation or containment?' in L. Barton and S. Walker (eds) *Social Crisis and Educational Research*, Beckenham: Croom Helm, pp. 75–97.

Troyna, B. (1989) 'A new planet? Tackling racial inequality in all-white schools and colleges' in G.K. Verma (ed.) *Education for All: a landmark in pluralism*, Lewes: Falmer, pp. 175–91.

Troyna, B. (1992) '"Can You See the Join?" An historical analysis of multicultural and anti-racist education policies' in D. Gill, B. Mayor and M. Blair (eds) *Racism and Education: structures and strategies*, London: Sage, pp. 63–91.

Troyna, B. (1993) *Racism and Education: Research Perspectives*, Buckingham: Open University Press.

Troyna, B. and Ball, W. (1985) 'Styles of LEA policy intervention in multicultural/anti-racist education', *Educational Review*, 17, 2, pp. 165–75.

Troyna, B. and Carrington, B. (1990) *Education, Racism and Reform*, London:

Routledge.

Troyna, B., and Hatcher, R. (1991)'"British schools for British citizens"?' *Oxford Review of Education*, 1, 3, pp. 287–99.

Troyna, B., and Hatcher, R. (1992) *Racism in Children's Lives: a study of mainly white primary schools*, London: Routledge.

Troyna, B. and Williams, J. (1986) *Racism, Education and the State*, London: Croom Helm.

Turner, B. (1986) *Equality*, London: Methuen.

Wainwright, M. (1993) 'Shire counties gain at cities' expense', *Guardian*, 9 July, p. 6.

Webb, A. (1991) 'Governors' perceptions of training needs' in M. Leicester (ed.) *Governor Training: perspectives post-ERA*, Coventry: University of Warwick Research Paper in Continuing Education, no. 1, pp. 11–19.

Weiler, H. (1990) 'Decentralisation in educational governance: an exercise in contradiction?' in M. Granheim, M. Kogan and U. Lundgren (eds) *Evaluation as Policymaking*, London: Jessica Kingsley, pp. 42–65.

Chapter 9: School Governors, 'Race' and Racism

Ben-Tovim, G., Gabriel, J., Law, I., and Stredder, K. (1982) 'A political analysis of race in the 1980s' in *'Race' in Britain*, ed. C. Husband, London: Hutchinson, pp. 303–16.

Bhaskar, R. (1989) *Reclaiming Reality*, London: Verso.

Blair, M. (1993) 'Where do we fit in the scheme of things? Black teachers and the myth of marketability', paper given to International Sociology of Education Conference, Sheffield.

Brehony, K.J. (1985) 'Popular control or control by experts? Schooling between 1880 and 1902' in *Crises in the British State 1880–1930*, ed. M. Langan and B. Schwarz, London: Hutchinson, pp. 256–73.

Brehony, K.J., and Deem, R. (1990) 'Charging for free education: an exploration of a debate in school governing bodies', *Journal of Education Policy*, 5 (4), 333–45.

Brown, R. (1988) *Group Processes*, Oxford: Blackwell.

Bryman, A. (1988) *Quantity and Quality in Social Research*, London: Unwin Hyman.

Cashmore, E. and B. Troyna (1990) *Introduction to Race Relations*, London: Falmer.

Cole, M. (1993) '"Black and ethnic minority" or "Asian, black and other minority ethnic": a further note on nomenclature', *Sociology* 27 (4): 671–3.

Craib, I. (1992) *Modern Social Theory*, 2nd edn, London: Harvester Wheatsheaf.

Deem, R. (1989) 'The new school governing bodies: are race and gender on the agenda?' *Gender and Education* 1 (3): 247–60.

Deem, R. and Brehony, K.J. (1993) 'Consumers and education professionals in the organisation and administration of schools: partnership or conflict?' *Educational Studies*, 19 (3): 339–55.

Deem, R., Brehony, K.J. and Hemmings, S. (1992) 'Social justice, social divisions and the governing of schools' in *Racism and Education*, ed. D. Gill and B. Mayor, London: Sage, pp. 208–25.

DES (Department of Education and Science) (1981) *West Indian Children in Our Schools*, London: HMSO (Rampton Report).

DES (1985) *Education for All*, London: HMSO (Swann Report).

Geddes, A. (1993) 'Asian and Afro-Caribbean representation in elected local government in England and Wales', *New Community* 20 (1): 43–57.

Golby, M. and S. Brigley (1989) *Parents as School Governors*, Tiverton: Fairway.

Gordon, P. (1992) Introductory essay in *'Race', Education and Society*, London: Sage.

Guy, W. and I. Menter (1992) 'Local management of resources: who benefits?' in *Racism and Education*, ed. D. Gill and B. Mayor, London: Sage, pp. 151–68.

Holdsworth, N. (1983) 'Governors display racist attitudes', *Times Education Supplement*, 23 April.

Keys, W. and Fernandes, C. (1990) *A Survey of School Governing Bodies*, Slough: NFER.

Le Grand, J. and Bartlett, W. (eds) (1993) *Quasi-Markets and Social Policy*, London: Macmillan.

National Consumer Council (1990) *Minority Ethnic Communities and School Governing Bodies*, London: NCC.

Porter, S. (1993) 'Critical realist ethnography: the case of racism and professionalism in a medical setting', *Sociology* 27 (4): 591–609.

Rogers, L. (1990) 'Moslems in bid to sack school head', *Evening Standard*, 17 December.

Sayer, A. (1992) *Method in Social Science*, London: Routledge.

Streatfield, D. and G. Jefferies (1989) *The Reconstitution of School Governing Bodies*, Slough: NFER.

Troyna, B. and B. Carrington (1990) *Education, Racism and Reform*, London: Routledge.

Whitty, G., Edwards, T., and Gewirtz, S. (1993) *Specialisation and Choice in Urban Education*, London: Routledge.

Chapter 10: School, Community and Ethnic Minority Parents

ACER (Afro-Caribbean Education Resource Centre) (1986) *Parents' Voice In Early Childhood Education*, London: ACER.

Ball, C., (1994) *Start Right: the importance of early learning*, London: Royal Society of Arts.

Brar, H., (1991) 'Teaching, professionalism and home–school links', *Multicultural Teaching*, 9 (3), 32–5.

DFE (Department for Education) (1991) *The Parents' Charter*, London: HMSO.

DFE, (1992) *Choice and Diversity* (White Paper), London: HMSO.

David, M. (1993) *Parents, Gender and Educational Reform*, Cambridge: Polity Press.

Epstein, D. (1993) *Changing Classroom Cultures*, Stoke-on-Trent: Trentham.

Gee, J. (1989) 'The narratization of experience in the oral style', *Journal of Education* (USA edn) 171 (1), 75–96.

Gillborn, D. (1990) *'Race', Ethnicity and Education*, London: Unwin Hyman.

Gillborn, D. (1993) 'Racial violence and harassment' in D.Tattum (ed.) *Understanding and Managing Bullying*, London: Heinemann.

Gillborn, D. (1994) *Racism and Anti-racism in Education*, Buckingham: Open University Press.

Hess, G. (1991) *School Restructuring, Chicago Style*, California: Corwin Press.

Jones, G., Bastiani, J., Bell, G. & Chapman, C. (1992) *A Willing Partnership*, London: Royal Society of Arts.

Mac an Ghaill, M. (1988) *Young, Gifted and Black*, Milton Keynes: Open University.

Macbeth A. (1989) *Involving Parents*, Oxford: Heinemann.

Macdonald, I., Bhavani, R., Khan, L. & John, G. (1989) *Murder in the Playground* (The Macdonald Report), London: Longsight.

Macleod, F. (1985) *Parents In Partnership: involving Muslim parents in their children's education*, Coventry: Community Education Development Centre.

McCarthy, C. (1990) *Race and Curriculum*, London: Falmer.

Mirza, H. (1992) *Young, Female and Black*, London: Routledge.

Musgrave, P. (1979) *The Sociology of Education*, London: Methuen.

Philips, R. (1989) 'The Newham Parents' Centre' in S. Wolfendale (ed.) *Parental Involvement: developing networks between school, home and community*, London: Cassell.

Pugh, G. and De'Ath, E. (1989) *Working Towards Partnership in the Early Years*, London: National Children's Bureau.

Rizvi, F. (1993) 'Williams on democracy and the governance of education' in D. Dworkin and L. Roman (eds) *Views Beyond the Border Country: Raymond Williams and Cultural Politics*, London: Routledge.

Showstack-Sasson, A. (1983) 'Dear Parent...' in A-M. Wolpe and J. Donald (eds) *Is There Anyone Here From Education?*, London: Pluto.

Thomas, D. (1986) *White Bolts, Black Locks*, London: Allen & Unwin.

Tizard, B., Blatchford, P., Burke, J., Farquhar, C. and Plewis, I. (1988) *Young Children at School in the Inner City*, London: Lawrence Erlbaum.

Tizard, B., Mortimore, J. and Burchell, B. (1988) 'Involving parents from minority groups' in J. Bastiani (ed.) *Working with Parents: a whole school approach*, Windsor: NFER-Nelson.

Tomlinson, S. (1984) *Home and School in Multicultural Britain*, London: Batsford.

Tomlinson, S. (1991) 'Home–school partnerships', in S. Tomlinson and A. Ross, *Teachers and Parents*, London: Institute of Public Policy Research.

Tomlinson, S. (1993) 'Ethnic minorities: involved partners or problem parents?' in P. Munn (ed.) *Parents and Schools: customers, managers or partners?*, London: Routledge.

Tomlinson, S. and Hutchison, S. (1991) *Bangadeshi Parents and Education in Tower Hamlets*, London: Advisory Centre for Education (ACE).

Troyna, B. and Hatcher, R. (1992) *Racism in Children's Lives*, London: Routledge.

Vincent, C. (1992) 'Tolerating intolerance? Parental choice and race relations: the Cleveland case', *Journal of Education Policy*, 7 (5), 429–33.

Vincent, C. (1993a) 'Community participation? The establishment of "City's" Parents' Centre', *British Educational Research Journal*, 19 (3), 227–41.

Vincent, C. (1993b) 'Education for the community?', *British Journal of Educational Studies*, 41 (4), 366–80.

Willis, P. (1990) *Common Culture*, Milton Keynes: Open University Press.

Wright, C. (1987) 'Black students, white teachers' in B. Troyna (ed.) *Racial Inequality In Education*, London: Tavistock.

Young, M., and Wilmott, P. (1957) *Family and Kinship in East London*, London: RKP.

Notes on Contributors

Sally Tomlinson is Professor of Educational Policy and Management at Goldsmiths' College, University of London. A member of the Editorial Board of *Ethnic and Racial Studies*, she has taught, written and researched in the area of race, ethnicity and education for twenty-five years, and her books include *Ethnic Minorities in British Schools* (1983), *Home and School in Multicultural Britain* (1984) and *Multicultural Education in White Schools* (1990).

Maurice Craft is Research Professor in Education at the University of Greenwich. Formerly Dean of Education and Pro-Vice-Chancellor at Nottingham University, he has also held senior academic posts in Australia and Hong Kong. Member of teacher education advisory groups for the Swann Committee and CRE, he has written widely on multicultural education, including *Education and Cultural Pluralism* (1984) and *Teacher Education in a Multicultural Society* (1987).

Carl Bagley has worked on several research projects on race: in relation to social policy, housing and education for Aston University, The Open University (where he obtained a doctorate), and the NFER. He also qualified as a community worker, and worked as an anti-racist strategist with Leeds City Council. He is currently researching parental choice in education on a three-year ESRC project at The Open University.

Kevin Brehony is a Senior Lecturer in Education at Reading university. Formerly a primary school teacher, he gained a PhD from The Open University. As well as work in historical sociology, he has published articles on school governors and education policy. He taught the *Ethnic Minorities and Community Relations* course for the Open University, and currently teaches on 'race' for an MA in School and Society.

Anna King is Senior Lecturer in Religious Studies and Philosophy at King Alfred's College, Winchester. Formerly Course Director of a UFC INSET project in multicultural education at Cambridge University, she has published in this field and in religious studies, including *The Multicultural Dimension of the National Curriculum* (1993), with Michael Reiss. A social anthropologist, she has engaged in extensive periods of fieldwork, particularly in northern India.

Heidi Mirza, Senior Lecturer in Social Science at South Bank University, has taught at Brown University, USA, and the University of London, and has been a researcher at the Thomas Coram Unit, Institute of Education, and Goldsmiths' College, University of London. She is currently carrying out research into the experience of black women in higher education, and is the author of *Young, Female and Black* (1992).

Peter Mitchell is a Lecturer in Education at the University of Cambridge, where his responsibilities include the teaching of religious studies and values in education. He was formerly a secondary school teacher in East London and a college of education lecturer. He has published articles in philosophy, ethics and religious education, and was Director of an ESRC-funded research project on Muslim attitudes to education in Britain.

Monica Taylor, a Senior Research Officer at the NFER and Editor of the *Journal of Moral Education*, undertook critical reviews of research on the education of ethnic minority pupils for the Rampton and Swann Committees, and has conducted research into personal and social education, religious education and multicultural/anti-racist education. Her most recent publications are on values education in Europe, and a directory of UK research and resources.

William H. Taylor, a Senior Lecturer in Education at Exeter University, has taught in schools and FE colleges in Glasgow, and in Universities in France, India, Nigeria, Tanzania and USA. He has pioneered initial and in-service courses in multicultural/anti-racist education in south-west England, using links with inner-city, multi-ethnic schools. His publications are mainly in comparative education, multicultural education, history and teacher education.

Barry Troyna is Reader in Education and Director of Research Development at the University of Warwick Institute of Education. Editor of the *British Educational Research Journal*, and school governor of a multi-ethnic primary school in Coventry, he has written widely on anti-racist education, and his most recent books include *Racism in Children's Lives* (1992), with Richard Hatcher, and *Racism and Education: research perspectives* (1993).

Gajendra Verma, Professor of Education, Dean of the Research and Graduate School in Education at the University of Manchester, and formerly at the Universities of Bradford and East Anglia, has researched and published extensively in applied psychology and in many areas of 'race', ethnicity and education. His latest publications include *Inequality and Teacher Education* (1993), and (with Peter Pumfrey) *Cultural Diversity and the National Curriculum* (1994).

Carol Vincent, a Lecturer in Special Education in the School of Education at The Open University, has also worked as a research officer, and has taught in mainstream primary and special schools in inner London. In 1993 she completed her PhD, which was an ethnographic study of home–school relations in primary education. Her other research interests include special education, 'race' and education, and local government.

Cecile Wright is a Senior Lecturer in Sociology at The Nottingham Trent University, and was formerly a Lecturer in Education at the University of Leicester. She has both carried out research and written extensively in the field of 'race', ethnicity and education, and her recent book *Race Relations in the Primary School* (1992) is based on an ethnographic study carried out in inner-city primary schools.

Suggested Reading

The reader will find an extensive bibliography for each chapter on pages 196–218, but the following introductory reading list may be helpful for those new to the field.

General
Jones, T. (1993) *Britain's Ethnic Minorities*, London: Policy Studies Institute.
Modood, T. (1992) *Not Easy being British: colour, culture, and citizenship*, London: Runnymede Trust and Trentham Books.
Skellington, R. with Morris, P. (1992) *Race in Britain Today*, London: Sage.

Policy and Practice
Craft, A. and Bardell, G. (Eds) (1984) *Curriculum Opportunities in a Multicultural Society*, London: Harper and Row.
Craft, M. 'Teacher education in multicultural Britain', in Thomas, J.B. (Ed) (1990) *British Universities and Teacher Education: a century of change*, London: Falmer.
Department of Education and Science (1985) *Education For All*, London: HMSO (The Swann Report).
Foster, P. (1990) *Policy and Practice in Multicultural and Anti-racist Education*, London: Routledge.
Fyfe, A. and Figueroa, P. (Eds) (1993), *Education for Cultural Diversity*, London: Routledge.
Grugeon, E. and Woods, P. (1990) *Educating All: multicultural perspectives in the primary school*, London: Routledge.
King, A.S. and Reiss, M.J. (1993) *The Multicultural Dimension in the National Curriculum*, London: Falmer.
Mac an Ghaill (1988) *Young, Gifted and Black*, Buckingham: Open University Press.
Mirza, H.S. (1992) *Young, Female and Black*, London: Routledge.
Tomlinson, S. (1990) *Multicultural Education in White Schools*, London: Batsford.
Tomlinson, S. (1993) 'Ethnic minorities: involved partners or problem parents?' in Munn, P. (Ed) *Parents and Schools: customers, managers and partners*, London: Routledge.
Troyna, B. (1993) *Racism and Education*, Buckingham: Open University Press.
Verma, G.K. and Pumfrey, P.D. (Eds) (1993), *Cross-Curricular Contexts, Themes and Dimensions in Secondary Schools*, London: Falmer.

Index